# CHRISTIAN ROMAN EMPIRE SERIES

Vol. 3

# THE BOOK
# OF THE POPES
## *(LIBER PONTIFICALIS)*

## *TO THE PONTIFICATE OF GREGORY I*

Translated with an introduction by
## Louise Ropes Loomis, Ph.D.

Evolution Publishing
Merchantville NJ
2006

Originally Published by
Columbia University Press, New York
1916


This edition ©2006 by Evolution Publishing
Merchantville, New Jersey.


Printed in the United States of America


ISBN 1-889758-86-8

**Library of Congress Cataloging-in-Publication Data**

Loomis, Louise Ropes, 1874-
  [Liber pontificalis.]
  The book of the popes : to the pontificate of Gregory I / translated with an
introduction by Louise Ropes Loomis.
      p. cm. -- (Christian Roman Empire series ; v. 3)
  Originally published: New York : Columbia University Press, 1916.
  ISBN 1-889758-86-8
  1.   Papacy--History--Sources. 2.   Catholic  Church--History--Sources. 3.
Popes--Biography--Early works to 1800. 4.  Church history--Primitive and early
church, ca. 30-600.  I. Title.
  BX950.E6L6 2006
  270.10922--dc22
  [B]

                                                            2006020125

# PREFACE TO THE 2006 EDITION

The Papacy, as an institution, claims a history stretching back to the earliest days of Christianity and a founder who was none other than the most illustrious of the Apostles, St. Peter. Though the first few centuries of the Roman See are generally shrouded in obscurity, ancient documents, such as the *Liber Pontificalis*, help to shed light not only on the Papacy itself, but also more broadly on the political, religious, social, military, and economic climate of the age.

The *Liber Pontificalis*, as a work of history, is intriguing and tantalizing, yet often unsatisfying. The earliest biographies offer only the briefest glimpses of the Popes in question and are often riddled with errors or provably spurious claims. The entries for those Popes who reigned during the 3rd and 4th centuries AD, though fuller and more detailed, are often possessed of similar defects. However, the biographies of the 5th and 6th century Popes, taking up fully half of the present volume, are undoubtedly the most valuable portion of the work from a historical perspective, both in terms of unique data they contain and the relative paucity of secular histories during the same period.

Covering up through the end of the 6th century AD, this translation by Louise Ropes Loomis represents only the beginning portion of the *Liber Pontificalis* which was continued haphazardly through the 15th century. As such, it coincides with the rise of Christianity from the catacombs to become the preeminent faith of the Mediterranean world and fits well within the scope of the present series. The footnotes, mostly derived from the authoritative 19th century commentaries by Mommsen and Duchesne, are most helpful in identifying and correcting the problematic sections of the work and otherwise providing context.

The handsome illustrations found throughout this edition are a novelty introduced in the 2006 edition and are taken from John Gilmary Shea's *Pictoral Lives of the Saints*, originally published in 1887.

—*Anthony P. Schiavo, Jr.*
*Merchantville, NJ*
*June 2006*

# ILLUSTRATIONS

# PREFACE

THE preparation of an English text of the *Liber Pontificalis*, of which the following pages furnish the first installment, is something more than the translation of a crabbed text, crowded with obscure references. Even of the great libraries in this country only about ten possess the original in the best working edition, if one may judge by library returns, and it is doubtful if many more copies of the complete text exist this side of the Atlantic. A document which long was viewed as of fundamental importance for the history of the Papacy has thus sunk so completely out of sight as to have become a rather rare curiosity to all but research students of medieval history. This is in part due to the character of the work, with its forbidding lists of items of local and temporary interest, in which only the trained archæologist can find his way, but it is also surely due to the fact that both texts and commentary have hitherto been in foreign languages and are to be found only in costly and rare volumes. The English version aims to overcome these difficulties. While the narrative portions of the text have been kept in full, lists of mere names and figures, especially in the case of ordinations, have been in part eliminated unless they were of distinct historical interest. The narrative, when no longer clogged with an undue amount of this material, will be found to run along with something of the swiftness of a medieval chronicle. The archæologist, who alone will miss the discarded portions, will turn to the original in any case. In the second place, sufficient apparatus has been given in the form of explanatory notes to make the narrative clear, while bibliographical references furnish a guide to the treatment of the more intricate problems. It is hoped, therefore, that in its new form — for the *Liber Pontificalis* has never before been translated into any other tongue — this quaint monument of curial historiography will be found to have retained enough of that charm of naïve simplicity, which the scholar appreciates in the original, to lure the general reader of history into a study of the important facts with which it deals.

It should be borne in mind, however, that this volume is not an attempt to present a history of the Papacy during the first six centuries. It is simply the presentation of an ancient text with enough commentary to make it intelligible. The text is that of the earliest history of the Papacy, but even were it provided with most exhaustive notes, it could never furnish by itself an adequate basis for a modern narrative. The historian of to-day has at his disposal other documents and archæological remains, which are often of greater importance for an understanding of these early pontificates than the meagre biography in the *Liber Pontificalis*. It was originally planned that a collection of such documents should form a part of the volume in which the *Liber Pontificalis* appears; but it now seems best to publish these documents in a separate and parallel volume, and so leave the way open to complete the *Liber Pontificalis*, or at least to carry it down to the heart of the Middle Ages.

A word should be said as to the point at which the text of the *Liber Pontificalis* is broken in this edition. When the translation was first undertaken it seemed unlikely that it would ever be continued further than in the present enterprise. Dr. Loomis, therefore, carried the text through the pontificate of Gregory I, as a point of general historical interest. Since there is now a possibility that the next section of the book may also be translated, the division has been put as near to the one originally planned as possible, including the pontificates immediately preceding Gregory.

Those who read this book will surely appreciate the arduous task which Dr. Loomis has here accomplished, and their appreciation will probably grow upon a closer acquaintance with the problems involved.

J. T. S.

# CHRONOLOGICAL LIST OF POPES

The dates of the first eighteen pontificates are so conjectural that they are not given here.

# INTRODUCTION

THE bishopric of Rome, favored by circumstance in many ways over the bishoprics of other cities, is fortunate also in this, that it possesses records dating almost from the age of its venerable foundation. The equally ancient sees of Jerusalem, Antioch and Alexandria have no memorials earlier than the catalogues of bishops which were set down by the historian Eusebius in the fourth century. Constantinople can trace its episcopal line no further back than the seventh century. On the other hand, Rome, for a variety of reasons which are still matters of controversy, was regarded as a peculiarly faithful custodian of apostolic tradition; the sequence of its bishops from Peter, the apostle, was cited even as early as the second century as guarantee of its claim to transmit the pure doctrine unalloyed. The episcopal lists of the second century were repeated and continued in succeeding centuries, the later records being expanded and enlarged, until in the sixth or seventh century the Liber Pontificalis, the first historical narrative or series of papal biographies, was compiled by a member of the papal court. Later yet every pope had his official annalist, who carried on the Liber Pontificalis, adding a new biography at the death of the pontiff. The chronicle was often bare and perfunctory, was now and then omitted altogether for long periods at a time, but was not finally abandoned until the age of Martin V in the fifteenth century.

Throughout the Middle Ages and until comparatively modern times the Liber Pontificalis was accepted as not only the oldest but as also the most authentic existing history of the papacy. Extracts from it were incorporated into church liturgies. It was quoted as an authority by countless historians and ecclesiastical writers from the eighth century to the eighteenth. It served as model for other chronicles, both secular and religious, in particular for the *Gesta Episcoporum* and the *Gesta Abbatum*, the records which were kept in cathedral chapters and monasteries of Western Europe during the later Middle Ages. Because of its unmistakable antiquity and because of the profound importance of its subject matter it was reckoned as a source of unimpeachable veracity and as one of the indisputable proofs of the primitive power and activity of the popes.

Modern scholarship, however, in the persons of Lipsius, Lightfoot, Waitz, Duchesne, Mommsen, and others, has laid its unscrupulous hands on this Liber Pontificalis, analyzed it and separated it into two parts, each differing from the other in origin and historical value. The latter portion, from the seventh century downward, is, as we have already indicated, simply the annals of the papal court, written up from time to time by the papal biographer. The narrative may be biassed or inaccurate, but it recounts events of which the narrator had for the most part some personal knowledge, from which he was in no case very far distant, and as such deserves considerable credence. It is, in fact, one of the few surviving sources for the turbulent centuries that followed the death of Gregory I. It presents no unusual problems beyond those offered by any history treating of an age so alien to our own.

The earlier portion, covering the era from St. Peter to the seventh century, and compiled first toward the end of that era, is of different quality. Although still admitted to be the oldest of all local church histories, based upon records earlier yet and of undoubted genuineness, it is itself a mesh of veritable fact, romantic legend, deliberate fabrication and heedless error. It deals with persons and things which seemed often almost as remote to the author as they do to us and of which he had only the scantiest and most fragmentary accounts; it describes achievements which he had little means of estimating justly and which he had sometimes the strongest motive to exaggerate or misrepresent. One can, therefore, observe in this single document a blending of most of the processes by which a history may be constructed, the use of sober, reliable, sometimes first-hand reports of events and again of marvelous legends, the creations of generations of enthusiasm and piety, the intentional manufacture of data for a definite purpose, the distortion of other data through prejudice or ignorance. This portion of the Liber Pontificalis is often fraudulent, often partisan, often naïvely devout and credulous. Yet the very frauds and uncorroborated assertions and mistakes and venerations have a value to us of a sort. It is interesting to know what could be believed about some of these matters in the sixth or seventh century. At bottom there is the residue of substantiated fact and credible tradition which continue to make even this part of the Liber Pontificalis indispensable, if not for the study of the policies of the immediate successors of Peter, yet for the history and archæology of Rome and the church in the earliest Middle Ages.

The translation which follows gives the text of this first portion[1] from the beginning to the life of Gregory the Great, with the omission toward the last of some formulæ and lists of church appurtenances which seem to possess only an archæological worth or interest. In order to make clearer the peculiar, heterogeneous character of our text, we may here consider more in detail the elements of which it was composed: first, the ancient, papal chronologies which preceded it and upon which it was based; second, the supplementary material with which the unknown author filled out the bare skeleton of names and dates furnished him by the chronologies and which distinguished his work from them.

The oldest papal lists of which we hear anything were written down, as we have already said, in the second century. About 150 A.D. Hegesippus, a Christian from Syria, perplexed by the fine-spun Gnostic theories of the nature and mission of Christ which were winning acceptance in the East, visited Rome and drew up a list of the Roman bishops to his own day in order to satisfy himself and his countrymen of the validity of the Roman form of doctrine. His list contained, perhaps, not only the names of the bishops but also the duration in years of each pontificate. Oral tradition would still be reasonably exact for the years since 100 A.D.; for the bishops who came before it would be able to supply the names and a rough calculation as to the length of their terms. Unhappily Hegesippus' list has not been preserved in its original

[1] On the termination of the first recension see pp. xxi and xxii, and notes to Vigilius below.

form. Eusebius, in his Church History, quotes from Hegesippus' writings his account of the visit to Rome and the securing of the list, but not the list itself, and the writings have perished. The list was used, however, by later chroniclers, Eusebius among them.

Twenty-five or thirty years afterwards, during the persecution of Marcus Aurelius, Irenæus came from Lyons to Rome and while there compiled another list of the Roman succession as far as Eleutherius, who was then in office. Irenæus was anxious to reconcile the warring sects which menaced the life of the church from within more seriously than the persecutions without. He wrote a great treatise, *Against the Heresies*, in which he exposed the fallacies of the heterodox and set forth systematically the whole Catholic scheme of the relations between God and man. To support his system he cited the unbroken line of the episcopate and the grace transmitted by the laying on of hands as well as the testimony of the Scriptures. Irenæus inserted in his episcopal list a few facts which he had learned at Rome about the early bishops. He says, for instance, that Linus, the second in office, was the man to whom St. Paul referred in his Epistle to Timothy, that Clement, the fourth bishop, had seen and heard both the apostles and that many others surviving at Rome in Clement's day had been taught by them. He also mentions the martyrdom of Telesphorus and, in another connection, the relations of Anicetus with Polycarp, who had known the apostle John, and the rise of heresies at Rome under Hyginus and Pius. The work of Irenæus is preserved only in fragments in the original Greek, but one of the fragments includes the passage with which we are concerned. In its time it exerted an immense influence on the formulation of dogmatic theology in both East and West.

In the third century the lists of the second century were transcribed and carried forward by at least two other hands. Hippolytus, bishop of Porto, who was banished for his faith to Sardinia in company with the Roman bishop, Pontianus, and whose marble statue now stands in the Lateran Museum, drew up about 235 A.D. a catalogue of the Roman succession as far as his own day. Hippolytus was a voluminous writer, interested not only in theology but also in ecclesiastical law and in chronography. He compiled a chronicle of the world from the creation to the year 234 A.D., with tables of the Roman emperors, kings of Macedon and Jewish high priests, the type of many a similar work in the centuries to follow. It is natural that he had his list of Roman bishops also. Unfortunately, although a large part of the chronicle has survived, the episcopal list itself, as Hippolytus prepared it, has been lost. It was incorporated in later lists, however, and in that way the substance of it has come down to us.

Another third century list of which we hear but which has likewise now disappeared in its original shape is said to have been the work of one Julius Africanus, a native of Palestine. This last list seems to have been more elaborate than any which preceded it and to have included the names of the emperors and consuls in office when the terms of the various bishoprics began and ended. The author probably gave these synchronisms accurately enough for the period with which he was acquainted and reckoned backward to secure the dates for the earlier age, using as a means the consular Fasti and the figures in the older papal lists.

From the fourth century onward the chronologies of the popes come gradually into more general circulation. The papacy by this time was an old, established institution of increasing importance, with a history in which it might take pride. The emperors were leaving Rome and from their distance no longer overshadowed the head of the church. In fact it became customary to couple lists of the popes with lists of consuls and kings and other secular magnates. Eusebius, the historian and friend of Constantine, inserted lists of the Roman bishops in both his Chronicle and his Church History, bringing them down to the year 325. His two lists disagree with one another in the figures for the length of some of the earlier pontificates, but give precisely the same names in the same order. They may have been taken from two different sources. They show that even at that date tradition and records were uncertain as to the years but were in accord as to the men. Toward the close of his chronologies Eusebius added the months to the years of some of the pontifical terms.

About the year 350 a collection of chronological and geographical lists and tables was compiled for the convenience of Christian residents in Rome, which must have been but one of many similar collections of that and later times. This particular collection has chanced to come down to us almost entire, and gives us a curious glimpse into the range of interests of the persons for whom it was written, such as a World's Almanac for 1915 would give to a student of our age living in the year 3500. Comprised in the collection were civil and court calendars, paschal tables, lists of the anniversaries of the burials of popes and martyrs, a topography of the city of Rome divided into districts, tables of Roman emperors and consuls and a list of the popes to the time of Liberius, fuller and more comprehensive than any which had gone before.

This last list has since become known as the Liberian Catalogue, so-called from the date of its composition, not from any connection with Liberius himself. It gave the length of each term from the beginning in years, months and days, the imperial and consular synchronisms, in the case of some popes the date of burial or deposition, and here and there it marked an event. Under Pius, for example, it mentioned the writing of *The Shepherd of Hermas*, probably because of the discussion in Liberius' day over the canonicity of the book. Under Pontianus, Lucius and Marcellinus it noted the troubles due to persecution, under Fabianus and Cornelius the outbreak of the Novatian schism and under Julius the five basilicas which he built. It committed the grave blunder of making two popes out of Cletus and Anencletus, different forms in different earlier chronologies of the same man's name. The major part was compounded from several of the previous lists. There is reason to think that Hippolytus' was one of those consulted. At any rate some one of these pattern lists gave apparently the duration of a few pontificates in days as well as in years and months and alluded now and then to events associated with particular names. The author of the Liberian Catalogue copied out these figures and references to events and added arbitrarily months and days to the years of all the terms from Peter downward in order to make his work appear more symmetrical. Two or three centuries later this Liberian Catalogue was transported outright into the Liber Pontificalis to form the groundwork for the period that it covered. The author of the Liber Pontificalis was content to take it as it stood, without troubling to go behind to any of the more primitive lists. Indeed he seems to have known them only through the medium of the Catalogue.

Henceforth lists of the popes are found with increasing frequency in the literature of the day, quoted by theologians in opposition to the novelties of the heretics, brought down to date by chroniclers and historians. Optatus and Augustine cited the unbroken papal line, the bishops of "the unique see," as witness against the Donatists. The unknown author of a poem against Marcion invoked them in support of his metrical arguments on behalf of orthodoxy. Jerome, who translated and continued the Chronicle of Eusebius, carried the catalogue on to 378. Prosper of Aquitaine, who lived at Rome under Leo I and continued Jerome's Chronicle to 453, Socrates, Sozomen and Theodoret, Greeks of the early fifth century, who undertook to supplement the Church History of Eusebius, all added their quota to the chronology of the popes. It is hardly necessary to enumerate the writers who later still reviewed the names of the bishops of Rome. They, of course, depended upon one or another of the preceding lists, and, though their dates and figures showed often a wide diversity, due to the carelessness or ignorance of copyists, they all followed some one of the forms already worked out.

The nameless priest or clerk who first compiled the Liber Pontificalis took, as we have said, his papal list for the first three and one half centuries, with few modifications, directly from the Liberian Catalogue. A few supplementary data and the outline for the following centuries he found in Jerome's Chronicle and the later compendiums. Into this framework of names and dates he proceeded to fit a large quantity of fresh material, in order to make his book more interesting and more instructive and to give it the character of a history rather than of a catalogue. This body of new material, which forms the distinguishing feature of the Liber Pontificalis as compared with the chronologies, must next be the subject of our attention. It has been dissected and examined of recent years by archæologists like De Rossi, as well as by the historians, Duchesne and Mommsen. We may summarize briefly in the succeeding two or three pages the results of their investigation.

1. The two prefatory letters, ostensibly composed by St. Jerome and Pope Damasus, by means of which the authorship of the whole first part of the Liber Pontificalis is ascribed to Jerome, are manifest forgeries of the sixth or seventh century. Our unknown

author invented them in the clumsy Latin of his time, hoping through them to give prestige to his own work. The practice was not uncommon in his day. The particular form which the letters took was suggested to him, no doubt, by an epistle of Jerome to Damasus, prefixed to the former's version of the Gospels, and by the correspondence which served as introduction to Jerome's Martyrology. Our author's acquaintance with the correspondence is proved by the fact that he took from one of those letters his figures for the number of martyrs that perished in the persecution of Diocletian in the time of Pope Marcellinus.

2. The names of the fathers of the popes and of their nations and birthplaces our author may have copied, at least for all that concerns the later popes, from some ecclesiastical record lost to us to-day. We know of no such source, but our author may have discovered it in some Roman archive, long since destroyed in the ruin of the ancient city. For the earlier popes he undoubtedly invented these details, in order that he might seem to possess as much information about them as about their successors.

3. The comparatively circumstantial biographies of St. Peter and St. Clement, and the account of the debate over the date of Easter under Victor he took from two fourth century productions, the *De Viris Illustribus* of Jerome and Rufinus' translation of the apocryphal *Recognitions* attributed to Clement. He may also have drawn from the letter of Gregory I to Eulogius of Alexandria. Unluckily these works were all too late to have much value as authorities on events of the first or second century.

4. The decrees for the organization and government of the church ascribed to the various bishops are practically all spurious until they reach the latter half of the fifth century. Our author evidently felt it necessary to record some achievement for every bishop in the whole long line, and therefore assigned to each in turn the institution of some ecclesiastical custom which obtained at the time he himself was writing. These statements have some worth as indicating the nature of procedure in the sixth or seventh century but little or none as bearing upon the earlier periods. Exceptions to this general rule are the decrees of Siricius and of Innocent I, which our author probably found in the official letters of those popes included in the Collection of Acts of Popes and

Councils compiled by Dionysius Exiguus at the opening of the sixth century. From this same collection he derived his knowledge of the so-called Apostolic Canons, to which he refers in the first of his prefatory letters, and of the acts of several apocryphal councils, such as the Council of Sinuessa before which Marcellinus professed his penitence and the two Roman synods of Sylvester, which passed measures to enhance to an incredible degree the powers of the bishop. Here also he obtained his untrustworthy accounts of the vicissitudes of Liberius and the trial of Xystus III. He apparently knew the genuine Acts of the Council of Chalcedon, for his report of that assemblage, though badly confused, is not marred by actual untruth. He makes no allusion to the general Council of Constantinople, held in 551, though we should expect some mention of it if he were acquainted with its proceedings. As for the Council of Sinuessa, it is now certain that no such gathering ever took place, but it is not clear whether or not Marcellinus was a renegade. The tale has perhaps some ground in fact, but it may, on the other hand, be the fabrication of a later party that wished to cast discredit on the pontificate.

5. The descriptions of persecutions and martyrdoms and of religious marvels, such as the discovery of the Holy Cross and the healing of Constantine, were culled from popular martyrologies and passions of the saints, almost all of which have since disappeared. They were merely pious stories, simple and uncritical, in which the heroic and legendary elements predominated over the historical. Our author seems to have felt a special ardor for the memory of the martyrs. He has three early popes, Clement, Anteros and Fabianus, each make provision for the collection of facts regarding them and out of the thirty-one first popes he has twenty-three win for themselves the martyr's crown. Few of these statements can be accepted unless corroborated by outside testimony.

6. The notices of churches built or repaired and of gifts offered by prelates or princes are a conspicuous feature of the biography of Sylvester, and thereafter are copious and frequent. They must have been copied, in part at least, from records or memoranda in the archives of the Roman see. The curious and imposing list of Constantine's donations bears marks of genuineness as a document,

although, in its present shape it is plainly corrupt in passages, the proper names being at times quite unintelligible. The donations enumerated in such lists are of genuine but obscure historical interest, either for the history of the Patrimony of St. Peter, if grants of estates, or for the history of art, if basilicas and appurtenances of worship. In the latter case they furnish valuable — if sometimes uncertain — evidence for the relation of Byzantine art to Roman in the early Christian period. The catalogue of Constantine's benefactions is reproduced entire in the translation, also the most notable items of the later lists. The student who wishes more will consult the original text.

7. The lists of episcopal ordinations, set like formulæ near the end of each biography, were also in all probability taken from records kept toward the close of our period in the Roman church. Indeed Gregory I alludes in one of his letters to such a record. Our author then introduced fictitious lists of ordinations into the early biographies in order to maintain the much desired appearance of uniformity and of completeness of information. All the lists, however, in spite of their official semblance, are so bare and brief and the figures in many cases are obviously so corrupt that they retain no value at the present day. Like the accounts of the provisions for the conduct of the church, they emphasize the part played by the bishop to the disparagement of that played by the other clergy or the laity. They show the autocratic or monarchical character of the Roman structure as it appeared to the eyes of its first historian.

8. The notices of the dates and places of burial or deposition of popes and martyrs were based partly on the Liberian Catalogue and partly on lists of saints' anniversaries and traditions connected with certain basilicas and cemeteries. When a bishop's name, however, did not appear in the well-known lists of saints, and no tradition associated him with any particular tomb, our author arbitrarily supplied him with date and place of sepulture. The natural spot for interring the first pontiffs was the Vatican; afterward the catacomb of Callistus. In fact, the bishops Anicetus and Soter are assigned in one text to the cemetery of Callistus some years before Callistus constructed it.

Having herewith baldly sketched the antecedents and sources

of the Liber Pontificalis, we must add a few words on the vexed
problem of the period of composition, the date when our anonymous cleric set about piecing it together out of its miscellaneous
elements. It is a problem upon which the most erudite authorities still disagree and which we can do hardly more than state in
abbreviated form, the arguments on either side being too lengthy
and technical to reproduce here. They are rendered especially
complicated by the fact of the variety and number of texts of the
Liber Pontificalis and by the difficulty of determining which text
represents the archetype or original draft of the work. As it hap-
pens, it has come down to us not only in three different versions
of the full text but also in two abridgments or epitomes. It is
now generally conceded that all forms of the complete text, in the
shape that we have them, are products of the seventh century.
The earliest recension or edition dates back perhaps to the first
quarter of the century, not long after the death of Gregory I.
Forty or fifty years later it was rewritten in a slightly more expan-
sive style and brought down to include the popes who had held
office since the first recension was finished. Shortly afterward a
third or composite version was constructed by a combination of
the two previous recensions, wherein some passages were borrowed
from the first and some from the second. Thenceforward no further
alterations were made in the biographies of the seven first centuries.
One or other of the three recensions was copied by later writers
with the additions necessary to carry on the narrative to date.

The question still in dispute is the age of the two epitomes.
The first or Felician Epitome, as it is called, breaks off with the
pontificate of Felix IV, 530 A.D. Certain scholars of great learning and distinction, such as Lipsius, Lightfoot and Duchesne, hold
that this epitome is a summary of an early text of the Liber Pontificalis which concluded at that point and was in fact composed
soon after Felix' death; or, in other words, that the original text
was about a century older than any full text which we possess at
the present day and that our author lived and wrote toward the
end of Theodoric's reign instead of under Heraclius. The second
or Cononian Epitome, which closely resembles the Felician but
continues on to the time of Pope Conon, 687 A.D., is also in the
opinion of these same scholars a résumé of the first text, supple-

mented by an abridgment of the latter part of one of the seventh century recensions. To illustrate this theory we may mention one or two of the simpler arguments. Duchesne contends that these epitomes show variations from the language of the seventh century versions that indicate their derivation from a different and older prototype, that the biographies of the popes of the period of Theodoric are written in a vivid and personal style as if by a contemporary and that Gregory of Tours, who died in 594, alludes in his history to a version of the Liber Pontificalis current in his time.

On the other hand, Waitz and Mommsen, scholars no less learned and distinguished, maintain that the two epitomes, in spite of their occasional divergences from the seventh century phraseology, are nevertheless founded upon the seventh century text and that, in consequence, the Liber Pontificalis itself is no older than the earliest of the recensions, that is, than the period of the disturbances after the death of Gregory I. They insist that the differences in language between the two epitomes and the full seventh century versions are not important enough to require a different source for the epitomes, that the increase in vivacity and in minuteness of description noticeable in the biographies of the age of Theodoric may be explained by the use on the part of the seventh century author of a sixth century chronicle since lost, and that passages in these same biographies contain mistakes and misunderstandings impossible to a contemporary. They pronounce the quotation from Gregory of Tours too vague and indecisive to be accepted as proof of his acquaintance with the Liber Pontificalis. Other writers of the age, men like Isidore of Seville and Pope Gregory himself, more deeply versed in Roman affairs than the Gallic Gregory could be, would inevitably have referred to the Liber Pontificalis if it had been in existence in their day. But, as we have said before, the arguments on either side of this controversy are far too elaborate to rehearse adequately here. Something more of them will be found in the notes appended to the text.

The following translation is based upon the text edited by Mommsen in the *Monumenta Germaniæ Historica*. He gives the full seventh century version with the variations between the three recensions or between them and either or both of the epitomes printed in parallel columns. Mere differences in individual manuscripts, caused by the errors or interpolations of copyists, he enumerates in his footnotes. I have preserved his method of setting the various readings of different classes of texts in parallel columns so that the extent of the variations might be easily seen, but have for the most part made no attempt to indicate, as he does, by a system of letters and numbers the text to which each reading belongs nor to convey an idea of the idiosyncrasies of single manuscripts. For a close study of the separate texts the reader must consult Mommsen himself.

The magnitude of Mommsen's undertaking may be better appreciated by noting in passing the age, number and location of the manuscripts which he thought essential to collate in preparing his edition. His text of the Felician Epitome he derived from three manuscripts, the oldest of which dates from the eighth century and is now in Paris, the other two being at Berne and Rome. The Cononian Epitome he found in two manuscripts, both of the ninth century, one in Paris and one in Verona. The first recension of the full seventh century text he obtained from nineteen manuscripts, the oldest of which belongs to the eighth century and is now in the Library at Lucca, the others are scattered in Paris, Rome, Florence, Milan and elsewhere. The second recension he took from twenty manuscripts, the oldest now in Naples, dating from the close of the seventh century, the remainder in Leyden, Cologne, Paris, Brussels, Treves and other places. The third or composite text he based upon eleven manuscripts. The earliest, now at Modena, goes back to the end of the seventh or the opening of the eighth century, but it consists only of excerpts. The oldest copy of the entire text is in the Vatican and dates from the tenth century.

For fuller discussions of the numerous, interesting topics connected with the Liber Pontificalis, its origin, character, and value, the student who wishes to pursue his investigations further is referred first of all to the voluminous and exhaustive introductions and notes attached to Duchesne's edition of the text, published a few years earlier than Mommsen's; also to Mommsen's briefer Prolegomena to his own edition, Lightfoot's volume on St. Clement of Rome in the series entitled *The Apostolic Fathers,* and Waitz' articles on the subject in the *Neues Archiv*, especially volumes IV, IX, X, and XI. A convenient summary of some of the researches of the greater scholars is afforded by Rosenfeld's monograph, *Über die Composition des Liber Pontificalis biz zu Constantin*. From these authorities and the others quoted from time to time in the text I have gathered my statements in this introduction and much of the material in my notes. In fact, without the guidance of Duchesne, I should often have been at a loss how to elucidate the text, my own notes being in many cases scarcely more than abridgments or paraphrases of his. The references in the notes are, for the most part, to these same works, the indispensable apparatus for any serious study of the Liber Pontificalis, to the Latin and Greek sources in English translation, whenever such translations exist, otherwise in the original, and finally to English books, accessible to most readers and likely to prove helpful for a general understanding of the subjects treated in the text.

L. R. L.

# THE BOOK OF THE POPES
## (*LIBER PONTIFICALIS*)

# I

## TO THE PONTIFICATE OF GREGORY I

# THE BOOK OF THE POPES

## (*LIBER PONTIFICALIS*)

### PREFACE

Jerome to the most blessed pope Damasus: [1]

We humbly beseech thy glorious holiness that as the apostolic see, which we understand is ruled by thy holiness,[2] . . . we bend in supplication and entreat that thou deign to impart to us in order the record of the deeds done in thy see from the principate of blessed Peter, the apostle, even to thine own day; that thus we may humbly ascertain which of the bishops of the aforesaid see attained the crown of martyrdom and which are judged to have transgressed the canons of the apostles.[3] Pray for us, most blessed pope. Given April 27. Received at Rome.

Damasus, bishop of the city of Rome, to Jerome.

The church rejoices already, drinking with satisfaction at thy fountain, and the thirst grows ever keener among its priests to hear of the past, in order that what is right may be recognized and what is wrong rejected. So all the record which the zeal of our see has been able to discover we send with gladness to thee, beloved. Pray for us unto the holy resurrection, brother and fellowpriest. Farewell in Christ, our God and Lord. Given May 23. Received September 26. Sent from Rome to Jerusalem.

---

[1] These letters are obvious forgeries, designed to give the authority of two great names to the ensuing narrative. The author is even naïve enough to attribute to Damasus and Jerome a history which covers a century or two beyond their time. See *Introduction*, pp. vii and viii.

[2] Some words are lost here. Traube suggests a reading: "that thou wouldest assist us by the authority vested in the apostolic see, which we understand," etc. Mommsen, *Liber Pontificalis*, p. 1.

[3] The collection of canons translated into Latin by Dionysius Exiguus at the beginning of the sixth century. Cf. Hefele, *Histoire des Conciles*, I, pp. 1203–1221 (H. Leclercq).

3

## I. Peter

| Blessed Peter,[1] the Antiochene, son of John, of the province of Galilee and the town of Bethsaida, brother of Andrew and chief of the apostles, | Blessed Peter, the apostle, and chief of the apostles, the Antiochene, son of John, of the province of Galilee and the town of Bethsaida, brother of Andrew, |
|---|---|

first occupied the seat of the bishop in Anthiocia [2] for 7 years. This Peter entered the city of Rome when Nero was Cæsar and there occupied the seat of the bishop for 25 years,

| 1 month and 8 days. | 2 months and 3 days. |
|---|---|

He was bishop in the time of Tiberius Cæsar and of Gaius and of Tiberius Claudius and of Nero.[3]

He wrote two epistles which are called catholic, and the gospel of Mark, for Mark was his disciple and son by baptism; afterwards the whole source of the four gospels, which were confirmed by inquiring of him, that is Peter, and obtaining his testimony; although one gospel is couched in Greek, another in Hebrew, another in Latin, yet by his testimony were they all confirmed.[4]

---

[1] As explained above in the *Introduction* (p. xii), when different versions of the narrative are found in the different epitomes or recensions of the *Liber Pontificalis*, the readings are set down, as here, in parallel columns, the older text being given first. Most of the following story of the life of the apostle is taken by the author of the *Lib. Pont.* from Jerome's *De Viris Illustribus*, c. 1 (ed. Richardson, pp. 6 and 7; *Texte und Untersuchungen zur Gesch. der altchristlichen Literatur*, vol. XIV). An excellent little hand book to consult for information on Jerome and the other church fathers who will be cited in the course of our text and notes is Bardenhewer's *Patrology*, translated by Strahan.

[2] Antioch, the ancient Antiochia. Corrupt or peculiar forms of proper names in the Latin text will be reproduced in the translation.

[3] Our author gives two incompatible traditions, the first that Peter did not come to Rome before the reign of Nero (*cf.* the late second century *Acta Petri et Pauli* in Tischendorf, *Acta Apostolorum Apocrypha*, p. 1, etc.), the second that after a pontificate of twenty-five years at Rome he was put to death under Nero. The latter is Jerome's version. The reader may find a discussion of the Petrine problem, with many further references, in the volume of this series devoted to the history of the Papacy.

[4] Duchesne suggests that the idea that the four gospels all issued from a single source was derived from the apsidal mosaics of fifth and sixth century churches which represented the four rivers of paradise all flowing out from one head. *Lib. Pont.*, vol. I, p. 119, n. 7.

He ordained two bishops, Linus and Cletus, who in person fulfilled all the service of the priest in the city of Rome for the inhabitants and for strangers; then the blessed Peter gave himself to prayer
and preaching, instructing the people.[1]

He disputed many times with Simon Magus both before Nero,
the emperor, and before the people, since by magic arts and trickery
Simon was drawing away those whom the blessed Peter was gathering into the faith of Christ. And while they debated once at great
length Simon was struck dead by the will of God.

He consecrated blessed Clement as bishop and committed to
him the government of the see and all the church, saying: [2] "As
unto me was delivered by my Lord Jesus Christ the power to gov-
ern and to bind and loose, so also I commit it unto thee, that thou
mayest ordain stewards over divers matters who will carry onward
the work of the church and mayest thyself not become engrossed
with the cares of the world but mayest strive to give thyself solely
to prayer and preaching to the people."

After he had thus disposed affairs he received the crown of martyrdom with Paul in the year 38 after the Lord's passion.[3]

He was buried also on the Via Aurelia, in the shrine of Apollo,
near the place where he was crucified, near the palace of Nero, in
the Vatican,[4] near the triumphal district,[5] on June 29.

---

[1] Rufinus, *Preface* to the apocryphal Clementine *Recognitions; cf. infra*, p. 7, n. 4.

[2] This passage is taken from the apocryphal *Epistle of Clement to James*, c. 2 and 5;
prefixed to the *Recognitions. Cf. infra*, p. 8, n. 2.

[3] Our author follows here the Paschal tables of the fifth century, according to which
Christ was crucified in the year 29. Duchesne, *op. cit.*, p. 119, n. 12. Eusebius'
*Chronicle* says that Peter and Paul died in the thirteenth year of Nero's reign, the
211th Olympiad, the year 2083 of the Jewish calendar, which would correspond to
our year 67 A.D. The persecution of Nero, however, took place in 64 A.D. The
earliest passage that may be construed as a reference to the martyrdom of the two
apostles at Rome occurs in the *First Epistle of Clement to the Corinthians*, written probably about 90–100 A.D. It is translated in the *Loeb Classical Library, Apostolic Fathers*,
vol. I. p. 17. *Cf.* also Lightfoot, *Apostolic Fathers*, Part I, for text and discussion.

[4] Vaticanus was the ancient name of the hill forming the prolongation of the Janiculum toward the north, and the Campus or Ager Vaticanus was the space between
the foot of the hill and the Janiculum and the Tiber. Here the word is used to denote
this low region stretching back from the river.

[5] Jerome says, "near the Via Triumphalis." The tomb of Peter, now covered by
the crypt of the modern basilica, was situated between the Via Aurelia and the Via Triumphalis, on the outskirts of the circus of Nero, near a temple of Cybele, which through

He held three ordinations, 7 deacons, 10 priests, 3 bishops,[1] in the month of December.

He held ordinations in the month of December, 3 bishops, 10 priests, 7 deacons.[2]

## II. LINUS

Linus, by nationality an Italian, from the province of Tuscany, son of Herculanus, occupied the see 11 years, 3 months and 12 days. He was bishop in the time of Nero from the consulship of Saturninus and Scipio (A.D. 56) until the year when Capito and Rufus were consuls (A.D. 67).

He was crowned with martyrdom.

He, by direction of the blessed Peter, decreed that a woman must veil her head to come into the church.[3]

He held two ordinations, 15 bishops, 18 priests.

He also was buried near the body of the blessed Peter in the Batican [4] about September 24.

a popular error was later called a temple of Apollo. Cf. Grisar, *Rome and the Popes in the Middle Ages*, I, pp. 277 ff.; C. Erbes, *Die Todestage der Apostel Paulus und Petrus und ihre Römischen Denkmäler*, in *Texte und Untersuchungen*, Neue Folge, IV.

[1] The three bishops were evidently Linus, Cletus and Clement. The number seven was attached to the deacons in order to ascribe to Peter the institution of the seven Roman deacons. Sozomen, the Greek historian, writing in the middle of the fifth century, mentions the curious fact that the Roman church never had more than seven deacons, a number which they considered sanctioned by the apostles. *Ecclesiastical History*, VII, c. 19; Eng. tr. in *Nicene and Post Nicene Fathers*, ser. 2, vol. II.

[2] One manuscript adds the following. "He first ordained the celebration of the mass to commemorate the Lord's passion, with bread and wine mixed with water and the Lord's prayer repeated alone and the sanctifying of the holy cross, a rite which the other holy apostles imitated for this celebration." The earliest detailed account of a Christian service is in Justin Martyr's *First Apology*, written for presentation to Antoninus Pius. It is translated in Cresswell, *Liturgy of the Apostolic Constitutions*, *Early Church Classics Series*.

[3] Linus is represented as associated with and acting under the direction of Peter. The ordinance may have been suggested by *I Corinthians*, xi. 5.

[4] A corruption, of course, for Vatican. In the seventeenth century some workmen digging near the tomb of Peter in the crypt of the present cathedral unearthed several ancient sarcophagi, one bearing an inscription in which the name Linus was thought to be decipherable. There were, however, no scholars at hand competent to verify the reading, the sarcophagus was not preserved where it could be studied, and De Rossi, the Italian authority on Christian epigraphy, is inclined to doubt the correctness of the report. Duchesne, *Lib. Pont.*, vol. I, p. 121, n. 3. Grisar, I, p. 279.

Pope St. Peter

Pope St. Clement I

## III. CLETUS

Cletus, by nationality a Roman, from the precinct Vicus Patricius,[1] son of Emilianus, occupied the see

7 years, 1 month and 20 days. | 12 years, 1 month and 11 days.

He was bishop in the time of Vespasian and Titus from

of Domitian |

the 7th consulship of Vespasian and the 5th of Domitian (A.D. 77) until the year when Domitian was consul for the 9th time and Rufus was consul with him (A.D. 83).

He was crowned with martyrdom.

He, by direction of the blessed Peter, ordained 25 priests[2] in the city of Rome

in the month of December. |

He also was buried near the body of the blessed Peter in the Batican, April 26.

And the bishopric was empty 20 days.


## IV. CLEMENT I

Clement, by nationality a Roman, from the district of the Celian Hill,[3] son of Faustinus, occupied the see 9 years, 2 months and 10 days. He was bishop in the time of Galba and Vespasian from the consulship of Tragalus and Italicus (A.D. 68) until the year when Vespasian was consul for the 9th time and Titus was consul with him (A.D. 79). He wrote many books in his zeal for the faith of the Christian religion[4] and was crowned with martyrdom.

[1] Near the modern Via Urbana, a region extending from the Viminal to the Esquiline.

[2] The number twenty-five was apparently chosen here in order to give apostolic sanction to the twenty-five titular or parish churches which existed in Rome at the close of the fifth century. *Cf. infra*, p. 38 and n. 3. On the actual slow development of the ecclesiastical organization see *Cambridge Medieval History*, vol. I, ch. vi.

[3] The author probably deduced the location of Clement's house from the situation of the church of San Clemente which stands between the Caelian and the Esquiline.

[4] The author may have in mind the ten books of the apocryphal *Recognitions* attributed to Clement and translated from Greek into Latin by Rufinus. The original Greek text has since been lost. Text by P. de Lagarde supersedes that of Migne, *Pat. Gr.*, vol. I. Translation, *Ante Nicene Fathers*, VIII.

He created 7 districts and assigned them to faithful notaries of the church that they might make diligent, careful and searching inquiry, each in his own district, regarding the acts of the martyrs.[1] He composed two epistles which are called catholic.

He, by direction of the blessed Peter, undertook the pontifical office of governing the church, even as Peter received the seat of authority from the Lord Jesus Christ; moreover in the epistle which he wrote to James [2] thou mayest learn in what manner the church was entrusted to him by the blessed Peter. Therefore Linus and Cletus are recorded before him for the reason that they were ordained bishops also by the chief of the apostles to perform the priestly ministry.

He held two ordinations in the month of December, 10 priests, 2 deacons and 15 bishops in divers places.[3]

He died a martyr

in the third year of Trajan.[4] 　　| in the third Trajan.

He also was buried in Greece,[5] November 24.

And the bishopric was empty 21 days.

---

[1] It seems far more likely that the seven ecclesiastical districts of Rome were the creation of Pope Fabianus in the third century. Our author is obviously anxious to give an early origin and a dignified function to the church notaries, a body to which he possibly belonged. *Cf. infra*, pp. 10, n. 3 and 24.

[2] This epistle was translated by Rufinus and early became prefixed to the pseudo-Clementine *Recognitions* just mentioned. In the Greek it is prefixed to the pseudo-Clementine *Homilies.* There is no reference here to the one authentic letter of Clement still preserved, written to the church of Corinth. Lightfoot, *St. Clement of Rome; Loeb Classical Library, The Apostolic Fathers*, vol. I.

[3] *I.e.* the priests and deacons were to serve in the city churches, the bishops in the dioceses about the city.

[4] Jerome also gives this as the date of Clement's death. *De Viris Illustribus*, c. xv; ed. Richardson, p. 17. A fragment of an inscription of the end of the fourth century has been discovered in the church of San Clemente, which was built over the site of Clement's own house. In this inscription the word MARTYR apparently follows the name of Clement.

[5] An allusion to the legend of the St. Clement, who was said to have been drowned in the Black Sea, and who became in time identified with Pope Clement of Rome. Duchesne, *Lib. Pont.*, vol. I, p. xci.

### V. ANENCLETUS

Ancclitus,[1] by nationality a Greek from Athens, son of Anthio-
cus, occupied the see

12 years, 10 months and 7 days. | 9 years, 2 months and 10 days.

He was bishop in the time of Domitian from the 10th consulship
of Domitian when Savinus was his colleague (A.D. 84) until the
year when Domitian was consul for the 17th time and Clement was
consul with him (A.D. 95).

He built and adorned the sepulchral monument[2] of the blessed
Peter, forasmuch as he had been made priest by the blessed Peter,
and other places of sepulchre for the burial of bishops. There he himself likewise was buried near the body of the blessed Peter, July 13.

He held 2 ordinations in the month of December, 5 priests, 3
deacons, 6 bishops in divers places.

And the bishopric was empty 13 days.


### VI. EVARISTUS

Euvaristus, by nationality a Greek

of Antioch,                                  |

son of a Jew named Judah, from the city of Bethlehem, occupied
the see

13 years, 7 months and 2 days. | 9 years, 10 months and 2 days.

---

[1] The fifth bishop of Rome was not Anencletus but Evaristus, who here comes
sixth. Anencletus and Cletus were two forms of the same name, and in the earliest
lists the bishop ordained by Peter was called by either one form or the other. The
compiler of the *Liberian Catalogue*, however, took the two forms for the names of two
different men and inserted them both into his list. The author of the *Lib. Pont.*
followed the *Liberian Catalogue*. For full explanation see Lightfoot, *Clement of Rome*
(*The Apostolic Fathers*), vol. I, p. 201 *et seq.*

[2] *I.e.* the tomb. The second century *Acta Petri et Pauli* (Tischendorf, *Acta Apostolorum Apocrypha*, p. 38) says that the bodies of the apostles were laid in a place outside the city for one year and seven months until their sepulchres were prepared for
them. These earliest tombs were small and inconspicuous and stood close among
pagan tombs in the same localities. In fact, remains of pagan tombs or columbaria
have been found so near to the resting places of both apostles as to be disturbed when
foundations were being laid for the heavy bronze baldachinos which cover the high
altars in both of the modern basilicas. The shrine of Peter was only large enough to

He was bishop in the time of Domitian and Nerva and Trajan, from the consulship of Valens and Vetus (A.D. 96) until the year when Gallus and Bradua were consuls (A.D. 108).

He was crowned with martyrdom.

He divided the parish churches in the city of Rome among the priests,[1] and ordained 7 deacons to keep watch over the bishop when he spoke, for the sake of the word of truth.[2]

He held 3 ordinations in the month of December, 17 priests, 2 deacons, 15 bishops in divers places.

He also was buried near the body of the blessed Peter in the Batican, October 27.

And the bishopric was empty 19 days.

## VII. ALEXANDER

Alexander, by nationality a Roman, son of Alexander, from the region of Caput Tauri,[3] occupied the see 10 years, 7 months and 2 days.

He was bishop in the time of Trajan until the year when Helianus and Vetus were consuls (A.D. 116).

He introduced the passion of the Lord into the words of the priest at the celebration of mass.[4]

---

contain niches or places for his immediate successors. Duchesne, *Lib. Pont.*, vol. I, p. 125, n. 2, and p. civ.

[1] Cletus is said to have ordained twenty-five priests to serve in the city, Evaristus to have assigned them their churches. *Cf. supra*, p. 7, and *infra*, p. 38, n. 2.

[2] Among the canons of the apocryphal council of Sylvester (*cf. infra*, p. 45, n. 1) is the following, which sheds some light on the passage here: "There shall be seven deacons to watch over the officiating bishop for the sake of the word of truth and catholic dogma and the wisdom of age, lest in speaking we say Father in place of Son or Holy Spirit in place of Father." Mommsen, *Lib. Pont.*, p. 9. On the institution of the seven Roman deacons see *supra*, p. 6, n. 1.

[3] Cf. Lanciani, *Ruins and Excavations of Ancient Rome*, p. 404. The district is mentioned again in the *Lib. Pont.* as the home of Anastasius II, and is said to be in the Fifth Region, which, if the reference be to the regions of Augustus, comprised a large part of the Esquiline Hill along the city wall. *Cf. infra*, p. 114. The boundaries of the seven ecclesiastical divisions, said to have been created by Fabianus (*Infra*, p. 24), are for the most part unknown. For an account of both civil and ecclesiastical divisions see Duchesne, *Mélanges d'Archéologie et d'Histoire*, vol. I, p. 126, Gregorovius, *History of Rome in the Middle Ages*, trans. Hamilton, vol. I, pp. 80–82. The latter gives the conjectural outlines of Fabianus' regions.

[4] *I.e.* Alexander introduced the passage beginning, "Qui pridie," into the liturgy

He was crowned with martyrdom and Eventius, the priest, and Theodulus, the deacon, were crowned together with him.

He appointed the blessing of the water of sprinkling and of salt in the dwellings of the people.[1]

He held 3 ordinations in the month of December, 6 priests, 2 deacons, 5 bishops in divers places.

He also was buried on the Via Nomentana, where he was beheaded,[2] not more than 7 miles from the city of Rome, May 3.

And the bishopric was empty 35 days.

## VIII. Xystus I

Xystus, by nationality a Roman, son of Pastor, from the district of the Via Lata, occupied the see 10 years,

3 months and 21 days.      |    2 months and 1 day.

He was bishop in the time of Adrian, until the year when Verus and Anniculus were consuls (A.D. 126).[3]

He was crowned with martyrdom.

He ordained that consecrated vessels should not be touched except by the ministering clergy.[4]

He ordained that no bishop who had been summoned to the

Roman          |

apostolic see should be received upon his return to his parish,

This, like all accounts of early papal decrees, is of course fabrication, an attempt to assign a definite, primitive origin to the order prevailing in the sixth century.

[1] An allusion to the custom of blessing private houses with a sprinkling of water and of blessing the salt which the owner offers.

[2] The "tomb of Alexander" is mentioned in an itinerary attributed to William of Malmesbury. The site of it, near the Via Nomentana, was rediscovered in 1855. But it is probable that there were two Alexanders and that the martyr has been erroneously identified with the pope. Duchesne, *Lib. Pont.*, vol. I, pp. xci *et seq.*

[3] *The Liberian Catalogue* (*cf. Introduction*, p. vi) gives the consular reckoning more exactly; viz. "from the consulship of Niger and Apronianus (A.D. 117) to the 3rd consulship of Verus when Ambibulus was consul with him (A.D. 126)." The text of the *Catalogue* is printed in Duchesne, *Lib. Pont.*, vol. I, pp. 2–9; also in Lightfoot's *Clement of Rome*, pp. 253–258.

[4] One of several decrees ascribed to these first popes emphasizing the sacredness of altar vessels and hangings. *Cf. infra*, pp. 16 and 91.

unless he brought with him the "formata" of general greeting from the apostolic see.[1] | unless he brought with him the letter of general greeting from the apostolic see, which is the "formata."

He ordained that at the beginning of mass the priest should chant to the people the hymn, "Sanctus, sanctus, sanctus, dominus deus Sabaoth," etc.[2]

He held 3 ordinations in the month of December, 11 priests, 4 deacons, 4 bishops in divers places.

He also was buried near the body of the blessed Peter in the Batican, April 3.

And the bishopric was empty 2 months.

## IX. TELESPHORUS

Telesphorus, by nationality a Greek, previously an anchorite, occupied the see 11 years, 3 months and 21 days. He was bishop in the time of Antoninus and Marcus.[3]

He ordained that the fast of seven weeks should be kept before Easter.[4]

He was crowned with martyrdom.

He appointed that at the season of the nativity of our Lord Jesus Christ | and that at the season of the Lord's nativity

[1] This seems to be a garbled form of an edict recorded in the acts of the spurious Council of Sylvester (*supra*, p. ix, *infra*, p. 45, n. 1), which required each bishop to take home with him a written report of the decisions of the council, so that they might be accurately known to the people. The ordinance as it stands in our text is unintelligible. Duchesne, *op. cit.*, p. 128, n. 4.

[2] The "Sanctus," like the "Sursum corda" and the opening words of the preface, "Vere dignum," etc., are included in every liturgy that has come down to us. They were perhaps in use even as early as Xystus. Duchesne, *op. cit.*, p. 128, n. 5.

[3] The *Liberian Catalogue* gives the consulships omitted here; viz. "from the consulship of Titianus and Gallicanus (A.D. 127) until the year when Cæsar and Balbinus were consuls (A.D. 137)."

[4] The fast before Easter was observed before the pontificate of Telesphorus. It is

Pope St. Evaristus

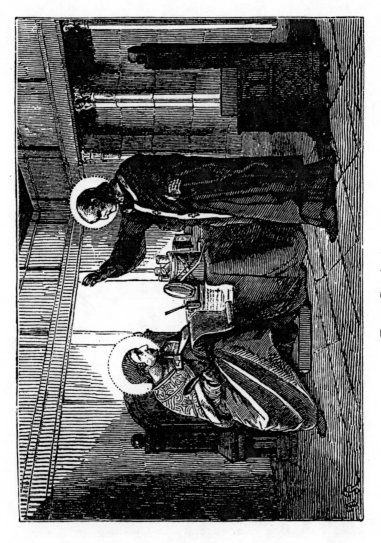

Pope St. Anicetus

masses should be celebrated during the night;[1] for in general no one presumed to celebrate mass before tierce, the hour when our Lord ascended the cross;

| and that at the opening of the sacrifice | and that before the sacrifice |

the angelic hymn should be repeated, namely, "Gloria in excelsis deo"

| etc., but only upon the night of the Lord's nativity.[2] | He was crowned with martyrdom. |

He also was buried near the body of the blessed Peter in the Batican, January 2.

He held 4 ordinations in the month of December, 12 priests, 8 deacons and 13 bishops in divers places.

And the bishopric was empty 7 days.


## X. Hyginus

Yginus, by nationality a Greek, previously a philosopher of Athens, whose ancestry I have not been able to ascertain, occupied the see

| 10 years, 3 months and 7 days. | 4 years, 3 months and 4 days. |

described by Irenæus a few years later as a custom of the ancestors, dating back nearly to apostolic times. The length, however, was at first variable. See the interesting discussion in Eusebius' *Church History*, lib. V, c. 24, trans. McGiffert, *Nicene and Post Nicene Fathers*, ser. II, vol. I, p. 243. Mommsen cites the passage here as an indication that the *Lib. Pont.* was not compiled until the seventh century. He points out that under Leo I, Gelasius and Gregory I the Lenten fast lasted only six weeks and that therefore our author must have written after the death of Gregory. *Lib. Pont.*, p. xvii. Cf. Introduction, p. xii.

[1] The night mass at Christmas is still a feature of the Roman ritual. The author of the *Lib. Pont.* is the earliest writer to allude to it. It can hardly have been instituted before the date of the Nativity was fixed during the fourth century.

[2] Pope Symmachus introduced the angelic hymn into all masses celebrated on Sundays or feast days. *Cf. infra*, p. 123. The institution applied, however, only to papal masses. The priests in Rome were forbidden to chant the "Gloria," except at Easter, as late as the eleventh century. In the early Gallican ritual the "Benedictus" was sung at the opening of mass instead of the "Gloria." Duchesne, *Lib. Pont.*, vol. I, p. 130, n. 5. Atchley, *Ordo Romanus Primus*, pp. 71-72.

He was bishop in the time of Verus and Marcus, from the consulship of Magnus and Camerinus (A.D. 138) until the year when Orfitus and

Camerinus were consuls.         | Priscus were consuls (A.D. 149).

He set in order the clergy and distributed ranks.[1]

He held 3 ordinations in the month of December, 15 priests, 5 deacons, 6 bishops in divers places.

He also was buried near the body of the blessed Peter in the Batican, January 11.

And the bishopric was empty 3 days.


## XI. Pius I

Pius, by nationality an Italian, son of Rufinus, brother of the shepherd,[2] from the city of Aquilegia,[3] occupied the see 19 years, 4 months

and 21 days.                    | and 3 days.

He was bishop in the time of Antoninus Pius, from the consulship of Clarus and Severus (A.D. 146).[4]

While he was bishop,

his brother                     |

Hermas wrote a book in which he set forth the commandment which the angel of the Lord delivered to him, coming to him in the garb of a shepherd and commanding him that

---

[1] A vague phrase. The author may merely intend to convey that Hyginus carried further the organization of the clergy into definite ranks and the assignment of special tasks and functions.

[2] Hermas, surnamed Pastor or Shepherd, from the title Pastor or Ποιμήν of his book. See in the text below. He was a second century writer whose treatise, which contained an account of a revelation from an angel, was once in such repute as to be read in the churches. It was composed originally in Greek but was early translated into Latin. Jerome says of it that in his day it was still read in the churches of Greece, although it had almost been forgotten among the Latins. *De Viris Illustribus*, c. x, ed. Richardson, p. 14. An English translation of *The Shepherd of Hermas* may be found in volume II of *The Apostolic Fathers* in the *Loeb Classical Library*.

[3] *I.e.* Aquileia.

[4] The second pair of consuls is here omitted; "until the year when the two Augusti were consuls (A.D. 161)." *Liberian Catalogue*.

the holy feast of Easter      |    Easter

be observed upon the Lord's day.[1]

He ordained that a heretic coming out from the heresy of the Jews should be received and baptised;[2] and he made a regulation for the church.

He held 5 ordinations in the month of December, 19 priests, 21 deacons, bishops 12 in number in divers places.

He also was buried near the body of the blessed Peter in the Batican, July 11.

And the bishopric was empty 14 days.[3]


## XII. Anicetus

Anicetus, by nationality a Syrian, son of John, from the town of Humisa,[4] occupied the see

9 years, 3 months and 3 days.    |    11 years, 4 months and 3 days.

He was bishop in the time of Severus[5] and Marcus, from the consulship of Gallicanus and Vetus (A.D. 150) until the year when Præsens and Rufinus were consuls (A.D. 153).

He forbade the clergy to grow long hair, following thus the precept of the apostle.[6]

He held 5 ordinations in the month of December, 19 priests, 4 deacons, 9 bishops in divers places.

---

[1] There is no mention of Easter in the book of Hermas.

[2] Duchesne cites the fact that Prudentius in his *Apotheosis* classes the Jews with the heretics. *Lib. Pont.*, vol. I, p. 132, n. 5.

[3] In manuscripts of the eleventh century the following sentences have been added to the life of Pius, drawn undoubtedly from the story of SS. Pudentiana and Praxedis (*Cf. Acta Sanctorum*, May, vol. IV, p. 299.) "He by request of the blessed Praxedis dedicated a church in the baths of Novatus in the Vicus Patricius to the honor of her sister, the holy Pudentiana, where also he offered many gifts and frequently he ministered, offering sacrifice to the Lord. Moreover he erected a font of baptism and with his own hand he blessed and dedicated it and many who gathered to the faith he baptised in the name of the Trinity." The church of Santa Pudenziana is mentioned in an epitaph of A.D. 384. For the Vicus Patricius, *cf. supra*, p. 7, n. 1.

[4] *I.e.* Emesa, an important city of northern Syria.

[5] An error for Verus. The chronology is mistaken. The pontificate was probably from 154-5 to 166-7. *Cf.* Hefele, *Hist. d. Conciles*, I, p. 136.

[6] Jerome alludes to a prohibition of this sort. *In Ezech.*, XLIV, 20. Quoted by Duchesne, *Lib. Pont.*, vol. I, p. 134, n. 3. *Cf. I Corinthians*, xi. 14.

He also died a martyr and was buried

| near the body of the blessed Peter in the Vatican, | in the cemetery of Calistus,[1] |

April 20.

And the bishopric was empty 17 days.

## XIII. SOTER

Soter, by nationality a Campanian, son of Concordius, from the city of Fundi,[2] occupied the see 9 years, 6 months and 21 days. He was bishop in the time of Severus,[3] from the consulship of Rusticus and Aquilinus (A.D. 162) until the year when Cetegus and Clarus were consuls (A.D. 170).

He ordained that no monk should touch the consecrated altar cloth or should offer incense in the holy church.[4]

He held 3 ordinations in the month of December, 18 priests, 9 deacons, 11 bishops in divers places.

He also was buried

| near the body of the blessed Peter, | in the cemetery of Calistus on the Via Appia,[5] |

April 22.

And the bishopric was empty 21 days.

## XIV. ELEUTHERIUS

Eleuther, by nationality a Greek, son of Habundius, from the town of Nicopolis,[6] occupied the see 15 years, 3 months and 2 days.

[1] This cemetery, if in existence at the time, was certainly not known by the name of Callistus, who was the fifth pope after Anicetus. *Cf. infra*, p. 21. The reading in the first column is probably the correct one.

[2] The modern Fondi.

[3] This should be Verus.

[4] Several manuscripts read "no nun" instead of "no monk." They are perhaps influenced by the passage in the life of Pope Boniface I. "Boniface decreed that no woman or nun should touch the consecrated altar cloth." *Infra*, p. 91. The author of the *Lib. Pont.* undoubtedly belonged to the secular clergy.

[5] *Cf. supra*, n. 1.

[6] The city of Nicopolis in Epirus at the entrance to the Gulf of Arta.

He was bishop in the time of Antoninus and Commodus until the year when Paternus and Bradua were consuls (A.D. 185).

He received a letter from Lucius, king of Britain, asking him to appoint a way by which Lucius might become a Christian.[1]

| He also decreed | He also confirmed again the decree |

that no kind of food

in common use

should be rejected especially by the Christian faithful, inasmuch as God created it; provided, however, it were rational food and fit for human kind.[2]

He held 3 ordinations in the month of December, 12 priests, 8 deacons, 15 bishops in divers places.

He also was buried near the body of the blessed Peter in the Batican, May 24.

And the bishopric was empty 15 days.


## XV. VICTOR

Victor, by nationality an African, son of Felix, occupied the see

| 15 years, 3 months and 10 days. | 10 years, 2 months and 10 days. |

He was bishop in the time of Cæsar Augustus,[3] from the 2nd consulship of Commodus when Gravio [4] was his colleague (A.D. 186) until the year when Lateranus and Rufinus were consuls (A.D. 197).

---

[1] The source of or ground for this extraordinary statement is quite unknown. It appears first here in the *Lib. Pont.* Bede and other medieval English chroniclers built up considerable legend upon it. Bede, *Ecclesiastical History*, I, c. 4, tr. Giles (Bohn's Library), p. 10.

[2] The apostle Paul had already prohibited the classification of certain foods as unclean. *Romans*, xiv; *Colossians*, ii. 16, 17; *I Timothy*, iv. 3, etc. Our author may have had in mind the Manichean practice of condemning wine and meat, of which much was heard in Rome in the fifth century.

[3] Severus.

[4] A corruption for Glabrio.

He appointed that the holy feast of Easter should be observed upon the Lord's day,

| | |
|---|---|
| as Eleuther had done. | as Pius had done.[1] |

He added acolytes to the clergy.[2]

He was crowned with martyrdom.

He also ordained that, at a time of necessity, any gentile who came to be baptised, wherever it might be, whether in a river or in the sea or in a spring

| | |
|---|---|
| or in a marsh, if only he pronounced the Christian confession of faith, | if only he said clearly the Christian confession of faith, |

should be thereafter a Christian in full standing.[3]

He held 2 ordinations in the month of December, 4 priests, 7 deacons, 12 bishops in divers places.

| | |
|---|---|
| He also summoned a council and an inquiry was made of Theophilus, bishop of Alexan- | He instituted an inquiry among the clergy concerning the cycle of Easter and the Lord's |

---

[1] The feast of Easter was celebrated on Sunday long before the time of Victor. See *supra*, p. 15. There was, however, a fresh discussion about this time as to the mode of determination of the date, of which Jerome preserves a reminiscence when he says that Victor wrote treatises "on the question of Easter and other matters." *De Viris Illustribus*, c. 34, ed. Richardson, p. 25. Eusebius has an interesting account of the disagreement between those who followed the Jewish custom and celebrated Easter on the Passover day, whenever in the week it fell, and those who insisted upon celebrating it on Sunday as the day of resurrection. *Church History*, V, cc. 23-25, trans. McGiffert, pp. 241-244. Jaffé (*Regesta*, vol. I, p. 11) gives a decree of the synod held at Rome between 190 and 194, which provided that the Lord's resurrection should be celebrated always upon Sunday. It seems likely that Victor actually excommunicated the Eastern churches which persisted in adhering to the Jewish calendar. On the importance of Victor's pontificate see Langen, *Geschichte der Römischen Kirche* and the volume on the early papacy in this series.

[2] There is some doubt as to the translation of this sentence. "Hic fecit sequentes cleros." It may also mean: "he instituted clergy in attendance," *i.e.* the notaries and subdeacons of the papal court as distinguished from the local or parish clergy connected with the different local churches. *Cf.* Duchesne, *Lib. Pont.*, vol. I, p. 137, n. 4, and Ducange, *Glossarium Mediæ et Infimæ Latinitatis*, under *Sequens*. Harnack, *Sources of the Apostolic Canons*, tr. Wheatley, p. 88, n. 3.

[3] Pope Gelasius in a letter written in 494 to the bishops of Lucania makes a similar provision for baptism in time of emergency. Mansi, *Conciliorum Amplissima Collectio*, vol. VIII, p. 37. Jaffé, *Regesta*, vol. I, p. 85, 636.

dria, concerning Easter and the first day of the week and the moon.

day for Easter and he gathered together the priests and the bishops. Then Theophilus, bishop of Alexandria, was questioned and in the assembly it was decided that the Lord's day between the 14th day of the moon in the first month and the 21st day of the moon should be kept as the holy feast of Easter.[1]

He was buried near the body of the blessed apostle Peter in the Batican, July 28.

And the bishopric was empty 12 days.

## XVI. ZEPHYRINUS

Zepherinus, by nationality a Roman, son of Habundius, occupied the see

18 years, 3 months and 10 days. | 8 years, 7 months and 10 days.

He was bishop in the time of Antoninus and Severus, from the consulship of Saturninus and Gallicanus (A.D. 198) to the year when Presens and Stricatus were consuls (A.D. 217).

He decreed that in the presence of all the clergy and the faithful laity every cleric, deacon or priest, should be ordained.[2]

He also made a regulation for the church,[3] that there should be vessels of glass before the priests in the church and servitors to hold them while the bishop was celebrating mass and priests standing about him. Thus mass should be celebrated and the clergy

---

[1] *I.e.* between full moon and the third quarter of the moon. The first month was March. The narrative here again is a confused memory of the great controversy over Easter. *Cf. supra*, p. 18, n. 1. The Theophilus who took part in the synod was bishop of Cæsarea. He has been mistaken for the later and more famous Theophilus of Alexandria. The present lunar method of reckoning the date was not worked out until the fifth century. Duchesne, *op. cit.*, p. 138, n. 6.

[2] So far as we have record, the ordination ceremonies of the clergy have always been public.

[3] The following passage is corrupt and obscure. It must be read freely in order to get any meaning from it. It deals apparently with the part played by the assisting clergy in the episcopal mass.

should assist in all the ceremony, except in that which belongs only to the bishop; from the consecration of the bishop's hand the priest should receive the consecrated wafer to distribute to the people.

He held 4 ordinations in the month of December, 14 priests, 7 deacons, 13 bishops in divers places.

He also was buried in his own cemetery near the cemetery of Calistus on the Via Appia, August 25.[1]

And the bishopric was empty 6 days.


## XVII. Callistus I

Calistus, by nationality a Roman, son of Domitius, from the district Urbs Ravennantium,[2] occupied the see

| 5 years, | 6 years, |

2 months and 10 days. He was bishop in the time of Macrinus and Theodoliobullus,[3] from the consulship of Antoninus (A.D. 218) and of Alexander (A.D. 222).

He was crowned with martyrdom.

He instituted a fast from corn, wine and oil upon the Sabbath day thrice in the year, according to the word of the prophet, of a fourth, of a seventh, and of a tenth.[4]

He built a basilica beyond the Tiber.[5]

He held 5 ordinations in the month of December, 16 priests, 4 deacons, 8 bishops in divers places.

---

[1] Later tradition fixed Zephyrinus' tomb in a small basilica over the catacomb of Callistus. Beginning with him the popes of the third century were buried in the cemeteries about the Via Appia, no longer in the resting place of the apostle Peter, which may have been full.

[2] A district beyond the Tiber peopled by settlers from Ravenna, the modern Trastevere.

[3] A corrupt form for Heliogabalus.

[4] *Zechariah*, VIII, 19. Some manuscripts give the reading, "in the fourth, the seventh and the tenth months." If one adds the fast of Lent, which took place during the first month, March, one has the fasts of the four seasons which are mentioned in early Roman liturgies and in the homilies of St. Leo. Duchesne, *Lib. Pont.*, vol. I, p. 141, n. 4.

[5] On or near the site of Santa Maria in Trastevere, which was called sometimes the church of Callistus as late as the eighth century.

Pope St. Zephyrinus

Pope St. Callistus I

He also was buried in the cemetery of Calipodius on the Via Aurelia at the third milestone,[1] October 14.

He constructed another cemetery on the Via Appia, where many priests and martyrs rest, which is called even to this day the cemetery of Calistus.

And the bishopric was empty 16 days.

## XVIII. URBANUS I

Urbanus, by nationality a Roman, son of Pontianus, occupied the see

| | |
|---|---|
| 9 years, 1 month and 2 days.[2] | 4 years, 10 months and 12 days. |
| He instituted sacred vessels of silver, | He had all sacred vessels made of silver, |

and he gave as an offering 25 patens of silver.[3]

| | | | |
|---|---|---|---|
| He also obtained glory as a confessor in the time of Diocletian.[4] | He was himself a confessor. | He was himself a confessor in the time of Diocletian. | He was himself a confessor at the time when Maximin and Africanus were consuls. |

He by his teaching turned many to baptism and faith and among them Valerianus, a man of high nobility, husband of the holy Cecilia.

---

[1] The catacomb of Calepodius on the Via Aurelia, of which few traces now are visible. The body of Callistus may have been hurriedly buried there because it was nearer to the scene of his martyrdom than his own cemetery. For the traditional account of his death see *Acta Sanctorum*, October, vol. VI, p. 430.

[2] The *Liberian Catalogue* says: "He was bishop in the time of Alexander, from the consulship of Maximus and Elianus (A.D. 223) until the year when Agricola and Clementinus were consuls (A.D. 230)."

[3] The number is intended probably to correspond to that of the parish churches, one paten for each church. Glass was also a favorite material for the sacred vessels at this early period. *Cf. supra*, pp. 7, n. 1; 19. Lowrie, *Christian Art and Archæology*, pp. 343, 357.

[4] A careless anachronism. The history of Pope Urban has been apparently confused with that of a confessor Urban, who may have lived under Diocletian.

These he guided even to the palm of martyrdom,[1]

| and many were crowned with martyrdom through his words. | and through his exhortations many were crowned with martyrdom. |

He held 5 ordinations in the month of December, 19 priests, 7 deacons, 8 bishops in divers places.

He also was buried in the cemetery of Pretextatus on the Via Appia.[2]

The blessed Tiburtius buried him, May 19.

And the bishopric was empty 30 days.

## XIX. PONTIANUS (230–235)

Pontianus, by nationality a Roman, son of Calpurnius, occupied the see

| 5 years, 2 months and 22 days. | 9 years, 5 months and 2 days. |

He was crowned with martyrdom. He was bishop in the time of Alexander, from the consulship of Pompeianus and Pelinianus (A.D. 231).

At that time Pontianus, the bishop, and Ypolitus, the priest,[3]

---

[1] The *Passion of St. Cecilia*, with some form of which the author of the *Lib. Pont.* was acquainted, was compiled, in the opinion of Mommsen, during the fifth century and probably in Africa. The following is the earliest version given in the *Acta Sanctorum* (May, vol. VI, p. 11). "Cecilia, a virgin of lofty rank, carried always the gospel of Christ hidden in her bosom. . . . She was espoused to a young man, Valerianus. . . . Valerianus . . . found the holy Urbanus, the bishop, who had already been twice a confessor and was in hiding among the tombs of the martyrs. . . . 'Dost thou call thyself that Urbanus whom the Christians entitle their pope? I hear that he is now condemned a second time and again he has betaken himself into hiding for the same cause.' . . . (Valerianus and Tiburtius, his brother,) were executed with the sword. . . . The holy Urbanus baptised in her (Cecilia's) house more than four hundred of both sexes. . . . Almachius commanded that Cecilia should be brought before him and he asked her, saying. . . . 'Of what state art thou?' Cecilia said, 'A free woman and a noble of high rank.' . . . The examiner beheaded (Cecilia)."

[2] Pope Urban was buried in the cemetery of Callistus, where his epitaph has been discovered. Another Urban, perhaps the confessor, was buried in the cemetery of Praetextatus and his name preserved by the neighboring church of San Urbano alla Caffarella. Duchesne, *Lib. Pont.*, vol. I, p. 143, n. 5.

[3] This is thought to be the famous Hippolytus, bishop of Porto, mentioned in the *Introduction*, p. iv, whose statue is now in the Lateran museum. A translation of his work, *On the Refutation of Heresies*, which treats of pagan science and philosophy,

were transported into exile by Alexander to the island of Bucina[1] in Sardinia during the consulship of Severus and Quintianus (A.D. 235). In that island he was maltreated and beaten with clubs and he died, October 30. In his place Antheros was ordained, November 21.

He held 2 ordinations in the month of December, 6 priests, 5 deacons, 6 bishops in divers places.

| And the blessed Fabianus brought him back in a boat and buried him in the cemetery of Calistus on the Via Appia.[2] And the bishopric was empty 10 days. | And the blessed Fabianus brought him back with clergy in a ship and buried him in the catacombs. | And he was buried in the cemetery of Calistus on the Via Appia. The bishopric was empty from the day of his burial until November 21. |

## XX. ANTEROS (235–236)

Antheros, by nationality a Greek, son of Romulus, occupied the see

| 1 month and 12 days. | 12 years, 1 month and 12 days. |

He was crowned with martyrdom at the time when Maximin and Africanus were consuls (A.D. 236).[3]

He collected carefully from the notaries the acts of the martyrs and of the readers and deposited them in the church,

| because at one time Maximus, a priest, had been a martyr.[4] | for the sake of one Maximinus a priest, who had been crowned with martyrdom. |

jugglery and priestcraft, as well as of Jewish and Christian heresies, is in the *Ante Nicene Fathers*, vol. V. *Cf.* Lightfoot, *Apostolic Fathers*, Part I, Vol. II, pp. 316–477.

[1] No island of this name is known near Sardinia. The word is probably garbled.

[2] The epitaph of Pontianus has disappeared, but on the doorway of the papal crypt among other graffiti the following words have been roughly scrawled: "Mayest thou live, Pontianus, . . . in God with all." They may have been written by a witness of his interment. Duchesne, *Lib. Pont.*, vol. I, p. 146, n. 8.

[3] The *Liberian Catalogue* says of Anteros simply that he died after a pontificate of forty days. His name does not occur in the lists of martyrs.

[4] No other clear reference to this martyred priest, Maximus or Maximinus, has

| | |
|---|---|
| He created one bishop in the city of Fundi, in the Campania, during the month of December. | He held one ordination, 1 bishop, in the month of December. |

He also was buried in the cemetery of Calistus on the Via Appia,[1] January 3.

And the bishopric was empty 13 days.


## XXI. FABIANUS (236–250)

Fabianus, by nationality a Roman, son of Fabius, occupied the see 14 years,

| | |
|---|---|
| 1 month and 10 days. | 11 months and 11 days. |

He was crowned with martyrdom. He was bishop in the time of Maximus and Africanus (A.D. 236) until the year when Decius was consul the 2nd time and Quadratus was his colleague (A.D. 250), and he suffered January 29.

He divided the districts among the deacons[2] and created 7 subdeacons to be associated with the 7 notaries, that they might faithfully compile the acts of the martyrs, omitting nothing.[3]

And he commanded many buildings to be erected throughout the cemeteries.[4]

And after his passion Moyses and Maximus, priests, and Nicostratus, a deacon, were seized and committed to prison.

At that time Novatus arrived from Africa and drew away from

---

come down to us. On the other hand there are numerous unidentified martyrs of the name in the Roman calendars and the date of his death falls during the persecution of Maximin. The author of the *Lib. Pont.* was in possession of a tradition or a history which has since been lost. Duchesne, *Lib. Pont.*, vol. I, pp. xcv–xcvi.

[1] His brief epitaph is in the papal crypt. Duchesne, *ibid.*, p. 147, n. 4.

[2] On the ecclesiastical divisions of the city, see *supra*, p. 10, n. 3.

[3] The seven subdeacons of Rome are mentioned in a letter of Cornelius written about two years after Fabianus' death to Fabius of Antioch. Eusebius, *Church History*, VI, c. 43, tr. McGiffert, *Nicene and Post Nicene Fathers*, Series 2, vol. I, p. 288. *Infra*, p. 35, n. 1. Harnack, *Sources of the Apostolic Canons*, tr. Wheatley, pp. 93–95. On the work of the notaries in preserving records of the martyrs see *supra*, p. 8, n. 1.

[4] De Rossi thinks that Fabianus continued the construction of the cemetery of Callistus both above and below ground. Duchesne, *Lib. Pont.*, vol. I, p. 149, n. 5.

the church Novatian and certain confessors.[1]  Afterwards Moyses died in prison, when he had been there 11 months; and therefore many Christians fled to divers places.

He held 5 ordinations in the month of December, 22 priests, 7 deacons, 11 bishops in divers places.

He also was buried in the cemetery of Calistus on the Via Appia,[2] January 20.

And the bishopric was empty 7 days.

## XXII. CORNELIUS (251–253)

Cornelius, by nationality a Roman, son of Castinus, occupied the see 2 years,

| | |
|---|---|
| 3 months and 10 days. | 2 months and 3 days.[3] |

He was crowned with martyrdom.

While he was bishop Novatus ordained Novatian without the church and Nicostratus in Africa.[4]  After this the confessors who had left Cornelius returned into the church together with Maximus, the priest, who had been with Moyses, and they became faithful confessors.  Then Cornelius, the bishop, was banished to Centumcellæ [5] and there he received a letter written and sent for his encouragement by Cyprian, which Cyprian wrote in prison to tell of Celerinus, the reader.[6]

[1] This passage and the allusion to the consecration of Novatian as antipope in the time of Cornelius refer to the beginnings of the Novatian schism which lasted two centuries and spread over the empire.  Novatus, Novatian and their adherents refused to readmit to communion those Christians who under stress of persecution had sacrificed to idols after being baptized.  Eusebius has an animated account of the discussion over this question at the close of the terrible persecution of Decius; *Church History*, VI, cc. 42–45, tr. McGiffert, pp. 285–291.

[2] The name and title of Fabianus are cut into the stone of the papal crypt in the catacomb of Callistus, close to those of Anteros.  The letters MTP, the abbreviation for martyr, have been added to the inscription, but they are not cut so deep and are probably by a later hand.  Duchesne, *ibid.*, p. 149, n. 8.

[3] The *Liberian Catalogue* adds, "from the 3rd consulship of Decius and the 2nd of Decius (A.D. 251) to the year when Gallus and Volusianus were consuls (A.D. 252)."

[4] *Cf.* n. 1 on this page.  Also for letters of Cornelius describing some of these events, Jaffé, *Regesta*, vol. I, p. 17, 106; p. 18, 111.

[5] The modern Civitavecchia.

[6] The *Passio Cornelii*, composed perhaps in the fifth century, thus expands this passage.  "At the same time the blessed Cyprian, the bishop, wrote to the blessed

He during his pontificate at the request of a certain matron, Lucina, took up the bodies of the apostles, blessed Peter and Paul, from the catacombs by night; first the body of the blessed Paul was received by the blessed Lucina and laid in her own garden on the Via Ostiensis,

| near the place | beside the place |

where he was beheaded ; the body of the blessed Peter was received by the blessed Cornelius, the bishop, and laid near the place where he was crucified, among the bodies of the holy bishops, in the shrine of Apollo, on the Mons Aureus,[1] in the Batican, by the palace of Nero, June 29.[2]

Afterwards he held one ordination, 8 priests, and walked by night from Centumcellæ.

---

Cornelius, while he was in custody, to tell of Celerinus, the reader, what stripes he had endured for the faith and confession of Christ." As a matter of fact Cyprian himself was not in prison when he wrote to Cornelius in exile. His letter has been preserved, along with others in which the sufferings of Celerinus are described. *Epp.*, lx, xxi, xxxix, *Corpus Scriptorum Ecclesiasticorum Latinorum*, vol. III, pp. 691–695, 529–532, 581–585; Eng. tr. in *Ante Nicene Fathers*, vol. V, *Epp.* lvi, xx, xxxiii; pp. 350–352, 298–299, 312–314. The tenor of the letter to Cornelius may be inferred from an extract. "It cannot be sufficiently expressed how great were the exultation and the joy here when we heard of your success and courage, that you had stood forth as a leader of confession to the brethren there, and that, moreover, the confession of the leader had been multiplied by the loyalty of the brethren; so that while you precede them to glory you have made many your companions in glory and have persuaded the people to confess by being first yourself prepared to confess on behalf of all."

[1] A popular name for the Janiculum, perhaps a corruption from Mons Aurelius. The name is perpetuated by the church of San Pietro in Montorio.

[2] A very ancient tradition, confirmed by an inscription of Damasus, ascribes to the bodies of the two apostles a temporary sojourn in a crypt known as "ad Catacumbas," beneath the present church of San Sebastiano on the Via Appia. Duchesne supposes that this sojourn took place during the persecution of Diocletian, that the sacred bodies were then removed from their tombs in the Vatican and on the Via Ostiense (*Cf. supra*, p. 5, *infra*, p. 57) and laid together in this more inconspicuous spot for the sake of safety. He argues that the author here is confusing the date when they were hidden away with the date of their restoration, that the persecution under Cornelius was the occasion of their concealment and that the peace under Constantine was in all likelihood the signal for their return to their venerated sepulchres. Duchesne, *op. cit.*, p. civ, and p. 151, n. 7. Also *infra* under Damasus, p. 81.

At that time Decius heard that he had received a letter from the blessed Cyprian, bishop of Carthage,[1]

| | | | |
|---|---|---|---|
| and he had him brought from Centumcellæ, | | He sent to Centumcellæ and brought out blessed Cornelius, | |
| and he summoned him before his presence at night | and he summoned him before his presence in Terlude,[2] in front of the temple of the palace, | and he summoned him before his presence with the prefect for the city in an interlude of the night, | and he summoned him before his presence with the prefect of the city in an interlude of the night, in front of the temple of Pallas, |
| and said to him: | and came near to him and said: | and said to him: | and said to him: |

"Hast thou determined to regard neither the gods nor the ordinances

| of our ancestors | of princes |
|---|---|

and to have no fear of our threatenings, that thou receivest and sendest letters harmful to the state?"

Cornelius, the bishop, answered and said: "I have received a letter concerning the crown of the Lord, not harmful to the state

| but rather succor to the soul." | but counsel to the spirit." |
|---|---|

| Then Decius ordered that he be beaten upon the mouth with | Then Decius, full of wrath, ordered that the blessed Cornelius | Then he ordered that he be beaten upon the mouth with a |
|---|---|---|

---

[1] The following account of the trial and execution of Cornelius by Decius is entirely apocryphal. Decius died almost two years before Cornelius and the latter perished in exile at Civitavecchia. The *Liberian Catalogue* preserves the earlier and authentic tradition: "being banished to Centumcellæ he there fell asleep in glory."

[2] A corrupt form. Some manuscripts read, "in Tellude," *i.e.* "in Tellure," the temple of Tellus where the Senate sometimes met. It stood near the forum of Nerva and the temple of Pallas (Minerva) was in the forum. *Cf.* Jordan, *Topographie der Stadt Rom*, Vol. II, p. 381.

| | | |
|---|---|---|
| a scourge and led to the temple of Mars [1] | be beaten upon the mouth with a scourge and led to the temple of Mars | scourge and led before the temple of Mars |

to worship and, if he would not worship, be beheaded. This was done.

　And he was beheaded

| | |
|---|---|
| by the temple of Mars | in the place aforesaid |

and became a martyr.

　And his body was taken up at night by the blessed Lucina and the clergy and was buried in a crypt in her own garden, near the cemetery of Calistus on the Via Appia,[2] September 14.

　And the bishopric was empty 66 days.

## XXIII. Lucius (253-254)

　Lucius, by nationality

| | |
|---|---|
| a Roman, son of Purphirius, | a Tuscan from the city of Luca, son of Lucinus, |

occupied the see 3 years,

| | |
|---|---|
| 8 months and 10 days. | 3 months and 3 days. |

He was crowned with martyrdom. He was bishop in the time of Gallus and Volusianus (A.D. 252), until the year when Valerian was consul for the third time and Gallicanus [3] was his colleague (A.D. 255). He was in exile. Afterwards by the will of God he returned in safety to the church.

　He ordained that in every place two priests and three deacons should abide with the bishop to be witnesses for him to the church.[4]

---

[1] There was a famous temple to Mars just outside the city wall, on the left of the Via Appia. From there it was a plausibly short distance to the cemetery of Callistus.

[2] The body of Cornelius was translated from Civitavecchia to a crypt close to the cemetery of Callistus. The inscription has been recovered. Duchesne, *Lib. Pont.*, vol. I, p. 152, n. 14.

[3] The name should be Gallienus.

[4] The system of private attendance upon the pope by members of the clergy, regular or secular, seems to have been first instituted by the council of 595 under Gregory I. Until that time the pope received personal service from laymen. Duchesne

He was also beheaded by Valerian, March 5.

| He, while on his way to his passion, gave authority to Stephen, archdeacon of his church.[1] | He gave authority over the whole church to Stephen, his archdeacon, while he was on his way to his passion. |

He held 2 ordinations in the month of December, 4 priests, 4 deacons, 7 bishops in divers places.

He also was buried

| in the cemetery of Calistus | near the cemetery of Calistus in a sandpit, |

on the Via Appia,[2] August 25.

And the bishopric was empty 35 days.

## XXIV. Stephen I (254–257)

Stephen, by nationality a Roman, son of Iobius, occupied the see

| 4 years, 2 months and 15 days. | 6 years, 5 months and 2 days. |

He was crowned with martyrdom.

He was bishop in the time of Valerian and Gallicanus and Maximus until the year when Valerian was consul for the 3rd time and Gallicanus for the 2nd time [3] (A.D. 255).

In [4] his time he was carried into exile; and afterwards by the

suggests that in ascribing this ordinance to Lucius our author may have been animated by the memory of the charge of adultery brought against Pope Symmachus later and the difficulty which that pope experienced in clearing himself for lack of witnesses. *Cf. infra*, p. 117, n. 2; Duchesne, *Lib. Pont.*, vol. I, p. 153, n. 2. There is no other record of an edict of the sort so early.

[1] This incident is probably taken from an apocryphal martyrology, or *Passion of Lucius*, now lost. Lucius is not usually reckoned among the martyrs, for although banished for a while he was permitted to return and died at Rome.

[2] A piece of the tablet which marked the tomb of Lucius and bears his name has been discovered in the course of excavation in the catacomb of Callistus. Duchesne, *ibid.*, p. 153, n. 5.

[3] Gallicanus should be Gallienus. The *Liberian Catalogue* gives the synchronism more exactly. "He was bishop in the time of Valerian and Gallienus, from the 2nd consulship of Volusianus and the first of Maximus (253) until," etc.

[4] The following paragraph is contained in only one manuscript of the composite seventh century text and is evidently an interpolation of that period. The early lists mention Stephen simply as bishop, not as martyr. Duchesne, *Lib. Pont.*, vol. I, p. 154, n. 1.

will of God he returned in safety to the church. And after 34 days he was tried by Maximian [1] and committed to prison with 9 priests and 2 bishops, Honorius and Castus, and 3 deacons, Xistus, Dionisius and Gaius. There in prison, near the arch of Stella,[2] he held a synod and all the vessels of the church he entrusted to the authority of his archdeacon, Xystus, and the money coffer. After 6 days he himself was brought forth under guard and beheaded.

He forbade priests and deacons to use their consecrated garments for daily wear save in church.

He held two ordinations in the month of December, 6 priests, 5 deacons, 3 bishops in divers places.

He also was buried in the cemetery of Calistus on the Via Appia, August 2.[3]

And the bishopric was empty 22 days.


### XXV. Xystus II (257–258)

Xystus, by nationality

a Greek,                |   a Roman,

previously a philosopher,[4] occupied the see

2 years, 11 months and 6 days.   |   1 year, 10 months and 23 days.

He was crowned with martyrdom.

He was bishop in the time of Valerian and Decius,[5] when there was the great persecution.

At that time he was seized

by Valerian                   |

and taken to offer sacrifice to demons. But he despised the com-

---

[1] An obvious anachronism.

[2] *I.e.* " Arcus Stillæ," an arch of the aqueduct (the dripping arch, *arcus stillans*); either the Porta Capena or the arch of Drusus. *Cf.* Jordan, *Topographie*, Vol. II, p. 380.

[3] The place of Stephen's burial is mentioned in all the liturgical calendars after 336 but his epitaph has not been found. Duchesne, *ibid.*, n. 4.

[4] There seems to have arisen some confusion between Pope Xystus and a Pythagorean philosopher, Sextius, whose *Sententiæ* were translated from Greek into Latin by Rufinus in the fifth century.

[5] The *Liberian Catalogue* omits the usual imperial synchronisms. The author of the *Lib. Pont.* supplies them, coupling Valerian and Decius as if they were contemporaries.

Pope St. Stephen I

Pope St. Felix I

mands of Valerian. He was beheaded and with him six others, all deacons, Felicissimus, Agapitus, Januarius, Magnus, Vincentius and Stephen, about August 6.[1]

And the priests kept charge [2] from the consulship of Maximus and Gravio (A.D. 255) until the year when Tuscus and Bassus were consuls (A.D. 258), from the consulship of Tuscus and Bassus until July 20, when

| | |
|---|---|
| there was the great persecution under Decius.[3] | the exceeding cruel persecution was raging under Decius. |

And after the passion of the blessed Xystus, on the third day, Lawrence, his archdeacon, suffered also, August 10, likewise the subdeacon Claudius and Severus, the priest, and Crescentius, the reader, and Romanus, the doorkeeper.[4]

He held 2 ordinations in the month of December, 4 priests, 7 deacons, 2 bishops in divers places.

He himself was buried in the cemetery of Calistus on the Via Appia and the aforesaid 6 deacons were buried in the cemetery of Prætextatus on the Via Appia, August 6.[5]

---

[1] A letter of Cyprian, written from Carthage a month or thereabout after these events, speaks of the news of the persecution at Rome. "But know that Xistus was martyred in the cemetery on August sixth and with him four deacons." The church at Carthage was expecting persecution also and Cyprian hopes "that every one of us may think less of death than of immortality." *Ep.* lxxxi, tr. *Ante Nicene Fathers*, vol. V, p. 408. According to tradition, Xystus was seated in a marble chair in the midst of a church service, when he was seized and carried away to the scene of his martyrdom. Duchesne, *Lib. Pont.*, vol. I, p. 156, n. 8. Felicissimus and Agapitus, the first two of the six deacons mentioned in the text, were interred, not with Xystus, but in the cemetery of Prætextatus, where their tombs may now be seen. Duchesne, *op. cit.*, p. 155, n. 4.

[2] *I.e.* during the vacancy in the bishopric following the execution of Xystus. Letters of Cyprian written at this juncture are addressed, "To the priests and deacons who are at Rome."

[3] The foregoing unintelligible tangle of dates is a garbled version of the passage in the *Liberian Catalogue*. Xystus was bishop "from the consulship of Maximus and Glabrio (A.D. 256) until the year when Tuscus and Bassus were consuls (A.D. 258), and he suffered August 6. And the priests kept charge from the consulship of Tuscus and Bassus until July 21 of the year when Æmilianus and Bassus were consuls (A.D. 259)."

[4] The later legends of St. Lawrence knew nothing of Claudius and Severus, though the memory of Crescentius and Romanus was sometimes recalled. The *Lib. Pont.* may preserve an earlier and more accurate tradition. *Cf. Acta Sanctorum*, August, vol. II, pp. 485–532.

[5] Duchesne prints the verse with which Pope Damasus later commemorated the

The aforesaid blessed Lawrence

| | | |
|---|---|---|
| was buried on the Via Tiburtina in a crypt in the Ager Veranus, August 10.[1] | was buried in the cemetery of Cyriaco in the Ager Veranus in a crypt with many other martyrs. | was buried on the Via Tiburtina in the cemetery of Cyriaces in the Ager Veranus in a crypt with many other martyrs, August 10. |

And the bishopric was empty 35 days.

## XXVI. DIONYSIUS (259–268)

Dionysius, previously a monk, whose family we have not been able to ascertain, occupied the see

8 years,                         | 6 years,

2 months and 4 days.

He was bishop in the time of Galienus, from July 22 of the year when Emilianus and Bassus were consuls (A.D. 259), to December 26 in the consulship of Claudius and Paternus (A.D. 269).

He assigned churches and cemeteries to the priests and appointed parishes in the diocese.[2]

He held 2 ordinations in the month of December, 12 priests, 6 deacons, 8 bishops in divers places.

He also was buried in the cemetery of Calistus on the Via Appia, December 27.

And the bishopric was empty 5 days.

---

tomb of Xystus in the papal crypt. *Op. cit.*, p. 156, n. 8.  See *infra*, p. 82 and n. 1. Four out of the six deacons were buried with Xystus in the cemetery of Callistus. *Supra*, p. 31, n. 1.

[1] The site of the present famous basilica of San Lorenzo in Agro Verano or fuori le Mura.   For the building of the basilica see *infra*, p. 61.

[2] Duchesne takes this sentence to mean that Dionysius carried out the parish organization of the city, assigning certain suburban cemeteries to certain urban churches, so that each church should have its special cemetery.  He also assigned the boundaries of the episcopal dioceses within the metropolitan diocese of the pope. The word "parochia," parish, was employed at this period to signify either a rural parish in the modern sense or the whole territory governed by a bishop.  *Lib. Pont.*, vol. I, p. 157, n. 3.

## XXVII. Felix I (269-274)

Felix, by nationality a Roman, son of Constantius, occupied the see

| | |
|---|---|
| 2 years and 10 months. | 4 years, 3 months and 25 days. |

He was crowned with martyrdom.[1]

He was bishop in the time of Claudius and Aurelian, from the consulship of Claudius and Paternus (A.D. 269), to the year when Aurelian and Capitulinus were consuls (A.D. 274).

He instituted the celebration of masses

| | |
|---|---|
| over the sepulchres | over the memorials |

of the martyrs.[2]

He held 2 ordinations in the month of December, 9 priests, 5 deacons, 5 bishops in divers places.

| | |
|---|---|
| He also was buried in his own cemetery on the Via Aurelia at the 2nd milestone, May 30. | He built a basilica on the Via Aurelia, where also he was buried, May 30, 2 miles from the city of Rome. |

And the bishopric was empty 5 days.

## XXVIII. Eutychianus (275-283)

Eutycianus, by nationality a Tuscan, son of Marinus, from the city of Luna,[3] occupied the see

8 years, 10 months and 4 days. | 1 year, 1 month and 1 day.

He was bishop in the time of Aurelian, from the 3rd consulship

---

[1] Pope Felix was not counted a martyr in the early lists and he was buried with his predecessors in the cemetery of Callistus. He is confounded here with two martyrs of the same name who were associated with a basilica on the Via Aurelia. Duchesne, *Lib. Pont.*, vol. I, pp. cxxv, 158, n. 3.

[2] The poet Prudentius is witness to the fact that at the end of the fourth century the custom existed of celebrating masses in memory of the martyrs "ad corpus," either in the cemeterial basilicas over the tombs or in the subterranean vaults themselves. *Peristephanon*, lib. xi, v. 171, etc. Quoted by Duchesne, *op. cit.*, p. 158, n. 2.

[3] The modern Luni.

of Aurelian when Marcellinus was his colleague (A.D. 275), until December 13 of the year when Carus was consul for the 2nd time and Carinus was consul with him (A.D. 283).

He ordained that fruit might be blessed upon the altar, but only beans and grapes.[1]

He in his time buried 342 martyrs in divers places with his own hand.[2] He also ordained that whenever anyone of the faithful buried a martyr, he should bury him in a dalmatic or a purple tunic and the report of it should be brought to himself (Eutychianus).

He held 5 ordinations in the month of December, 14 priests, 5 deacons, 9 bishops in divers places.

And he was crowned with martyrdom.[3]

He also was buried in the cemetery of Calistus on the Via Appia, July 25.[4]

And the bishopric was empty 8 days.


## XXIX. Gaius (283–296)

Gaius, by nationality a Dalmatian, of the family of Dioclitian, the emperor, son of Gaius, occupied the see 11 years, 4 months

and 9 days.          | and 12 days.

He was bishop in the time of Carus and Carinus, from December 17 in the 2nd consulship of Carus when Carinus was his colleague (A.D. 283), until April 22 of the year when Diocletian was consul for the 4th time and Constantius for the 2nd time (A.D. 296).

---

[1] Prayers for the blessing of the first fruits are found in various early Roman liturgies. They had, of course, both Jewish and pagan archetypes. The bean and grape have been from ancient times the chief food crops of the Italian people. Duchesne, *Lib. Pont.*, vol. I, p. 159, n. 1.

[2] No persecution of importance is recorded under Eutychianus. Whether this sentence and the following refer to the original burying of martyrs or to the translation of their bodies is impossible to say. They may both be entirely apocryphal.

[3] There is no other record of Eutychianus' martyrdom. The words may be an interpolation.

[4] His inscription is in the papal crypt. Duchesne, *op. cit.*, p. 160, n. 6.

He decreed

| | |
|---|---|
| that whoever was worthy to be bishop must rise from door-keeper through each rank, step by step, to the higher place. | that all the offices in the church should be thus held in turn : whoever was worthy to be bishop must first be doorkeeper, reader, exorcist, acolyte, sub-deacon, deacon, priest and then be ordained bishop.[1] |

He divided the districts among the deacons.

He fled from the persecution of Diocletian into the crypts,

| | |
|---|---|
| and while dwelling there died a confessor. | and while dwelling there was crowned with martyrdom after 8 years.[2] |

He held 4 ordinations in the month of December, 25 priests, 8 deacons, 5 bishops in divers places.

He, after 11 years, was crowned with martyrdom in company with Gavinius, his brother, on account of the daughter of Gavinius, the priest, whose name was Susanna.

He also was buried in the cemetery of Calistus on the Via Appia, April 22.[3]

And the bishopric was empty 11 days.

[1] Pope Cornelius, writing thirty years before this of Novatian and the schism in the Roman church, gives the earliest known enumeration of the seven ranks in the hierarchy of the order. "This avenger of the Gospel then did not know that there should be one bishop in the catholic church; yet he was not ignorant — for how could he be? — that in it there were forty-six priests, seven deacons, seven subdeacons, forty-two acolytes, fifty-two exorcists, readers and doorkeepers." Eusebius, *Church History*, VI, c. 43, tr. McGiffert, p. 288. See under Pope Sylvester, *infra*, p. 46. On the institution of the graded hierarchy see *Cambridge Medieval History*, vol. I, pp. 150–152.

[2] The legend of Gaius' martyrdom is not authenticated. His name is not in the early martyrologies and the persecution of Diocletian did not begin until seven years after his death. We have in our text, however, three different versions of the legend, the last connecting him with the passion of St. Susanna. In fact she is sometimes said to have been a niece of Gaius. *Acta Sanctorum*, February, vol. III, p. 62; August, vol. II, p. 631; Duchesne, *Lib. Pont.*, vol. I, p. xcviii.

[3] The tablet which marked his tomb was discovered in fragments and put together by De Rossi. Duchesne, *op. cit.*, p. 161, n. 7.

### XXX. MARCELLINUS (296–304)

Marcellinus, by nationality a Roman, son of Projectus, occupied the see

8 years, 2 months and 25 days. | 9 years, 4 months and 16 days.

He was bishop in the time of Diocletian and Maximian, from July 1 in the 6th consulship of Diocletian and the 2nd of Constantius (A.D. 296) until the year when Diocletian was consul for the 9th time and Maximian for the 8th (A.D. 304). At that time was a great persecution, so that within 30 days 17,000 Christians of both sexes in divers provinces were crowned with martyrdom.[1]

For this reason Marcellinus himself was haled to sacrifice, that he might offer incense, and he did it.

And after a few days,[2] inspired by penitence, he was beheaded by the same Diocletian and crowned with martyrdom for the faith of Christ in company with Claudius and Cyrinus and Antoninus,

> and the blessed Marcellinus on his way to his passion adjured Marcellus, the priest, that he should not fulfil the commands of Diocletian.

---

[1] This exaggerated estimate seems to be founded upon a misconception of a statement in the apocryphal Preface to Jerome's *Martyrology*. Mommsen, *Lib. Pont.*, p. 41, note on l. 5.

[2] A single manuscript contains the following more detailed account. "And after a few days a synod was held in the province of Campania in the city of Sessana, where with his own lips he professed his penitence in the presence of 180 bishops. He wore a garment of haircloth and ashes upon his head and repented, saying that he had sinned. Then Diocletian was wroth and seized him and bade him sacrifice to images. But he cried out with tears, saying, 'It repenteth me sorely for my former ignorance,' and he began to utter blasphemy against Diocletian and the images of demons made with hands. So, inspired by penitence, he was beheaded," etc. Sessana is a corrupt form of the name Sinuessa. The modern town is called Rocca di Mandragone. See on the story of this council and the apostasy of Marcellinus, *Introduction*, p. ix. Petilianus, a Donatist bishop, with whom Augustine had a controversy, is the earliest authority for Marcellinus' defection. Duchesne, *Lib. Pont.*, vol. I, p. lxxiv; Mommsen, *Lib. Pont.*, pp. liv, lv. Petilianus says that Marcellinus not only offered incense but also surrendered the sacred books to be burned. Augustine in reply is non-committal. At any rate, he remarks, "it is no affair of ours. For they have borne their own burden, whether it was good or whether it was evil. We ourselves believe it was good; but whatever it was it was theirs." Augustine, *Contra Litteras Petiliani;* Migne, *Pat. Lat.*, vol. 43, cols. 323, 328.

And afterwards the holy bodies lay in the street for an example to the Christians 26 days by order of Diocletian.

Then the priest Marcellus and the other priests and the deacons took up the bodies by night with hymns and buried them on the Via Salaria in the cemetery of Priscilla in a chamber which is well known unto this day, as Marcellinus himself had commanded,

when in penitence he was being | haled to execution, in the crypt | near the body of the holy Criscentio, |

April 25.[1]

He held 2 ordinations in the month of December, 4 priests, 2 deacons, 5 bishops in divers places.

From that day the bishopric was empty 7 years, 6 months and 25 days while Diocletian was persecuting the Christians.

## XXXI. MARCELLUS (308–309)

Marcellus,[2] by nationality a Roman, son of

Marcellus, | Benedictus,

from the district of the Via Lata, occupied the see

4 years. | 5 years, 7 months and 21 days.

He was bishop in the time of Maxentius, from the 4th consul-

---

[1] The crypt of San Crescenzio in the cemetery of Priscilla is marked on seventh century itineraries of the holy places in the environs of Rome. The grave of Marcellinus, however, has not been identified.

[2] Eusebius, Jerome, Augustine and the authors of the *Roman Index* and other early lists omit either Marcellus or Marcellinus from their chronologies. There was evidently some tendency to confuse the similar names. The *Liberian Catalogue*, however, gives both and the *Lib. Pont.* copies it. Duchesne holds that Marcellinus was ignored by the compilers because of the disgrace which he brought upon his office. *Lib. Pont.*, vol. I, pp. lxxiii, lxxiv. Mommsen argues and supports his contention by the chronology of the *Lib. Pont.* itself, that Marcellus was not included in the episcopal lists because he was never regularly ordained bishop but merely performed some of the duties of the head of the church during the seven years of interregnum that followed the execution of Marcellinus. *Lib. Pont.*, pp. liii–lv.

ship of Maxentius when Maximus was his colleague, until after the consulship.[1]

He

made request of a certain matron, whose name was Priscilla,[2]
and

established a cemetery on the Via Salaria, and he appointed 25 parish churches[3] as dioceses[4] in the city of Rome to provide baptism and penance for the many who were converted among the pagans and burial for the martyrs.[5]

He ordained 25 priests in the city of Rome and 2 deacons, in the month of December, and 21 bishops in divers places.

He was seized by Maxentius and held in confinement, because he set the church in order, and imprisoned that he might deny his bishopric and degrade himself by sacrifices to demons. Then, forasmuch as he continually despised and scorned the words and commands of Maxentius, he was condemned to the stable.[6]  But, although he served many days in the stable, he did not cease his

---

[1] The years 308–309, which the author attempts to designate here, were years of some confusion in the consulate. Maxentius did not recognize the regular officials and the usual formulæ were not preserved.

[2] The name of Priscilla, introduced in a few manuscripts, is an anachronism, suggested undoubtedly by the well-known cemetery on the Via Salaria. That cemetery is much older than Marcellus. A few other manuscripts give the name Novella as that of Marcellus' foundation and De Rossi has proved the existence of such a cemetery across the Via Salaria facing the cemetery of Priscilla.  Duchesne, *op. cit.*, p. 165, n. 4.

[3] Marcellus may have found it necessary to reorganize the churches after the persecution and the vacancy in the episcopate.  See *supra*, pp. 7, n. 2; 21, n. 3.  For a brief account of the twenty-five parish churches of Rome in the fifth century see Frothingham, *Monuments of Christian Rome*, pp. 39–41.  Gregorovius, *History of Rome*, tr. Hamilton, vol. I, pp. 267–282.

[4] This passage may be compared with *supra*, p. 32 and n. 2, to show how variable was still the meaning of terms like "parish" and "diocese," which have since become so exact.

[5] Each parish church in the city was at first apparently connected with a suburban cemetery or catacomb, where its dead, whether martyrs or not, were buried.  Later the service of the cemeteries became so arduous that monasteries were established adjacent to take charge of them.  *Cf. infra*, p. 163, n. 1.

[6] The reference here seems to be to the public stables maintained as part of the service of the imperial post.  The story of the sufferings of Marcellus cannot be corroborated from other sources but is not in itself inconsistent with what facts we know of this turbulent period.

service to the Lord with prayers and fastings.  Moreover in the ninth month all his clergy came by night and removed him by night from the stable.  A certain matron and widow, whose name was Lucina, who had lived with her husband Marcus 15 years and had been 19 years a widow, received the blessed man ; and she dedicated her house as a church in the name of the blessed Marcellus [1] and there day and night the Lord Jesus Christ was confessed with hymns and prayers.  But Maxentius heard of it and sent and seized the blessed Marcellus a second time and gave orders that in that very church

a second time                        |

boards should be laid down and the animals of the stable should be collected and kept there and the blessed Marcellus should tend them.  And he died in the service of the animals, clad only in a hair shirt.

And the blessed Lucina took his body

and he was buried                    | and buried it

in the cemetery of Priscilla on the Via Salaria, January 16.[2]

And the bishopric was empty 20 days.

Lucina herself was condemned by proscription.


## XXXII. Eusebius (309 or 310)

Eusebius, by nationality a Greek, previously a physician, occupied the see

2 years, 1 month and 25 days.    | 6 years, 1 month and 3 days.

He was bishop in the time

of Constantine.[3]               | of Constans.

[1] The modern church of San Lorenzo in Lucina.   The association with St. Lawrence was achieved in the fifth century.

[2] The epitaph erected by Pope Damasus (see *infra*, p. 82, n. 1) over the grave of Marcellus is printed by Duchesne; *op. cit.*, p. 166, n. 10.  It alludes to a rebellious faction in the church and to an apostate who denounced the pope to the tyrant Maxentius and brought about his banishment.   It does not mention the manner of his death.

[3] The author of the *Lib. Pont.* has inserted the name of Constantine and the succeeding sentence into the text as allusions to the legend of the discovery of the True Cross by the Jew Cyriacus.  The Latin version of the legend is in the *Acta Sanctorum*,

While he was bishop the cross of our Lord Jesus Christ was found, May 3, and Judas was baptised, who is also Quiriacus.

He discovered heretics in the city of Rome and reconciled them by the laying on of hands.[1]

He held

| 3 ordinations | 1 ordination |

in the month of December, 13 priests, 3 deacons, 14 bishops in divers places.[2]

He also was buried in the cemetery of Calistus

| in a crypt | |

on the Via Appia, October 2.

And the bishopric was empty 7 days.


## XXXIII. MILTIADES (311–314)

Miltiades, by nationality an African, occupied the see 4 years, 7 months and 8 days, from July 7 in the

| 9th consulship of Maximin un-til the 2nd consulship of Maxentius, | 9th consulship of Maxentius until the 2nd consulship of Maximus, |

which was in the month of September, when Volusianus and Rufinus were consuls (A.D. 311).[4]

He decreed that no one of the faithful should in any wise keep fast upon the Lord's day or upon the fifth day of the week, because the pagans celebrated those days as a sacred fast.[5]

May, vol. I, p. 445. The other legend, which attributed the discovery of the Cross to the empress Helena, became eventually the more popular in the West.

[1] The rite employed by the early Roman church in the reconciliation of heretics seems to have been very similar to that of confirmation. Duchesne, *Lib. Pont.*, vol. I, p. 167, n. 3.

[2] Eusebius was pope for four months only, from April to August. He, therefore, could have held no ordinations in December.

[3] The tomb of Eusebius is in a special chamber of the catacomb of Callistus, at some distance from the large chamber where the third century popes are buried.

[4] The consular synchronisms are confused here and in the *Liberian Catalogue*, partly because Maxentius recognized a different set of consuls from the regularly elected officials and both the *Catalogue* and our author attempt to name them all. Our author omits the latter part of his clause, "until January 11 in the year when Volusianus and Annianus were consuls (A.D. 314)."

[5] Sunday fasting has been forbidden in the church since the rise of the dualist sects

And he discovered Manicheans in the city.[1]

He appointed that consecrated offerings should be sent throughout the churches from the bishop's consecration; these are called the leaven.[2]

He held 1 ordination in the month of December, 7 priests, 5 deacons, 11 bishops in divers places.

He was buried in the cemetery of Calistus on the Via Appia

in a crypt

December 10.

And the bishopric was empty 16 days.

## XXXIV. SYLVESTER (314-335)

Sylvester, by nationality a Roman, son of Rufinus, occupied the see 23 years, 10 months and 11 days.

He was bishop in the time of Constantine and Volusianus, from February 1 until January 1 in the consulship of Constantius and Volusianus.[3]

He was an exile on Mount Syraptin,[4]

who testified by that observance their abhorrence of the material world. Thursday also is rarely a fast day, although the reason for the latter rule is not so clear. Duchesne, *Lib. Pont.*, vol. I, p. 168, n. 2.

[1] This famous dualist sect had arisen some thirty years before the pontificate of Miltiades. For a convenient account of its history and doctrines see "Manicheanism," Harnack and Conybeare, *Encyclopædia Britannica*, 11th edition.

[2] An obscure passage which has given rise to much debate over the possible use of leaven in the Host. See "Fermentum," Ducange, *Glossarium Med. et Inf. Lat.* Duchesne quotes a letter of Pope Innocent I to Decentius, which evidently refers to the same custom. "And the priests of these (parish) churches, because they are prevented by their charges from assembling with us on the Lord's day, receive through acolytes the leaven prepared by us, in order that they may not suppose themselves divided from our communion on that great day; but I do not think it right to do this for the parishes (rural), because the sacred elements ought not to be carried a long distance, nor do we send them to the priests situated at the various cemeteries, for those priests have the right and privilege of preparing them." Duchesne, *op. cit.*, p. 169, n. 4. Mansi, *Amplissima Collectio*, vol. III, p. 1028. As late as the eighth century the Host was sent about in Rome from the pope's altar, as here described, on Holy Thursdays. Atchley, *Ordo Romanus Primus*, pp. 106–108.

[3] The *Liberian Catalogue* says: "He was bishop in the time of Constantine, from the consulship of Volusianus and Annianus (A.D. 314), January 31, to December 31 in the year when Constantius and Albinus were consuls (A.D. 335)."

[4] This form of the name is found in the fifth century Armenian text of the legend

driven by the persecution of
Constantine,

and afterward he returned and baptised with glory Constantine
Augustus, whom the Lord cured

through baptism

of leprosy, from whose persecution he had fled when he was in
exile. He built a church in the city of Rome, in the garden of one
of his priests who was called Equitius, and he appointed it as a
parish church of Rome, near the baths of Domitian, and even unto
this day it is called the church of Equitius.[1] There also he offered
the following gifts:[2]

> a silver paten,[3] weighing 20 pounds,[4] the gift of Constantine
> Augustus.

He gave likewise:

of the miraculous healing of Constantine. In the two epitomes of the *Lib. Pont.* and
in the second recension it is written Seracten or Soracten, with the evident intention of
identifying the spot with the well known mountain near Rome. Duchesne believes
that the Constantinian legend originated early in the fifth century in the Syrian or
Armenian communities of the Eastern church. *Lib. Pont.*, vol. I, pp. cix–cxx.
The most trustworthy account of the actual baptism of the emperor is furnished by
Eusebius in his *Life of Constantine*, tr. Richardson, *Nicene and Post-Nicene Fathers*,
ser. 2, vol. I, pp. 555–556. The ceremony took place shortly before the illustrious
convert's death, near Nicomedia in Asia Minor. Cf. Coleman, *Constantine the Great
and Christianity* for literature on this and associated topics.

[1] The church is now generally known as San Martino ai Monti. Remains of Sylvester's edifice still exist below the present structure. The baths here called by Domitian's name are more usually styled the baths of Trajan or the baths of Titus.

[2] On the value of this and subsequent lists of real and movable property bestowed
upon the churches see *Introduction*, pp. ix–x. Duchesne has a lengthy discussion of the
questions involved. In the course of it he prints an interesting document of the year
471, a deed of gift of lands, precious vessels and other articles from a man and his
wife to a church near Tivoli. The deed is strikingly similar in phraseology and arrangement to the lists of the *Lib. Pont.; op. cit.*, pp. cxl–cliv. Of course the churches
were plundered many times over in the centuries that followed.

[3] The paten of this early period, as represented in the mosaic of San Vitale in Ravenna, for example, was a large, flat bowl and was used to hold the consecrated Host
for the bishop and his assistants, the bread for the laity being broken and distributed in
bags. An ordinary church or an altar in a large church owned but one paten, though
a number of chalices. The paten, however, might also hold the consecrated oil or
chrism, as below. Duchesne, *op. cit.*, p. cxliv; Lowrie, *Christian Art and Archæology*, pp. 343–354.

[4] The Roman pound, nearly equal to twelve ounces avoirdupois.

2 silver beakers,[1] weighing each ten pounds;

a golden chalice, weighing 2 lbs.;

5 chalices for service,[2] weighing each two lbs.;

2 silver pitchers,[3] weighing each ten lbs.;

1 silver paten, overlaid with gold, for the chrism, weighing 5 lbs.;

10 chandeliers,[4] weighing each eight lbs.;

20 bronze lamps, weighing each ten lbs.;

12 bronze candelabra, weighing each three hundred lbs.; [5]

2 silver pitchers, weighing each ten lbs.;

1 silver paten overlaid with gold, for the chrism, weighing 5 lbs.;

10 chandeliers, weighing each eight lbs.;

20 bronze lamps, weighing each ten lbs.;

12 bronze candelabra, weighing each three hundred lbs.;

the Valerian manor in the Sabine region,[6] which yields 80 solidi; [7]

the Statian [8] manor in the Sabine region, which yields 55 sol.;

---

[1] The "scyphus" or beaker was a large vessel, shaped like a goblet, in which the wine was placed for consecration on the altar and from which it was poured into the smaller chalices for distribution to the congregation. At least this is Duchesne's theory; *ibid.*, p. cxliv. Sometimes, however, the term "chalice" is used to denote the vessel of honor for the altar. For the shape see the illustrations in Lowrie, *op. cit., passim.*

[2] The "chalices for service" were used to carry the wine to the laity.

[3] The "ama," pitcher or flagon, was a large receptacle which, in Duchesne's opinion, was set to receive the offerings of wine presented by the faithful. Lowrie suggests that it contained the wine and water which were mixed for the Eucharist. *Op. cit.*, p. 347.

[4] The churches of this and later centuries were illuminated by a wealth of lamps, chandeliers, candlesticks and candelabra, suspended from the roof or standing upon the floor. A large variety of terms is employed to enumerate the different kinds and shapes of lights, an exact translation of which is now impossible. The lamps and chandeliers found at Pompeii are smaller and far less sumptuous than these products of fourth century workmanship. Lowrie, *op. cit.*, pp. 349–352. It will be noticed that no lights were placed upon the altar. The officiating priest still stood behind it, facing the people, and illumination came from overhead or from the sides.

[5] Or thirty pounds. The figures throughout these lists vary in different manuscripts.

[6] It is impossible to locate most of the lands mentioned in the lists. The word "fundus," here translated manor, means a farm or piece of country property.

[7] The solidus was a gold coin introduced by Constantine and worth at this time about $3.50 in our money.

[8] A small hamlet called Stazzano perpetuates the name to-day.

the manor of Duæ Casæ in the Sabine region, which yields
40 sol.;

the Percilian manor in the Sabine region, which yields 20 sol.;

the Corbian manor in the region of Cora,[1] which yields 60 sol.;

a house in the city, with a bath, in the Sicinine district,[2] which
yields 85 sol.;

a garden within the city of Rome in the district of Ad Duo
Amantes,[3] yielding 15 sol.;

a house in the district of Orfea within the city,[4] which yields
58 and one third sol.

He made a regulation for the whole church. Likewise in his
time was held a council

with his approval             | at his bidding

in Nicea in Bithynia, and there were gathered together 318 catholic
bishops,

and 208 others unable to attend |

sent their signatures.

And they set forth in full the

holy,                            |

catholic and unspotted faith and condemned Arrius and Fotinus
and Sabellius and their disciples.[5]

And after consultation with Augustus he assembled 277

bishops                         |

---

[1] The modern village of Cori in the Campagna.

[2] It is impossible to identify all of the city districts enumerated in the lists. The
Sicinine district, however, was in the neighborhood of the church of Santa Maria
Maggiore, which was known in the fourth century as the "basilica Sicinini." Duchesne,
*op. cit.*, p. 188, n. 11.

[3] Probably in the vicinity of the Esquiline Hill, not far from the church of San
Martino, like the houses mentioned before and after.

[4] A "lake of Orfeus" is included in the region of the Esquiline by topographers of
the fourth century. A church of Santa Lucia in Orphea stood later near the church
of San Martino.

[5] This is, of course, the great Council of Nicea. The idea that Photinus and Sabellius, as well as Arius, were condemned by the council originated with the authors of
the popular, unhistorical lives of Sylvester, who were concerned to make their hero
crush as many errors as possible.

in the city of Rome [1] and he condemned a second time Calistus and Arrius and Fotinus and Sabellius; and he decreed that an Arian priest who became convinced of his error should not be received except by the bishop of his particular locality; and that the chrism should be consecrated only by the bishops; and he established the privilege of the bishops, that they should anoint those who had been baptised [2] to avert the propagation of heresy.[3]

He furthermore decreed that a priest might anoint with the chrism one who had been baptised and taken from the water, in case of the approach of death.

He decreed that no layman should presume to bring a charge against one of the clergy.[4]

He decreed that deacons should wear dalmatics [5] in church and napkins of mixed wool and linen over their left arms.[6]

He decreed that no member of the clergy should enter a court for any cause whatever or plead his case before a civil judge, unless it were in a church.[7]

He decreed that the sacrifice of the altar should be performed not upon a cloth of hair nor one that was colored, but only upon

[1] On this Council of Rome see *Introduction*, p. ix. The records of the council and of the canons promulgated by it and by Sylvester at this time are fabrications of the age of Symmachus, intended to provide sanction for episcopal claims and to exalt the episcopal office in general. They are the oldest set of apocryphal canons in existence dealing with matters of church discipline. Duchesne, *op. cit.*, p. cxxxiv.

[2] *I.e.* administer the sacrament of confirmation.

[3] A free translation of an enigmatical clause, "propter hereticam suasionem."

[4] On its face an impossible decree. The councils of this and later periods issued stipulations as to the methods to be employed in bringing suit against members of the higher clergy.

[5] The dalmatic worn by a Roman deacon as well as by a bishop at this time, a long, flowing tunic with wide sleeves, is pictured in many church frescoes and mosaics. It was, as the name indicates, originally an Oriental garment, introduced into Rome during the second century and worn in public first apparently by the emperor Commodus. It was distinguished by a purple stripe, which ran over each shoulder and down to the bottom of the skirt on both sides and sometimes around the edge of the sleeve. Pope Symmachus (498–519) granted to St. Cæsarius of Arles the privilege of clothing his deacons in dalmatics like those worn by the deacons at Rome. Lowrie, *op. cit.*, pp. 394–396.

[6] The towel or napkin carried by the deacon for use in his part of the service became in course of time the maniple. Lowrie, *op. cit.*, pp. 410–413.

[7] The word translated civil is "cinctum," *i.e.* clad in official robes. This spurious decree represents an effort to oblige the clergy to bring their suits to the episcopal courts. There is no parallel to it in authentic records. Duchesne, *op. cit.*, p. 190, n. 23.

linen sprung from the earth, even as the body of our Lord Jesus Christ was buried in pure linen cloth; [1]

thus mass should be celebrated. |

He decreed that anyone who wished to advance or make progress in the church must be a reader 30 years,[2] an exorcist 30 days,[3] an acolyte 5 years, a subdeacon 5 years,

a custodian of the martyrs 5 |
years,[4]                        |

a deacon 7 years, a priest 3 years; that he must be approved on every hand, even by them who are without, and must have good witness borne to him, the husband of one wife,[5] who had herself received the blessing of the priest, and that thus he might attain to the rank of bishop; that he must not enter upon a greater or superior office, but accept modestly the order of rank by years, and he must have the goodwill and favor of all the clergy with no one anywhere in the clergy

or among the faithful              |

[1] Mosaics of the sixth and seventh centuries in the churches of San Vitale and San Apollinare in Classe in Ravenna show the early table altar set with chalice and bread and covered with a white linen cloth.

[2] Some manuscripts give, "first a doorkeeper, then a reader," etc. There is much variation in the figures throughout the passage. An authentic decree of Pope Zosimus in 418 states what was undoubtedly the .accepted system. A man who had been dedicated to the church from infancy must remain a reader until his twentieth year. If an adult desired to enter the clergy, he must serve as reader and exorcist for five years. Thereafter he must be acolyte and subdeacon four years and deacon five years. From the priesthood he might be elevated to the bishopric if his life were holy and he had been married but once, not to a widow, and had never been a penitent. Duchesne, *op. cit.*, p. 191, n. 25; Mansi, *Amplissima Collectio*, vol. IV, p. 347; Jaffé, *Regesta*, vol. I, p. 50, 339. *Cf. supra*, p. 35 and n. 1.

[3] Two manuscripts read, "afterward an exorcist for the time required by the pontiff;" two others, "afterward an exorcist for the time which the bishop may appoint." Mommsen, *Lib. Pont.*, p. 51, notes.

[4] It seems probable that the care of the tombs of the martyrs in the vicinity of Rome was entrusted to subdeacons at the opening of the sixth century. Gregory of Tours often speaks of the "martyrarii" who performed a similar duty in the church of Gaul. Duchesne, *ibid.*, n. 25.

[5] Early in the fourth century both popes and councils took the position that no man could be ordained who had been married more than once or had espoused a widow. Duchesne, *ibid.*, n. 26.

opposed to him.  He held 6

| ordinations | orders |

of priests and deacons in the month of December, 42 priests, 27 deacons at different times in the city of Rome, 65 bishops in divers places.

In his time Constantine Augustus built the following basilicas and adorned them :

the Constantinian basilica,[1] where he offered the following gifts :
a ciborium of hammered silver, which has upon the front the Savior seated upon a chair, in height 5 feet, weighing 120 lbs., and also the 12 apostles, who weigh each ninety pounds and are 5 feet in height and wear crowns of purest silver ; further, on the back, looking toward the apse are the Savior seated upon a throne in height 5 feet, of purest silver, weighing 140 lbs., and 4 angels of silver,[2]

| | |
|---|---|
| which weigh each 105 lbs. and are 5 feet in height and have jewels from Alabanda[3] in their eyes and carry spears ; | which are each 5 feet in height upon the sides and carry crosses and weigh each 105 lbs. and have jewels from Alavanda in their eyes ; |

[1] San Giovanni in Laterano.  As early as 313 a council called to try the case of the Donatist heretics under Pope Miltiades met "in the house of Fausta in the Lateran."  Jaffé, *Regesta*, vol. I, p. 28, 313.  Fausta was the wife of Constantine.  The basilica erected on the site was first called Constantinian in the record of the Roman synod of 487.  Mommsen, *op. cit.*, p. xxvii and n. 4.  Needless to say no vestiges of this first basilica are visible in the present structure.  The former fell to the ground in 877 and was rebuilt once in the tenth century, twice in the fourteenth and thoroughly "restored" in the seventeenth and nineteenth.  For a description of the several basilicas ascribed in our text to Constantine see Gregorovius, *History of Rome*, vol. I, pp. 88–112.

[2] The figure of Christ seated in the midst of his apostles was represented often in the catacombs and on the sarcophagi of the fourth century.  The mosaic of the apse of the church of Santa Pudenziana dates from the end of that century.  Christ enthroned between angels was, for some reason, a subject less frequently chosen.  A nave mosaic of San Apollinare Nuovo at Ravenna, built for Theodoric about the year 500, shows the latter scene, the attendant angels carrying spears, as here.  This ciborium of Constantine was destroyed by Alaric's Gauls and replaced by one given by the emperor Valentinian in the pontificate of Xystus III.  See *infra*, p. 95, n. 1.

[3] A city in Caria, now Arab-Hissar.

the ciborium itself weighs 2025 lbs. of wrought silver; a vaulted ceiling of purest gold;[1]

the ciborium itself weighs 2025 lbs.;

the ciborium itself, where stand the angels and the apostles, weighs 2025 lbs. of wrought silver;

and a lamp of purest gold, which hangs beneath the ciborium, with 50 dolphins[2] of purest gold, weighing each 50 lbs., and chains which weigh 25 lbs.;

a lamp of purest gold beneath the ciborium with 50 dolphins and a chain which weighs 25 lbs.;

a lamp of purest gold which hangs beneath the ciborium, with 50 dolphins, which weighs with its chain 25 lbs.;

4 crowns[3] of purest gold with 20 dolphins, weighing each fifteen lbs.;

a vaulting for the basilica of polished gold, in length and in breadth 500 lbs.;[4]

7 altars of purest silver, weighing each 200 lbs.;

7 golden patens, weighing each thirty lbs.;

16 silver patens, weighing each thirty lbs.;

7 goblets of purest gold, weighing each 10 lbs.;

A single goblet of coral set all about with prases and jacinths and overlaid with gold, which weighs in all 20 lbs. and 3 ounces;

20 silver goblets, weighing each fifteen lbs.;

2 pitchers of purest gold, weighing each fifty lbs. and holding each 3 medimni;[5]

20 silver pitchers, weighing each ten lbs. and holding each one medimnus;

---

[1] *I.e.* the vault of the ciborium from which depended the great lamp next described.

[2] An ornament of lamps or chandeliers, shaped like a dolphin; probably each dolphin held a light.

[3] *I.e.* circular chandeliers with pendant lights.

[4] The readings of this clause vary a little but none are quite intelligible. The vaulting is that of the half dome of the apse.

[5] The medimnus or μέδιμνος was the Greek bushel, comprising about twelve gallons or one and one half English bushels.

40 smaller chalices of purest gold, weighing each one lb.;

50 smaller chalices for service, weighing each 2 lbs.;

For ornament in the basilica:

a chandelier of purest gold before the altar, wherein burns pure oil of nard, with 80 dolphins, weighing 30 lbs.;

a silver chandelier with 20 dolphins, which weighs 50 lbs., wherein burns pure oil of nard;

45 silver chandeliers in the body of the basilica,[1] weighing each 30 lbs., wherein burns the aforesaid oil;

on the right side of the basilica 40 silver lamps, weighing each 20 lbs.;

25 silver chandeliers on the left side of the basilica, weighing each 20 lbs.;

50 silver candelabra in the body of the basilica, weighing each 20 lbs.;

3 jars of purest silver, weighing each 300 lbs., holding 10 medimni;

7 brass candlesticks before the altars, 10 feet in height, adorned with figures of the prophets overlaid with silver, weighing each 300 lbs.;

and for maintenance of the lights there he granted:

the Gargilian estate in the region of Suessa,[2] yielding every year |

400 sol.;

the Bauronican estate in the region of Suessa, yielding 360 sol.;

the Aurian estate in the region of Laurentum,[3] yielding 500 sol.;

the Urban estate in the region of Antium,[4] yielding 240 sol.;

---

[1] *I.e.* the central nave. The right side mentioned next would be the right aisle, reserved at this time for women communicants, the left side the left aisle reserved for men.

[2] The modern Sessa in Latium. There is a village of Garigliano in that region now.

[3] The modern Torre Paterno in Latium. From the opening of the second century to the close of the fourth the ancient villages of Laurentum and Lavinium united to form one municipality.

[4] The modern Porto d'Anzio in Latium. Antium was a city in the fifth century

the  Sentilian  estate  in
 the  region  of  Ardea,[1]
 yielding  240  sol. ;

the estate of Castis in the region of Catina,[2] yielding 1000 sol. ;
 the  estate  of  Trapeæ  in  the  region  of  Catina,  yielding
  1650 sol. ;
 2 censers of purest gold, weighing 30 lbs. ;
  a gift of spices before the altar, every year 150 lbs.
The  holy font where Constantine Augustus was baptised [3]

by the same bishop Silvester   |

of stone of porphyry, overlaid on every side within and without and above and as far as the water with purest silver,
 3009 lbs.

In  the  centre  of  the  font  is  a  porphyry  column,  which  bears  a
 golden  basin  of  purest  gold,  weighing  52  lbs.,  where  is  a

flame and where    |

in the Easter season
burns balsam, 200 lbs., and the wick is of asbestos.
At the edge of the font

in the baptistery    |

is a golden lamb pouring water, which weighs 30 lbs. ;
to the right of the lamb the Savior of purest silver, 5 feet in
 height, weighing 170 lbs., and to the left of the lamb
 John, the Baptist, of silver, 5 feet in height, holding an
 inscribed scroll which bears these words : "Behold the
 Lamb of God, Behold, Who Taketh Away the Sins of
 the World," weighing

125 lbs. ;    |  100 lbs. ;

and its bishop attended the synods at Rome.  It suffered severely and dwindled in
size during the later disorders.
 [1] The colony of Ardea is mentioned as late as 223 A.D., but it sent no bishops to
the Roman councils of the fifth century.  It was evidently declining in population
in the interval.  Duchesne, *op. cit.*, p. 192, n. 39.
 [2] The modern Poggio Catino southwest of Rieti.
 [3] The most venerable part of the present Lateran baptistery is hardly older than
the end of the fourth century and most of it dates only from Xystus III.  See *infra*,
p. 96.  The stone font, however, is the original one stripped of its primitive decorations.

7 silver stags pouring water,[1] weighing each 80 lbs.;

a censer of purest gold set with 49 prases, weighing 15 lbs.

He bestowed upon the holy font:

the estate of Festus,

> the keeper of the
> sacred bed-cham-
> ber, which Con-
> stantine Augustus
> gave him,

in the region of Penestre,[2] yielding 300 sol.;

the estate of Gaba in the region of Gabii,[3] yielding 202 sol.;

the estate of Pictæ in the aforesaid region, yielding 205 sol.;

the Statilian[4] estate in the region of Cora, yielding 300 sol.;

an estate in Sicilia Taurana, in the region Paramnense,[5] yielding 500 sol.;

within the city of Rome houses and

> gardens,      |      granaries,

yielding 2300 sol.;

the estate of Bassus, yielding 120 sol.;

the estate of Laninæ in the region of Cartioli,[6] yielding 200 sol.;

the estate of Caculæ in the region of Momentum,[7] yielding 50 sol.;

---

[1] The stags may have been set around the font with the water running into it from their mouths. In the Roman baths water often flowed in jets from animal heads.

[2] Probably a corrupt form for Præneste, the modern Palestrina. A second century inscription in honor of one Valerius Priscus Festus has been found in the neighborhood. Duchesne, *op. cit.*, p. 192, n. 47.

[3] The modern Castiglione, twelve miles from Rome.

[4] There was a "gens Statilia," to which belonged Titus Statilius Taurus, the friend of Augustus.

[5] Duchesne thinks this may be Palermo. *Op. cit.*, p. 193, n. 51.

[6] Probably Carsioli, near the modern village Carsoli in Latium.

[7] This perhaps should read Nomentum, the modern Mentana, to which the Via Nomentana led.

the Statian estate in the Sabine region,[1] yielding 350 sol. ;

the estate of Murinæ in the Appian Alban region,[2] yielding 300 sol. ;

the estate of Virgo in the region of Cora, yielding 200 sol. ;

beyond the sea :

in the provinces of Africa :

the estate of Iuncis in the Mucarian region,[3] yielding 800 sol. ;

the estate of Capsis in the region of Capsa,[4] yielding 600 sol. ;

the estate of Varia Sardana in the Mimnian region,[5] yielding 500 sol. ;

the estate of Camaræ in the region of Crypta Lupi,[6] yielding 405 sol. ;

the estate of Numæ in the region of Numidia,[7] yielding 650 sol. ;

the estate of Sulphorata in the region of Numidia, yielding 720 sol. ;

the estate of Walzari, an olive plantation in the region of Numidia, yielding 810 sol. ;

| in Greece : | also in Greece, in the region of Crete : |
|---|---|
| the estate of Cefalina | |
| in Crete, | |
| yielding 500 sol. ; | |

---

[1] *Cf. supra*, p. 43, n. 8.

[2] *I.e.*, in the Alban Hills near the Via Appia. A district still called Morena lies between the Via Appia and the Via Latina.

[3] Possibly the region of the Macæ, a people living near the North coast. There were African bishops entitled "Iuncensis," but the situation of their diocese is not known. Duchesne, *op. cit.*, p. 193, n. 55.

[4] A city in the southwestern part of the modern country of Tunis. The place is now called Gafsa.

[5] A bishop of Mina, in the province of Mauretania, attended the council of Carthage in 525. Duchesne, *ibid.*, n. 57.

[6] A corruption, perhaps, of Syrtica Leptis, *i.e.* the city of Leptis in the Regio Syrtica, the modern Tripoli.

[7] The province of Numidia, which covered much the same territory as the modern Algiers.

in Mengaulus: [1]

the estate of Amazon, yielding 222 sol.

At the same time Constantine Augustus built

by request of Silvester, the
bishop,

the basilica of blessed Peter, the apostle, in the shrine of Apollo,[2]
and laid there the coffin with the body of the holy Peter;[3] the
coffin itself he enclosed on all sides with bronze, which is unchange-
able: at the head 5 feet, at the feet 5 feet, at the right side 5 feet,
at the left side 5 feet, underneath 5 feet and overhead 5 feet: thus
he enclosed the body of blessed Peter, the apostle, and laid it
away.

And above he set porphyry columns for adornment [4] and other
spiral columns which he brought from Greece.

---

[1] A corrupt form. Duchesne accepts the suggestion of M. Vignoli that the island of
Gaulus is intended, the modern Gozzo near Malta. *Op. cit.*, p. 193, n. 60.

[2] The great Constantinian basilica of St. Peter stood with some alterations and
many additions until it was torn down by the popes of the Renaissance to make way
for the present edifice. The mosaic of the triumphal arch, which represented Constantine offering a model of the church to Christ, seems to have kept its place to the
last and the stamp of the emperor was on the bricks of which the basilica was built.
For a good brief description of old St. Peter's see Frothingham, *Monuments of Christian
Rome*, pp. 25–29; Lanciani, *Destruction of Ancient Rome*, pp. 31–32; Duchesne, *op. cit.*,
pp. 193–194, n. 61. The last-named quotes from some of the surviving contemporary
descriptions of the church and reproduces a ground plan published by Alfarano in 1590.
There is a mass of literature on the subject to which it is impossible to refer here.
On the site see *supra*, p. 5, n. 5.

[3] The following rather confused description of the tomb of St. Peter is the oldest
and also the fullest in existence. The sarcophagus itself, enclosed still to all probability
in Constantine's bronze casing, lies in a small subterranean chamber connected by a
deep vertical shaft with the confession beneath the present high altar. In 1594, when
the foundations of this altar were being laid, Pope Clement VIII and three cardinals
saw at the bottom of the shaft, which the architect had laid open, a cross of gold lying
upon the tomb, but the pope ordered the shaft immediately filled up and it has never
since been opened. Whether the cross was the one placed there by Constantine is not
certain. The tomb was early made inaccessible, undoubtedly to protect it from in-
vading marauders.

[4] The porphyry columns apparently supported the ciborium above the altar, the
spiral columns next mentioned formed a line or colonnade in front of the confession,
separating it from the nave. Several of the latter may still be seen, adorning niches in the
pillars that support the cupola of the present cathedral, and one is venerated in a side
chapel. They served as models evidently for the huge bronze spiral columns of the

He made also a vaulted roof [1] in the basilica, gleaming with polished gold, and over the body of the blessed Peter, above the bronze which enclosed it, he set a cross of purest gold, weighing 150 lbs., in place of a measure,[2] and upon it were inscribed these words: "CONSTANTINE AUGUSTUS AND HELENA AUGUSTA THIS HOUSE SHINING WITH LIKE ROYAL SPLENDOR A COURT SURROUNDS,"[3]
inscribed in

clear,        |

enamelled letters upon the cross.

> He gave also [4] 4 brass candlesticks, 10 feet in height, overlaid with silver, with figures in silver of the acts of the apostles, weighing each 300 lbs.;
>
> 3 golden chalices, set with 45 prases
>
> > and jacinths,       |
>
> > weighing each 12 lbs.;
> 2 silver jars, weighing 200 lbs.;
> 20 silver chalices, weighing each 10 lbs.;

modern baldachino. They were preserved with particular reverence because of a tradition that arose in the Middle Ages to the effect that they had originally stood in the Temple at Jerusalem. They are represented in Rafael's cartoon of the healing of the impotent man at the Gate Beautiful.

[1] *I.e.* the vaulting of the apse.

[2] "In mensure locus," an unintelligible expression. Other manuscripts give "in mensuram loci," which might mean that the cross was as large as the chamber allowed.

[3] The inscription is recorded nowhere else and, as it stands here, is obviously incomplete. De Rossi suggests the insertion of three words and the alteration of one ending which would make it read, "Constantine Augustus and Helena Augusta beautify with gold this royal house which a court, shining with like splendor, surrounds." Mommsen, *op. cit.*, p. 57, n. on line 13. Duchesne thinks that the "royal house" is the subterranean tomb chamber, which during the fourth century was probably accessible to the devout and not impenetrably sealed until the invasions of the fifth century; in that case the surrounding court would be the basilica itself. Duchesne, *op. cit.*, p. 195, n. 67.

[4] Orosius relates that during Alaric's sack of Rome in 410 the precious vessels of St. Peter's were deposited for safe keeping in the house of an aged, consecrated virgin. They were discovered by the barbarians but before they were carried off Alaric learned that they were the property of the apostle and restored them all in state to the basilica. *Historia adversum Paganos*, lib. *VII*, c. 39, ed. Zangemeister, Teubner, pp. 292–293.

2 golden pitchers, weighing each 10 lbs.;

5 silver pitchers, weighing each 20 lbs.;

a golden paten with a turret of purest gold and a dove,[1]
adorned with prases, jacinths and pearls,

| white stones,

215 in number, weighing 30 lbs.;

5 silver patens, weighing each 15 lbs.;

a golden crown before the body, that is a chandelier, with
50 dolphins, which weighs 35 lbs.;

32 silver lamps in the body of the basilica, with dolphins,
weighing each 10 lbs.;

for the right of the basilica 30 silver lamps, weighing each
8 lbs.;

the altar itself of silver overlaid with gold,

| adorned on every side with gems, 400 in number, | with 210 | adorned on every side with 210 |
|---|---|---|

prases, jacinths and pearls, weighing 350 lbs.;

a censer of purest gold adorned on every side with jewels,

60 in number, |

weighing 15 lbs.

Likewise for revenue, the gift which Constantine Augustus
offered to blessed Peter, the apostle, in the diocese of the East:

in the city of Anthiocia:[2]

the house of Datianus, yielding 240 sol.;

the little house in Cæne,[3] yielding 20 and one third sol.;

the barns in Afrodisia, yielding 20 sol.;

the bath in Ceratheæ, yielding 42 sol.;

the mill in the same place, yielding 23 sol.;

the cook shop in the same place, yielding 10 sol.;

---

[1] Vessels shaped like small turrets or towers and like doves were used to enshrine
the Host.

[2] Antioch, it will be remembered, was traditionally the seat of Peter's first bishopric.
See *supra*, p. 4.

[3] Cæne, Afrodisia and Ceratheæ are all quarters of the city of Antioch.

the garden of Maro, yielding 10 sol.;

the garden in the same place, yielding 11 sol.;

near the city of Anthiocia:

the property Sybilles, a gift to Augustus, yielding 322 sol.,

150 decades [1] of papyrus,

200 lbs. of spices,

200 lbs. of oil of nard, |

35 lbs. of balsam;

near the city of Alexandria:

the property Timialica, given to Constantine Augustus by

Ambrosius,         | Ambronius,

yielding 620 sol.,

300 decades of papyrus,

300 lbs. of oil of nard,

60 lbs. of balsam,

150 lbs. of spices,

50 lbs. of Isaurian storax;

the property of Eutymus, who left no heir, [2] yielding 500 sol.,

70 decades of papyrus;

in Egypt: [3]

near the city of Armenia, [4] the property of Agapus, which he gave to Constantine Augustus;

the property of Passinopolis, yielding 800 sol.,

400 decades of papyrus,

50 medimni of pepper,

100 lbs. of saffron,

150 lbs. of storax,

200 lbs. of spices of cinnamon,

300 lbs. of oil of nard,

100 lbs. of balsam,

---

[1] The decade was apparently a package containing ten sheets.

[2] The property had, therefore, reverted to the imperial exchequer.

[3] After 386 A.D. Egypt did not form part of the administrative division of the Orient, as here, but constituted a separate division alone. Duchesne, *op. cit.*, p. cl.

[4] I do not know what city is meant here.

> 100 bags of flax,
> 150 lbs. of cariophylum,[1]
> 100 lbs. of Cyprian oil,
> 1000 fine stalks of papyrus;
> the property which Hybromius gave to Constantine Augustus, yielding 450 sol.,
> 200 decades of papyrus,
> 50 lbs. of spices of cinnamon,
>
> 200 lbs. of oil of nard, |
>
> 50 lbs. of balsam;
> in the province of the Euphrates, near the city of Cyrus:[2]
> the property of Armanazon, yielding 380 sol.;
>
> the property of Obariæ, |
> yielding 260 sol. |

At the same time Constantine Augustus[3] built the basilica of blessed Paul, the apostle, at the bidding of Silvester, the bishop, and laid his body away there in bronze and enclosed it, as he did the body of the blessed Peter.[4] And to this basilica he offered the following gifts:

> near Tarsus[5] in Cilicia:
> the island of Cordionon, yielding 800 sol.

All the consecrated vessels of gold and silver and bronze he set there, as in the basilica of blessed Peter, the apostle, so also he ordained them for the basilica of blessed Paul, the apostle. More-

---

[1] Perhaps a corruption for "carpheotum," a superior kind of frankincense.

[2] Perhaps Cyrrhus, a city in Syria.

[3] One manuscript reads, "Constantine Augustus and Lord Constantius Augustus built" etc. If Constantine really built the first basilica of St. Paul, it was a small and unpretentious edifice. In 386 the emperors Valentinian II, Theodosius and Arcadius ordered the erection of a great church on the site, which was completed early in the fifth century. It was destroyed by fire in 1823 and the present basilica of San Paolo fuori le Mura is almost entirely a latter-day reconstruction.

[4] The empty sarcophagus of St. Paul was unearthed during the work of rebuilding the present church. It is of marble and bears an inscription in fourth century letters, "PAULO APOSTOLO ET MARTYRI." The tomb lay farther outside the city walls than that of St. Peter and was rifled probably during the Saracen invasion, if not before.

[5] It was evidently thought appropriate to endow the church of Paul of Tarsus with lands in the vicinity of his birthplace.

over he placed a golden cross over the tomb of blessed Paul, the apostle, weighing 150 lbs.

near the city of Tyre:

the property of Comitum, yielding 550 sol.;

the property of Tymia, yielding 250 sol.;

the property of Fronimusa, yielding 700 sol.,

70 lbs. of oil of nard,

50 lbs. of spices,

50 lbs. of cinnamon;

near the city of Egypt:

the property of Cyrios, yielding 710 sol.,

70 lbs. of oil of nard,

30 lbs. of balsam,

70 lbs. of spices,

30 lbs. of storax,

150 lbs. of oil of myrrh;

the property of Basilea, yielding 550 sol.,

50 lbs. of spices,

60 lbs. of oil of nard,

20 lbs. of balsam,

60 lbs. of saffron;

the property of the island Maccabes, yielding 510 sol.,

510 stalks of fine papyrus,

300 bags of flax.

At the same time Constantine Augustus constructed a basilica in the Sessorian palace,[1] where also he

placed and               |

enclosed in gold and jewels some of the wood of the holy cross of our Lord Jesus Christ, and he dedicated the church under the name by which it is called even to this day, Hierusalem.[2] In that church

---

[1] The Sessorian palace is known to have been a residence of the empress Helena. Two inscriptions in her honor have been discovered there. In spite of alterations and mutilations the present basilica still shows traces of its origin as a private hall. Duchesne, *op. cit.*, p. 196, n. 75.

[2] The title is now Santa Croce in Gerusalemme. In the fifteenth century an inscription was still legible beneath the apsidal mosaic, which commemorated the pay-

he offered the following gifts : | he offered these gifts :

4 candlesticks of silver burning before the holy wood, like to the number of the 4 gospels, weighing each 80 lbs. ;

50 silver chandeliers, weighing each 15 lbs. ;

a goblet of gold, weighing 10 lbs. ;

5 golden chalices for service, weighing each one lb. ;

3 silver goblets, weighing each 8 lbs. ;

10 silver chalices for service, weighing each 2 lbs. ;

a golden paten, weigh-|
ing 10 lbs. ; |

a silver paten overlaid with gold and set with jewels, weighing 50 lbs. ;

a silver altar, weighing 250 lbs. ;

3 silver pitchers, weighing each 20 lbs. ;

and all the land

about the palace he gave | near the palace itself,
as an offering to the |
church ; |

likewise the property of Sponsæ on the Via Lavicana,[1] yielding 263 sol. ;

near the city of Laurentum[2] the property of Patræ, yielding 120 sol. ;

near the city of Nepeta[3] the property of Anglesis, yielding 150 sol. ;

near the aforesaid city the property of Terega,[4] which yields 160 sol. ;

---

ment of a vow by Valentinian, Placidia and Honoria Augusti to the "holy church Hierusalem." As for the relic of the cross, St. Cyril of Jerusalem, writing about 348, says that fragments of the sacred wood were dispersed through all the world. Duchesne, *ibid*.

[1] Or Labicana. One of the main roads leading over the Esquiline Hill to the Latin town of Labicum.

[2] *Cf. supra*, p. 50, n. 1.

[3] The modern Nepi in the upper border of the Roman province.

[4] The spot may have taken its name from the river Treia, which flows by Nepi. Duchesne, *op. cit.*, p. 196, n. 79.

near the city of Falisca,[1] the property of Herculus, which
he gave to Augustus and Augustus gave to the church
of Hierusalem, yielding 140 sol. ;

near the city of Tuder [2] the property of Angulæ, yielding
153 sol.

At the same time he built the basilica of the holy martyr Agnes [3]
at the request of

Constantia,[4]

his daughter, and a baptistery in the same place,[5] where both his
sister, Constantia, and the daughter of Augustus were baptised

by Silvester, the bishop,

where also he presented the following gifts :

a paten of purest gold, weighing 20 lbs. ;

a golden chalice, weighing 10 lbs. ;

a chandelier of purest gold with 30 dolphins, weighing
15 lbs. ;

2 silver patens, weighing each 20 lbs. ;

5 silver chalices, weighing each 10 lbs. ;

30 silver chandeliers, weighing each 8 lbs. ;

---

[1] Now Civita Castellana.

[2] Now Todi, in Umbria.

[3] The church of Sant' Agnese on the Via Nomentana, erected over the traditional
tomb of the virgin martyr, was rebuilt by Honorius I in the seventh century, so that it is
now uncertain if any part of the present structure belongs to the age of Constantine.

[4] The name of Constantine's daughter was Constantina. Originally an acrostic
inscription in the apse of the basilica commemorated the dedication of the church in
her name. Constantine's sister was Constantia. Duchesne, *op. cit.*, p. 196, n. 80.

[5] The small, circular building, now known as the church of Santa Costanza, was
used originally as a mausoleum but may have been intended also as a baptistery.
The huge porphyry sarcophagus, at present in the Vatican Museum, stood in a niche
in the wall facing the entrance and a baptismal font may have occupied the central
space under the dome. The arrangement would then have been similar to that in the
Lateran baptistery, and the shape of the two buildings, with their double apsed vestibules,
is not unlike. At any rate there is no vestige of another baptistery in the vicinity.
There is no unimpeachable account of the baptism of the princesses of Constantine's
house, but it is not, of course, improbable that such a ceremony took place. Am-
mianus Marcellinus tells us that in the year 360 the body of Helena, one of Constantine's
daughters, was sent to Rome to be buried on the Via Nomentana, outside the city,
where her sister Constantina already lay. *Roman History*, XXI, 1 ; tr. Yonge, Bohn's
Library, p. 244.

40

| chandeliers of brass; | lamps of brass metal; | chandeliers of brass metal; |

40 candelabra of brass overlaid with silver and adorned with reliefs;

a golden lamp with 12 wicks,

which weighs 20 lbs., |

over the font, weighing 15 lbs.;

likewise a gift

for revenue: |

all the land about the city of Fidelinæ,[1] yielding 160 sol.;
on the Via Salaria as far as the ruins, all the land

of the holy Agnes, |

yielding 105 sol.;
the land of Mucus, yielding 80 sol.;
the property of Vicus Pisonis, yielding

350 sol.; | 250 sol.;

the land of Casulæ, yielding 100 sol.

At the same time

Constantine Augustus | he

built the basilica of blessed Lawrence, the martyr,[2] on the Via Tiburtina in the Ager Veranus over the burial crypt, and he made stairs of ascent and of descent to the body of the holy martyr Lawrence. In that place he erected an apse and adorned it with

[1] Probably Fidenæ, the modern Castel Giubileo, five miles from Rome, near the Via Salaria.

[2] The present church of San Lorenzo in Agro Verano is formed by the union of two ancient basilicas, which were thrown into one by Honorius III in the thirteenth century. The smaller of these two, which contains the present choir and covers the resting-place of the saint, may owe its foundation to Constantine. Little beside the columns of the lower floor can, however, with safety be ascribed to him, for the building was restored at the beginning of the fifth century and again rebuilt, with the addition of the galleries, at the close of the sixth. See *infra*, p. 89, n. 3; p. 168, n. 2. The description given here is interesting as one of the earliest of a confession or tomb chamber of a martyr in a basilica erected "ad corpus." The basilica was placed so that its altar stood directly over the tomb, which was reached by steps leading down below the altar.

porphyry and the spot over the tomb he enclosed with silver and beautified it with railings of purest silver, which weighed 1000 lbs.; and before the tomb itself within the crypt he set:

> a lamp of purest gold with 10 wicks, weighing 20 lbs.;
>
> a crown of purest silver with 50 dolphins, weighing 30 lbs.;
>
> 2 bronze candlesticks, 10 feet in height, weighing each 300 lbs.;

> before the body of the blessed Lawrence, the martyr, images overlaid with silver to show his passion and silver lamps with 6 wicks, weighing each 15 lbs.

In the same locality : [1]

> the property of one Quiriaces, a religious woman, which the fisc had seized in the time of the persecution, the estate of Veranus,[2] yielding 160 sol.;
>
> the property of Aqua Tuscia on one side, yielding 153 sol.;
>
> the property of Augustus in the Sabine region, yielding to the name of the Christians[3] 120 sol.;
>
> the property of Sul-
> furatæ [4] yielding 62
> sol.;
>
> the property of Micinæ belonging to Augustus, yielding 110 sol.;

---

[1] Here, as in the case of the lands bestowed on Sant' Agnese, the estates, so far as their situation can now be determined, lay in the neighborhood of the basilica upon which they were conferred.

[2] This is the land upon which the basilica stood. Duchesne thinks that a passage like this, alluding to a well-known persecution with no mention of emperor or date, is certainly taken from a source at least as old as the first half of the fourth century. *Op. cit.*, p. cl.

[3] Duchesne believes that this passage also indicates the use of some primitive source, that the expression, "name of the Christians," to signify the Christian community antedates the persecution of Diocletian. The property here mentioned was perhaps a part of the possessions of the church restored to it by the Edict of Milan.[2] Duchesne, *ibid.*, pp. cl, cli.

[4] The name may be derived from some sulphurous springs on the Via Tiburtina, sixteen miles from Rome. Duchesne, *op. cit.*, p. 198, n. 89.

the property of Termulæ, yielding

65 sol. ;          | 60 sol. ;

the property of Aranæ, yielding 70 sol. ;

the property of Septi-
mitus, yielding 130
sol.

The gift which he offered :

a golden paten, weigh-
ing 20 lbs. ;

2 silver patens, weigh-
ing each 30 lbs. ;

a goblet of purest gold,
weighing 15 lbs. ;

2 silver goblets, weigh-
ing each 10 lbs. ;

10 silver chalices for
service, weighing
each 2 lbs. ;

2 silver pitchers, weigh-
ing each 10 lbs. ;

30 silver lamps, weigh-
ing each 20 lbs. ;

a jar of silver weigh-
ing 150 lbs., holding
2 medimni.

At the same time Constantine Augustus built a basilica to the blessed martyrs Marcellinus, the priest, and Peter, the exorcist, at Inter duas Lauros; also a mausoleum where his mother, Helena Augusta, was buried on the Via Lavicana, at the 3rd milestone.[1] And in this place,

At the same time Constantine Augustus built a basilica on the Via Lavicana at Inter duas Lauros to blessed Peter and Marcellinus, the martyrs; also a mausoleum where the most blessed Augusta, his mother, was buried in a sarcophagus of porphyry, and he offered there :

[1] The remains of the mausoleum of the empress Helena and the catacomb of Santi Pietro e Marcellino may be seen about two miles from the Porta Maggiore at a place

both for love of his mother and
for veneration of the saints, he
offered votive gifts :

> a paten of purest gold, weighing 35 lbs. ;
> 4 silver candlesticks overlaid with gold, 12 feet in height,
> weighing each 200 lbs. ;
> a golden crown, that is a chandelier, with 120 dolphins,
> weighing 30 lbs. ;
> 3 golden chalices, weighing each 10 lbs., set with prases and
> jacinths ;
> 2 golden pitchers, weighing each 40 lbs. ;
> an altar of purest silver, weighing 200 lbs. ;

before the tomb of the blessed
Helena Augusta, which is of porphyry carved with images,[1]

> 20 silver chandeliers, weighing each 20 lbs.

Likewise for the aforesaid holy | Likewise in the basilica of the
martyrs he gave to the basilica | saints Peter and Marcellinus he
as a gift : | gave as a gift :

> an altar of purest silver, weighing 200 lbs. ;
> 2 patens of purest gold, weighing each 15 lbs. ;
> 2 silver patens, weighing each 15 lbs. ;
> a large goblet of

> > the purest

> > gold,

now called Tor Pignattara on the Via Casilina, which was formerly the Via Labicana.
The basilica has completely disappeared. An imperial palace stood near by, "ad
Duas Lauros," near the two laurels, in the time of Septimus Severus and was the scene
of the assassination of Valentinian III in 455. The mausoleum is octagonal in shape
and surmounted with a dome. In the sixteenth century Bosio saw the ruins of a great
courtyard and portico about it, all of which have now vanished. Eusebius says that
the body of the empress was transported in state to Rome for burial. *Life of Constantine*, Richardson, *Nicene and Post-Nicene Fathers*, Ser. 2, vol. I, p. 532.

[1] The huge porphyry sarcophagus which was found in the mausoleum of Helena
was removed in the twelfth century to the Lateran by Pope Anastasius IV, who des-
tined it for his own sepulchre. Pius VI transferred it to the Vatican, where it now
stands near the sarcophagus from the mausoleum of Constantina. It is adorned with
figures in relief, chiefly battle scenes.

whereon the name of |
Augustus was engraved, |

weighing 20 lbs.;
a smaller goblet of gold, weighing 10 lbs.;
5 silver goblets, weighing each 12 lbs.;
20 silver chalices for service, weighing each 3 lbs.;
4 silver pitchers, weighing each 15 lbs.;
every year 900 lbs. of pure oil of nard,
100 lbs. of balsam,
100 lbs. of spices for incense for the aforesaid holy martyrs, blessed Marcellinus and Peter;
the estate of Laurentum near the aqueduct, with a bath, and
all the land from the Porta Sessoriana

| | | |
|---|---|---|
| as far as the Via Penestrina, and from the Via Itineris Latinæ as far as Mount Gabus; [1] | the travellers' road as far as the Via Latina near Mount Gabus, Mount Gabus itself; | and the travellers' road as far as the Via Latina near Mount Albius, Mount Albius itself; |

the property of Helena Augusta, yielding 1220 sol.;
the island of Sardinia[2] with all the property

belonging to that island, |

yielding 1024 sol.;

the island of                              |

Mesenum[3] with the property

belonging to that island, | belonging to it, all of it.

yielding 810 sol.;

---

[1] It is impossible to form an exact idea of the area meant by this obscure description, though the general location is clear enough. The "aqueduct" may be either the Alexandrine or the Claudian, both of which pass near the Via Prænestina and the Via Latina. Mount Gabus or Monte Cavo may be any one of the hollow hillocks or craters which dot the Campagna. Duchesne, *op. cit.*, p. 199, n. 91.

[2] The whole island cannot have been conveyed to the basilica. Our author has in all likelihood omitted a list of the particular properties on the island.

[3] Duchesne suggests that the peninsular of Misenum is intended. That is so nearly an island that it might well pass for one in common speech. *Op. cit.*, p. 199, n. 93.

the island of Matidia, which is Mount Argentarius,[1] yielding
600 sol.;

the property in the Sabine region, which is called Duæ Casæ,
at the foot of Mount Lucretius,[2] yielding 200 sol.

At the same time Constantine Augustus

by request of Silvester, the
bishop,

built a basilica in the city of Hostia[3] near Portus, the harbor city
of Rome, to the blessed apostles Peter and Paul and to John the
Baptist, where he offered the following

gifts:

a silver paten, weighing 30 lbs.;
10 silver chalices, weighing each

two lbs.;                        |    5 lbs.;

2 silver pitchers, weighing each 10 lbs.;
30 silver

chandeliers,                     |  lamps,

weighing each 5 lbs.;
2 silver goblets, weighing each 8 lbs.;
a single silver paten for the chrism, weighing 10 lbs.;
a bowl of silver for baptism, weighing 20 lbs.;
the island which is called Assis,[4] which lies between Portus
and Hostia;
all the property along the sea as far as Digitus Solis,[5] yielding

655 sol.;                        |  300 sol.;

the property of the Greeks in the region of Ardea, yielding 80
sol.;

[1] Monte Argentaro on the coast of Tuscany, also a peninsular almost cut off from
the mainland.

[2] Mount Lucretilis, now known as Monte Genaro, made famous by Horace.

[3] Ostia. Modern excavations on the site of the ancient city have not so far revealed any Christian church or monument. Portus is, of course, the modern Porto
on the right bank of the Tiber.

[4] This is apparently the island of the delta, formed by the two branches of the Tiber
at its mouth, but the name occurs nowhere else.

[5] Unknown.

the property of Quiritus in the region of Hostia, yielding 311 sol.;

the property of Balneolum in the region of Ostia, yielding 42 sol.;

the property Nymfulæ, yielding 30 sol.

Likewise that which Gallicanus [1] offered to the aforesaid basilica of the holy apostles Peter and Paul and of John the Baptist; he offered the following:

a silver crown with dolphins, weighing 20 lbs.;

a silver chalice carved in relief, weighing 15 lbs.;

a silver pitcher, weighing 18 lbs.;

the estate Mallianum [2] in the Sabine region, yielding 115 and one third sol.;

the estate Picturæ

in the region of Vellitræ,[3] yielding 43 sol.;

the estate of the Suri on the Via Claudia in the region of Veii,[4] yielding 56 sol.;

the Gargilian estate in the region of Suessa,[5] yielding 655 sol.

At this time Constantine Augustus built the basilica of holy John the Baptist in the city of Alba[6] and offered there the following:

[1] The *Acts of St. Gallicanus*, composed later than the *Lib. Pont.* and in part based upon it, ascribed to him the building of a basilica and hospital at Ostia. It seems likely that the legendary saint is a reminiscence of the historical character Pammachius, the proconsul and senator, who built a church and hospital at Porto toward the end of the fourth century and also the church over the house of the martyrs John and Paul on the Cœlian Hill at Rome. The charitable institution at Porto is the earliest of the kind known. The site has been explored sufficiently to show the general plan: a basilica opening off a square court with rooms and halls for the poor and sick arranged about it. Duchesne, *op. cit.*, p. 199, n. 99. Frothingham, *Monuments of Christian Rome*, pp. 48, 49.

[2] Magliano, the present seat of the bishopric of Sabinum.

[3] Velitræ, now Velletri in Latium.

[4] The ancient Etruscan town stood near the site of the modern village of Isola.

[5] A property of the same name and situation is included among the lands bestowed upon the Lateran basilica. *Supra*, p. 49.

[6] Albano in Latium. Some traces of Constantine's basilica are said to be still

a silver paten, weighing 30 lbs.;

a goblet of silver gilt, weighing 12 lbs.;

10

silver                 |

chalices for service, weighing each 3 lbs.;

2 silver pitchers, weighing each 20 lbs.;

the property of the Lake of Turnus[1] with the adjacent fields, yielding

the estate of Molæ,[2] |
yielding
60 sol.;

50 sol.;
the property

at Alba with the     |

Lake of Alba,[3] yielding 250 sol.;
the estate of Mucus, yielding

160 sol.;            |       170 sol.;

all the empty barracks or houses belonging to the municipality[4] in the town of Alba,

everything in the neighborhood | were offered as gifts to the holy
of the church of Constantine, | church of Constantine;
was offered by Augustus; |

the property of Hortus, yielding 20 sol.;
the property of Tiberius Cæsar, yielding 280 sol.;

visible. De Rossi has proved that the Christian church of Albano originated probably in the camp of the Second Parthian Legion, which was stationed there during the third century. Duchesne, *op. cit.*, p. 199, n. 103.

[1] The Laghetto di Turno, with its recollections of the Æneid, lies about two miles from Albano. Funeral inscriptions have been found there testifying to the existence of a rural Christian community in the sixth century. Duchesne, *op. cit.*, p. 200, n. 104.

[2] A place called Il Molo is now about a mile from Albano.

[3] The famous Lago di Albano.

[4] These are undoubtedly the buildings left empty by the departure of the Second Parthian Legion and the population of camp-followers and dependents. See *supra*, p. 67, n. 6. The word translated barracks is "schenica" or "scenica," which here has its original Greek sense of tents or camps, rather than its ordinary Latin association with theatres and actors.

the property of Marinæ,[1] yielding 50 sol. ;

the estate of Nemus,[2] yielding 280 sol. ;

the property of Amartianæ in the region of Cora, yielding 150 sol. ;

the Statilian property, yielding 70 sol. ;

the Median property, yielding 30 sol.

At the same time Constantine Augustus built a basilica of the apostles within the city of Capua,[3] which he called the Constantinian basilica, and there also he offered the following gifts :

2 silver patens, weighing each 20 lbs. ;

3 silver goblets, weighing each 9 lbs. ;

15 chalices for service, weighing each 2 lbs. ;

2 silver pitchers, weighing each 10 lbs. ;

4 bronze candlesticks, 10 feet in height, weighing each 180 lbs. ;

30 silver chandeliers, weighing each 5 lbs. ;

30 bronze chandeliers ;

And he offered certain property :

the Statilian estate in the region of Menturnæ,[4] yielding 315 sol. ;

a property in the region of Gaeta,[5] yielding 85 sol. ;

the property of Paternum in the region of Suessa, yielding 150 sol. ;

the property of Ad Centum[6] in the region of Capua, yielding 60 sol. ;

a property in the region of Suessa Gauronica,[7] yielding 40 sol. ;

the property of Leo, yielding 60 sol.

[1] At Marino, near Albano.

[2] The place may have some connection with the Lake of Nemi.

[3] There are no visible remains of Constantine's church in the modern Santa Maria di Capua.

[4] Minturnæ, a town in Latium, the ruins of which are to be seen near the modern Trajetta.

[5] The ancient Caieta, now Gaeta in Latium.

[6] This name does not signify, as might be supposed, "At the hundredth milestone," for Capua is 132 miles from Rome by way of the Via Appia, 138 by the Via Latina. Duchesne, *op. cit.*. p. 200, n. 114.

[7] Unquestionably a corruption for Suessa Aurunca, the full title in ancient times of the modern Sessa.

At the same time Constantine Augustus built a basilica in the city of Naples,[1] to which he offered the following :

2 silver patens, weighing each

15 lbs. ;          | 25 lbs. ;

2 silver goblets, weighing each ten lbs. ;
15 chalices for service, weighing each 2 lbs. ;
2 silver pitchers, weighing each fifteen lbs. ;
20 silver lamps, weighing each 8 lbs. ;
20 bronze lamps,

weighing each 10 lbs.   |

He built likewise an aqueduct, 8 miles in length ; he built also a forum

in the same city [2]          |

and he offered the following gift :

the property of Macarus, yielding 150 sol. ;
the Cimbrian property, yielding 105 sol. ;
the property of Sclina, yielding 108 sol. ;
the property of Afilæ, yielding 140 sol. ;
the property of Nymfulæ, yielding 90 sol. ;
the property of the island[3] with the fortress, yielding 80 sol.

At the same time the blessed Silvester established his parish church[4] in the city of Rome in the Third District, near the baths of Domitian, which are called also the baths of Trajan ; the parish church of Silvester, to which Constantine Augustus gave :

[1] The basilica may have stood on the site of the church of Santa Restituta, the medieval cathedral of Naples.

[2] A Neapolitan inscription in honor of Constantine has been discovered and two in honor of Helena, but they contain no allusion to public works of this sort. Duchesne, *op. cit.*, p. 200, n. 116.

[3] Possibly the island of Nisida between Naples and Pozzuoli, called in classic times "Nesis" or Νῆσος, *i.e.*, "the island," without other name.

[4] The church already described on p. 42. The Third District may be either the civil or ecclesiastical division, for the Third Region of Augustus comprehended this neighborhood. The list of precious vessels and lamps is not dissimilar to the inventory already given for this church, although the latter is longer. The two lists of lands of the church are, however, quite different, as may be seen by comparison. The author may have made two sets of extracts from the same document or may have drawn from two different documents of different dates. Duchesne, *op. cit.*, p. 200, n. 119.

a silver paten, weighing 20 lbs. ;

a silver pitcher, weighing 10 lbs. ;

2 silver goblets, weighing each 8 lbs. ;

10 silver chandeliers, weighing each 5 lbs. ;

16 bronze candelabra, weighing each 40 lbs. ;

5 silver chalices for service, weighing each 2 lbs. ;

the Percilian estate in the Sabine region, yielding 50 sol. ;

the Barbatian estate in the region of Ferens,[1] yielding 35 and
one third sol. ;

the Statian estate in the region of Tribula,[2] yielding 66 and
one third sol. ;

the estate of Beruclæ in the region of Cora, yielding 40 sol. ;

the Sulpician estate in the region of Cora, yielding 70
sol. ;

the estate of Taurus in the region of Beii,[3] yielding 42 sol. ;

the Sentian estate in the region of Tibur,[4] yielding 30 sol. ;

the Ceian estate in the region of Penestre,[5] yielding 50
sol. ;

the estate of Termulæ in the region of Penestre, yielding 35
sol. ;

the property of Cylon in the region of Penestre, yielding 59
sol.

He offered also all that was requisite to the parish church of
Equitius.

This Silvester held 6 ordinations in the month of December, 42
priests, 26 deacons, 65 bishops in divers places.

He was buried in the cemetery of Priscilla[6] on the Via Salaria,

[1] Ferentinum, now Ferentino, a small town on the Via Latina.

[2] Trebula was the name of three Italian towns, one in Campania, now Maddaloni,
the others in Sabinum, one of which is now Monte Leone, the last has disappeared.
Duchesne is of the opinion that the second of the three is meant here. *Op. cit.*, p. 200,
n. 122.

[3] Veii.

[4] The modern Tivoli.

[5] Præneste, now Palestrina.

[6] The little church which stood over the catacomb of Priscilla was known as the
church of St. Sylvester in the early Roman topographies drawn up for the guidance of
pilgrims. The Itinerary ascribed to William of Malmesbury mentions Sylvester's
marble tomb. The site is vacant and grassgrown to-day. Duchesne, *op. cit.*, p. 200,
n. 123.

three miles from the city of Rome, December 31. He verily died catholic and a confessor.[1]

And the bishopric was empty 15 days.

## XXXV. Marcus (336)

Marcus, by nationality a Roman, son of Priscus, occupied the see 2 years, 8 months and 20 days. He was bishop in the time of Constantine, during the consulship of Nepotianus and Facundus (A.D. 336), from February 1 until October 1.

He ordained that the bishop of Hostia, who consecrates the bishop, should wear the pallium and that by him the bishop of the city of Rome should be consecrated.[2] And he made regulations for the whole church.

He built two basilicas, one on the Via Ardeatina, where he is buried,[3] and one in the city of Rome, in Pallacinis.[4]

[1] These words testify to the unusual veneration for the memory of Pope Sylvester. In 1632 a silver "corona" of ancient workmanship, bearing a votive inscription to "the holy Silvester," was found in a garden adjacent to Sylvester's parish church, San Martino ai Monti. Duchesne thinks that the offering may have dated from the latter half of the fifth century. The spurious lives of the pope, with their miracles and marvels, may have increased popular reverence but the feeling seems to have existed before the legends. Unfortunately, in spite of the length and importance of Sylvester's pontificate, there are no authentic documents left to furnish us with an idea of the part he actually played in the stirring events of his day or with more than the vaguest notion of the situation at Rome under Constantine. Duchesne, *op. cit.*, p. 201, n. 125.

[2] In the time of Augustine the bishop of Ostia regularly performed the ceremony of consecrating the pope and he retains that right to this day. Duchesne, *Lib. Pont.*, vol. 1, p. 203, n. 2. The use of the pallium or scarf by the bishop seems to have been derived from the use of the pallium as badge of office by the civil magistrates of the fourth and fifth centuries, as depicted on consular diptychs of the period. The earliest writer to refer to the ecclesiastical pallium is St. Isidore of Pelusium about 440. He speaks of the symbolical significance of the garment as of something well known. In the sixth century Symmachus and succeeding popes sent pallia to other bishops. Frescoes and mosaics of that century at Rome and Ravenna uniformly portray these scarves on the shoulders of bishops. Their use was not confined to archbishops until the ninth century. Lowrie, *Christian Art and Archæology*, pp. 407–410.

[3] The small cemeterial church of Santa Balbina near the catacomb of Callistus. It has now disappeared.

[4] The modern church of San Marco. It is impossible to attribute anything in the present edifice to the fourth century. The mosaic in the apse dates only from the reconstruction of the church in the ninth century. However, Pope Hadrian IV in 794 cited the mosaics and paintings in the basilica of his day as proofs of the use of images at Rome in the time of the Council of Nicea. Mansi, *Amplissima Collectio,*

Pope St. Sylvester

Pope St. Julius I

\* \* \* \* \* \* \* \*[1]

He also was buried in the cemetery of Balbina on the Via Ardeatina, which he himself had supervised and built, October 6. And the bishopric was empty 20 days.

## XXXVI. JULIUS I (337–352)

Julius, by nationality a Roman, son of Rusticus, occupied the see 15 years, 2 months and 6 days. He was bishop in the time of Constantinus, son of Constantine, the heretic, from the consulship of Felicianus (A.D. 337) and of Maximin.[2] He endured many tribulations and was in exile 10 months and after the death of this Constantinus he returned in glory to the seat of blessed Peter, the apostle.[3]

He built 2 basilicas, one

in the city of Rome,

near the forum,[4]

and another across the Tiber[5]  |  and another on the Via Flaminia,

vol. XIII, p. 801. The name of the region where the church was built is as old as Cicero, who says that Sextus Roscius was killed on his way from dinner "ad balneas Pallacinas," near the Pallacine baths. *Pro Roscio*, VII, 18. Duchesne, *op. cit.*, p. 203, nn. 5 and 6.

[1] A catalogue of gifts bestowed by the emperor Constantine upon the church of Santa Balbina and the list of the clergy ordained by Marcus have been omitted. Hereafter such lists, unless possessing unusual interest or value, will not be included in the translation. Those already furnished will serve as types.

[2] The *Liberian Catalogue* has this, "in the time of Constantine, from the consulship of Felicianus and Titianus (A.D. 337), from February 6 to April 12 in the year when Constantius was consul for the fifth time and Constantius was Cæsar (A.D. 352)."

[3] The author of the *Lib. Pont.* has inserted here a sentence which would be more appropriate in the history of Liberius, the next pope, who was in fact driven into exile through the influence of an heretical emperor. Pope Julius, on the contrary, was supported throughout his pontificate by the orthodox Constans and after the latter's death by Magnentius. He played an authoritative part in the doctrinal controversies which in his day were distracting the Eastern branch of the church.

[4] The church was rebuilt by Pelagius I in honor of the apostles, Philip and James, and is now known as Santi Apostoli. *Infra*, p. 162, n. 2. It stands on the edge of the ancient forum of Trajan.

[5] The modern basilica of Santa Maria in Trastevere, rebuilt by Gregory IV in the ninth century and by Innocent II in the twelfth. It is called in the *Lib. Pont.* the basilica of Julius until the eighth century, when it is styled the basilica of Mary. The first church on the site was probably erected by Callistus but, built in an era of perse-

and 3 cemeteries, one on the Via Flaminia, another on the Via Aurelia and another on the Via Portuensis.[1]

He made a regulation that no member of the clergy should plead any case in public except in a church,[2] and that the information which concerns all in the faith

of the church　　　　　　　|

should be collected by notaries, and that all documents should be duly recorded in church by the chief of the notaries; whether bonds or instruments or deeds of gift or of exchange or of delivery or wills or rescripts or manumissions of a member of the clergy, they should be recorded in church within the sacred archives.[3]

＊　　　＊　　　＊　　　＊　　　＊　　　＊　　　＊　　　＊4

He also was buried on the Via Aurelia in the cemetery of Calepodus [5] at the third milestone

from the city of Rome,　　　|

April 12.

And the bishopric was empty 25 days.

---

cution, it was perhaps only a small and unobtrusive hall of meeting. See *supra*, p. 20, n. 5.

[1] The first of these three suburban foundations was the great basilica of San Valentino, two miles beyond the city gate of the same name. It is mentioned in the early pilgrim itineraries as a church of exceptional size and beauty but by the fourteenth century it was already in ruins and now hardly a vestige is left above ground. Recent excavations have disclosed the pavement of the nave and apse and have revealed among other objects an epitaph set up in 359, only seven years after the death of Julius. The second of the extramural churches was probably built above the cemetery of Calepodio, where Julius was buried, the third may have been the basilica of Felix, now also disappeared.

[2] A repetition of the apocryphal decree already ascribed to Sylvester. *Supra*, p. 45, and n. 7.

[3] An attempt to require all members of the clergy to register deeds, wills and other legal documents in the episcopal court instead of in the municipal. There is no other account of such a decree. Our text may record a custom or a policy which grew up gradually rather than a formal enactment. It is likely that there was jealousy between the ecclesiastical and civil tribunals and some overlapping of jurisdiction. Duchesne, *Lib. Pont.*, vol. I, p. 206, n. 10.

[4] List of ordinations.

[5] Pope Callistus had been buried there. *Supra*, p. 21, n. 1.

## XXXVII. LIBERIUS (352–366)

Liberius, by nationality a Roman, son of Augustus, occupied the see 6 years, 3 months and 4 days. He was bishop in the time of Constantius, son of Constantine, to Constantius Augustus III.[1]

He was sent into exile by Constantius because he refused to consent to the heresy of Arius, and he was in exile 3 years. And Liberius summoned together the priests and by their counsel ordained in his stead Felix, the venerable priest and bishop.[2] And Felix held a council and found two priests, Ursacius and Valens by name, in sympathy with Constantius Augustus, the Arian, and in the council of the 48 bishops he expelled them.[3]

[1] The *Liberian Catalogue* ends here with the date of the opening of the pontificate of Liberius, 352.

[2] The history of Liberius and Felix, as given in our text, is a strange medley of facts and legend. The actual occurrences seem to have been the following. Liberius, early in his pontificate, was required by the emperor to recognize the Eastern Arian bishops as members of the same communion. On his refusal he was condemned to exile and spent three years in banishment in Thrace. The Roman clergy meanwhile bound themselves by oath to accept no other bishop during his lifetime. However, the archdeacon Felix shortly afterward came to an understanding with the emperor and was ordained bishop in Liberius' stead and accepted by most of the clergy in the city. The Roman people, on the other hand, remained loyal to Liberius and demanded his recall of Constantius, when the latter visited the city in 357. Liberius now proved willing to give certain pledges of tolerance and returned to Rome in 358 to receive an enthusiastic welcome. It was planned at first that Liberius and Felix should share the duties and prerogatives of the bishopric but outbreaks of violence followed the attempt at compromise and Felix was compelled to leave the city. Later he tried to get possession of the basilica of Julius, Santa Maria in Trastevere, but was forced to retire. He died in November, 365. Liberius was inclined to be forgiving and restored the adherents of Felix to their original posts, but many of his party were less placable. On the death of Liberius in 366 a schism broke out, the bitter enemies of Felix chose Ursinus as pope, the moderates, who had upheld the pacifist policy of Liberius, chose Damasus. See *infra*, pp. 79–80. For a discussion of the process by which the legendary version of these incidents has been evolved and Felix has been transformed from a heretic supplanter of Liberius to an orthodox saint installed by Liberius' own hands, as in our text, see Duchesne, *Lib. Pont.*, vol. I, pp. cxx–cxxv. A summary of Liberius' correspondence with Constantius and with other bishops on these matters may be found in Jaffé, *Regesta*, pp. 33–35, 208–228.

[3] The real Ursacius and Valens were bishops of Belgrade and Eszek respectively and the chief representatives of the Arian sect in the West. They had been condemned by the Council of Sardica under Pope Julius but were readmitted to communion by Felix in fulfilment of his agreement with the emperor. The story given in the *Lib. Pont.* is therefore an exact reversal of the truth. Duchesne, *op. cit.*, p. 208, n. 6.

But after a few days Ursacius and Valens were impelled by zeal to beseech Constantius Augustus to recall Liberius from exile that he might maintain one single communion

| | |
|---|---|
| but without baptising a second time.[1] | apart from the second baptism. |

Then authority was sent by Catulinus, the commissioner,[2] and Ursacius and Valens went together to Liberius.  And Liberius accepted the commands

of Augustus

that he should extend the one

single

communion to the heretics, provided only that they should not administer the second baptism.

Then they recalled Liberius from exile.

And on his return

from exile

Liberius dwelt in the cemetery of the holy Agnes in the household of the sister

| | |
|---|---|
| of Constantius | of Constans |

Augustus,[3] as if he thought that through her intervention or at her request he might come again into the city.

Then Constantia Augusta, who was faithful to the Lord Jesus Christ, would not make request of Constantius Augustus, her brother, because she understood his design.

At that time Constantius, in company with Ursacius and Valens, assembled some men who belonged to the dregs of the Arians and, pretending that he had held a council, sent and recalled Liberius from the cemetery of the blessed Agnes.  And that same hour

[1] *I.e.* Liberius was not expected to demand the second baptism of all Catholics who chose to join the Arian sect, as the Arians themselves did.

[2] The title here translated commissioner is "agentem in rebus," *i.e.* one of the agents of the imperial police instituted by Diocletian.  They were employed often on business connected with the general administration.

[3] The fact that Liberius decorated the tomb of St. Agnes may have given rise to the idea of his sojourn at the basilica and the existence of the mausoleum of Constantina in the neighborhood may have suggested the addition of the princess.  As a matter of fact no princess of the name of Constantia or Constantina was living in 358. Constantina, daughter of Constantine, died in 354.  Duchesne, *op. cit.*, p. 208, n. 10.

Constantius Augustus entered Rome and held a council with the heretics and likewise with Ursacius and Valens and expelled Felix from the bishopric, for he was catholic, and reinstated Liberius.

From that day forward there was a persecution of the clergy, so that priests and clergy were slain in church and were crowned with martyrdom.[1]    But Felix, after he was deposed from the bishopric, dwelt on his own estate on the Via Portuensis and there he slept in peace, July 29.[2]    Liberius entered the city of Rome, August 2, and he was in accord with Constantius, the heretic.

Nevertheless Liberius was not baptised a second time,

but he gave his consent.    |

And he held the basilicas of the blessed Peter and of the blessed Paul and the basilica of Constantine for 6 years,[3] and there was a great persecution in the city of Rome, so that the clergy and the priests could enter neither a church nor a bath.

This Liberius decorated with slabs of marble the sepulchre of holy Agnes, the martyr.

Now all the years of Felix are included within the term of Liberius.[4]    He

built the basilica of his own name    |
near the Macellum of Libia [5] and    |
held 2 ordinations.

---

[1] The extent of the disorder may be inferred from the fact that at the Council of Rimini in 359 there was no representative from the church of Rome.

[2] The antipope Felix II is here confused with a popular saint Felix, of whom nothing is now known but the fact that he was revered in a basilica on the Via Portuensis, perhaps the very basilica erected just before these events by Pope Julius I. *Supra*, p. 74, n. 1.   Felix II died November 22, 365.   For a different but equally erroneous version of his death and burial see *infra*, pp. 78, 79.   Duchesne, *op. cit.*, pp. cxxiii, cxxiv, 209, n. 13.

[3] Liberius lived for eight years after his restoration, 358–366.

[4] This sentence would seem to imply that at the date when it was written there was no separate account of Felix II, such as now follows the life of Liberius, and that the separate account was an interpolation of one of the later editors of the *Lib. Pont.*   The untrustworthy character of the account makes this supposition plausible.

[5] Or "near the market of Livia."   The famous church of Santa Maria Maggiore. The framework of the structure, the columns and the mosaics of the nave may still go back to Liberius.   The church was the battleground of the warring factions under Damasus and underwent a thorough restoration at the hands of Xystus III.   *Infra*, p. 94, n. 1.

\*       \*       \*       \*       \*       \*       \*       \* [1]

And he was buried on the Via Salaria in the cemetery of Priscilla.[2]

September 9.                          | April 25.

And the bishopric was empty 6 days.


## XXXVIII.  Felix  II  (355–358)

Felix, by nationality a Roman, son of Anastasius, occupied the see 1 year, 3 months and 2 days.

He declared [3] that Constantius, son of Constantine, was a heretic and had been baptised a second time by Eusebius,

bishop of Nicomedia,                 | of Nicomedia near Nicomedia,

in the villa which is called Aquilone.[4]  And for this declaration, by order of the same Constantius Augustus, son of Constantine Augustus, he was crowned with martyrdom and beheaded.

He built a basilica on the Via Aurelia,[5]

---

[1] List of ordained clergy.

[2] The location of the tomb of Liberius within the cemetery is unknown.  Duchesne gives an epitaph in verse, copied by a pilgrim of the seventh century, which from internal evidence he thinks may have been the inscription over the grave of Liberius. *Op. cit.*, p. 209, n. 19.

[3] For the unreliability of the succeeding narrative see *supra*, p. 75, n. 2, p. 77, nn. 2 and 4.  On p. 77 Felix is depicted as dying peacefully and being buried on the Via Portuensis.  Here he defies the emperor, suffers martyrdom and is buried in his basilica on the Via Aurelia.  As in the preceding account he was confused with a saint of the same name who was honored on the Via Portuensis, so here he is confused with two other saints, also of the same name, who shared a basilica on the Via Aurelia.  It is possible that the story of his martyrdom was drawn from a Passion of one of the older saints. Pope Felix I had also been identified with one of them.  *Supra*, p. 33, n. 1.  Duchesne, *Lib. Pont.*, vol. I, pp. cxxiii, cxxiv.

[4] The name is taken from the *Chronicle* of St. Jerome, who says that Constantine, not Constantius, was baptised near Nicomedia and died soon afterward at a villa called Acyron in the same neighborhood.  Jerome, *Chronicon*, ed. Helm, in *Eusebius' Werke*, vol. VII, pt. 1, p. 234.  (*Die Griechischen Christlichen Schriftsteller der ersten drei Jahrhunderte.*)  Our author is here trying to defend the story of Constantine's baptism at Rome (*supra*, pp. 42, 50) by explaining away Jerome's statement that he was baptised in the East.  He says not only that Constantius, "son of Constantine," was the one baptised at Nicomedia but also that it was an heretical, second baptism.

[5] The basilica of the two saints Felix on the Via Aurelia may have been built by Felix II.  Its site has not been discovered.

two miles from the city,
where also he is buried,

while he was filling the office of priest, and he bought land around
the site of that same church, which he bestowed upon the church
which he had built.

\* \* \* \* \* \* \* \*1

| He also was be-headed, with many clergy and faithful, secretly near the walls of the city, beside the aqueduct of Trajan, | He also suffered in the town of Cora,² | He also suffered in the town of Cora, with many clergy and faithful, secretly near the walls of the city, beside the aqueduct of Trajan, |
| November 11, and thence the Christians with Damasus, the priest, stole away his body by night, | November 11, and thence his body was stolen away by priests and clergy | November 11, and thence his body was stolen away at night by priests and clergy together with Da-masus, the priest, |
| and they buried him in his aforesaid ba-silica on the Via Aurelia, November 15, | and was buried in the basilica which he himself had built on the Via Aurelia, No-vember 20, at the second milestone. | and was buried in his aforesaid basilica, which he himself had built on the Via Au-relia, November 20, at the second mile-stone, in peace. |
| in peace. | | |

And the bishopric was empty 38 days.

## XXXIX. Damasus (366–384)

Damasus, by nationality a Spaniard, son of Antonius, occupied
the see 18 years, 3 months and 11 days. And at the time of his
ordination ³ Ursinus was ordained also because of a dissension;

¹ List of ordinations.

² Cori in the Campagna. The festival of yet another St. Felix was celebrated in
the country districts near Rome. There may have been a tradition of his martyrdom
at Cori.

³ This and the following sentence do not appear in the two earliest abridgments

and a council of priests was held and they appointed Damasus, inasmuch as the multitude was powerful and very numerous, and thus Damasus was appointed. And they sent Ursinus from the city and appointed him bishop of Naples; and Damasus abode in the city of Rome as bishop over the apostolic see.

He was bishop in the time of Julian.[1]

| He built two basilicas, one to the blessed Lawrence near the theatre,[2] and the other on the Via Ardeati- | He built two basilicas, one near the Via Ardeatina, | | At the same time he built two basilicas, one, near the theatre, to the holy Lawrence, | He built two basilicas, one, near the theatre, to the holy Lawrence, and the other on the Via Ardeati- | He built a basilica near the theatre to the holy Lawrence, |
|---|---|---|---|---|---|

of the *Lib. Pont.* Duchesne regards them as interpolations, inserted to make the history of Damasus correspond as closely as possible to that of Pope Symmachus. (*Cf.* the election under Symmachus of the antipope Laurentius, *infra*, p. 116.) Some of the phrases in the two narratives are strikingly similar. Damasus' election was, of course, contested by Ursinus and his adherents (For the general situation see *supra*, p. 75, n. 2), but the deciding factor was not a church council but the civil government, which after some hesitation pronounced in favor of Damasus and sentenced Ursinus to exile. Ursinus was not granted a bishopric or any other compensation, as was Laurentius, the rival of Symmachus. Duchesne, *Lib. Pont.*, vol. I, p. 213, nn. 3–5.

[1] Our author is here attempting to continue the imperial synchronisms of the *Liberian Catalogue*. His attempt is not successful, since the reign of Julian fell altogether within the pontificate of Liberius.

[2] The basilica of San Lorenzo in Damaso, which stands not far from the theatre of Pompey. A dedicatory inscription, still preserved, seems to imply that the building was erected on the site of Damasus' father's house. Damasus himself had been elected pope in the church consecrated to St. Lawrence "in Lucina," and for that reason, perhaps, chose the great Roman martyr for the patron of one of his own churches. On either side of the original structure were porticos in which were stored the archives and library of the Roman see. Excavations in the palace of the Cancelleria have recently revealed fragments of the ground plan of one of these porticos. Damasus and his father before him had been connected with the custodianship of the archives and Damasus may, therefore, have been interested in providing an adequate home for them. They appear to have remained there until their removal, a century or more later, to the Lateran. Duchesne, *op. cit.*, p. 213, n. 7. Frothingham, *Monuments of Christian Rome*, p. 46.

| | | | | | |
|---|---|---|---|---|---|
| na,[1] where he is buried, | where he is buried. | | | na, where he is buried in the catacombs, | |
| and one over the Catacombs,[2] where lay the bodies of the holy apostles, Peter and Paul, | | He dedicated the marble slab, whereon the bodies of Peter and Paul, the apostles, lay, | and the other over the Catacombs, where lay the holy bodies of the apostles, Peter and Paul, | and he dedicated the marble slab, whereon lay the bodies of the apostles, that is the blessed Peter and Paul, | and the other over the Catacombs, where lay the holy bodies of the apostles, Peter and Paul, |
| and there he beautified with verses the very marble slab whereon the holy bodies lay.[3] | | and he embellished it with verses. | and there he beautified with verses the very marble slab whereon the holy bodies lay. | and he beautified it with verses. | and there he beautified with verses the very marble slab whereon the holy bodies lay. |

[1] Mommsen calls the passage, "on the Via Ardeatina . . . and one," an ancient interpolation taken from the account later on of Damasus' burial place and introduced here where it only confuses the sense. *Lib. Pont.*, p. 83, note on l. 7. The location of the cemetery of Damasus, near that of Domitilla, is known but all sign of his basilica has disappeared.

[2] The basilica of San Sebastiano on the Via Appia, built to commemorate the tomb of the martyr Sebastian, and the "Platonia," the crypt where the bodies of Peter and Paul are said to have lain during the persecution begun by Valerian. See *supra*, p. 26, n. 2; Lanciani, *Pagan and Christian Rome*, pp. 345–347. The basilica has since been completely rebuilt.

[3] The inscription of Damasus at this spot was often copied by pilgrims. It is

He searched out many bodies of the saints and found them and marked them with verses.[1]

He made a regulation for the church.

He was accused

spitefully                                      |

and charged with adultery and a synod was called and he was justified by 44 bishops, who also condemned Concordius and Callistus, the deacons, his accusers, and

expelled                                      | ejected

them from the church.[2]

He appointed the basilica which he had built as a parish church in the city of Rome.[3]

\*       \*       \*       \*       \*       \*       \*       \* 4

He appointed that the psalms should be chanted day and night in all the churches and he gave this command to priests and bishops

---

printed by Duchesne, *op. cit.*, p. civ, n. 1. The following is a rough rendering in English.

"This place, you should know, was once the dwelling of saints;
  Their names, you may learn, were Peter and likewise Paul.
  The East sent hither these disciples, as freely we confess.
  For Christ's sake and the merit of His blood they followed Him among the stars
  And sought the realms of heaven and the kingdoms of the righteous.
  Rome was deemed worthy to preserve them as her citizens.
  May Damasus offer them these verses, new stars, in their praise!"

[1] At the time when the *Liber Pontificalis* was written the beautiful inscriptions of Damasus still marked almost all of the numerous shrines and tombs of saints and martyrs that filled the environs of the city and were the resorts of pilgrims and sightseers. Already the identity of some sepulchres had been confused, others had been buried deep and altogether forgotten and his work of restoration and identification came in the nick of time. Frothingham, *op. cit.*, pp. 45, 46. De Rossi has made a collection of the Damasian inscriptions as far as they can be recovered. *Inscriptiones Christianæ Urbis Romæ*, vol. II.

[2] Pope Damasus was accused in his old age of some grave offence, but the charge was brought by a converted Jew, not by his deacons, and the case was tried before the prefect of Rome, not before a church council. The emperor Gratian intervened and Damasus was acquitted. The nature of the indictment is not known, but it seems unlikely to have been adultery. Damasus was about seventy-five years old at the time. Duchesne, *op. cit.*, p. 214, n. 15.

[3] *I.e.* San Lorenzo in Damaso. It is mentioned as a "titulus," or parish church, in the documents of the Roman synod of 499.

[4] Lists of gifts to the basilica and of ordinations.

Pope St. Damasus

Pope St. Celestine I

and monasteries.[1]   He also was buried on the Via Ardeatina in his own basilica, December 11, near his mother and his sister.[2]

And the bishopric was empty 31 days.

## XL. SIRICIUS (384–399)

Siricius, by nationality a Roman, son of Tiburtius, occupied the see 15 years.   He made a regulation for the whole church

| | |
|---|---|
| and sent it through the provinces.[3] | against all the heresies and sent it throughout the entire world, that it might be preserved in the archives of every church for a defense against all heresies.[4] |

He ordained

| | |
|---|---|
| that without the leaven consecrated by the bishop of the district no priest could perform the rite of consecration.[5] | that no priest could perform masses during all the week, unless he received from the bishop of the particular district the consecrated sign which is called the leaven. |

[1] This decree is an interpolation, suggested by the existence in later times of two apocryphal letters written ostensibly by Damasus and St. Jerome to one another on the subject of Jerome's edition of the Psalter.   The earliest text of the *Liber Pontificalis* attributed the institution of the recitation of the Psalms to Celestine I.   See *infra*, p. 92.   Duchesne, *op. cit.*, p. 214, n. 17.

[2] *Cf. supra*, p. 81, n. 1.   Damasus' own epitaph and the tender one he wrote for his young sister Irene, whose death robbed him of the fear of death, have both survived.   His mother's has been lost.   Duchesne, *op. cit.*, p. 215, n. 18.

[3] The following letters written by Siricius and containing general instructions for the government of the church are still preserved: one to the bishop of Tarragona giving fifteen canons for the churches in Spain, Gaul and Carthage, another to the church in Africa reporting the decrees of the synod held at the Vatican in 386 and others to the bishops in Illyria and to the orthodox throughout the provinces respecting the need of care in ecclesiastical appointments.   Jaffé, *Regesta*, vol. I, pp. 40–41, 255, 257, 258, 259, 263.

[4] The author of this reading had, perhaps, in mind a letter addressed by Siricius to the church at Milan on the subject of the heretic emperor Jovinian.   Jaffé, *op. cit.*, p. 41, 260.

[5] A repetition in substance of the decree of Miltiades.   *Supra*, p. 41, n. 2.

He found Manicheans

in the city [1]

and dispatched them into exile and ordained that

> they should not partake of com-
> munion with the faithful, be-
> cause the holy body of the Lord
> ought not to be mutilated in a
> polluted mouth.  He ordained
> that

if any Manichean were converted and returned to the church he
should in no wise be admitted to communion, except he were kept
in the restriction of a monastery as one guilty every day of his
life, that so he might afflict himself with fastings and prayers and
prove himself under every trial until the day of his death and thus
through the clemency of the church might obtain his viaticum.

He ordained that a heretic

should be reconciled        | should be received

through the imposition of hands in the presence of the whole
church.[2]

*       *       *       *       *       *       *       * [3]

[1] The second notice of Manicheans in Rome.  (Cf. supra, p. 41 and n. 1.)   That
they were active in the time of Siricius we know from the writings of Augustine, but
that Siricius undertook any such campaign against them as is indicated here is extremely doubtful.   At least Augustine says nothing of it.   Leo I, a half century later,
entered the lists against them, procured the exile of some and the reconciliation of
others to the church, but his labors in this direction are not mentioned in the *Liber
Pontificalis*.   Duchesne, *Lib. Pont.*, vol. I, p. 216, n. 3.

[2] This is perhaps the first of the numerous episcopal decrees cited in the *Liber
Pontificalis* known to be derived from a specific and authoritative documentary source.
It is evidently based upon the letter of Siricius to Himerius of Tarragona.   "At the
opening of your letter you stated that many who had been baptised by the impious
Arians were hastening to adopt the Catholic faith and that some of our brethren would
have them baptised a second time; but that is not permissible . . . for we admit
Novatians and other heretics . . . to the community of Catholics by merely the invoca-
tion of the sevenfold Spirit and the laying on of the episcopal hand."   Mansi, *Amplissima Collectio*, vol. III, p. 655.   *Cf. Introduction*, p. viii, and *supra*, p. 83, n. 3.   The
method of reinstating a heretic was first prescribed, according to our author, by Eusebius.   *Supra*, p. 40 and n. 1.

[3] List of ordinations.

He also was buried in the cemetery of Priscilla on the Via Salaria,[1] February 22.

And the bishopric was empty 20 days.

## XLI. ANASTASIUS I (399–401)

Anastasius, by nationality a Roman, son of Maximus, occupied the see 3 years and 10 days.

He ordained that whenever the holy gospels were read the priests should not sit but stand with bowed heads.[2] He made a regulation for the church.

He built also the basilica which is called the Crescentian in the Second District on the Via Mamurtini in the city of Rome.[3]

And he ordained

| | |
|---|---|
| that no cleric from beyond the sea | that no one from beyond the sea |

should be received

                | into the ranks of the clergy

unless he showed the signature of 5 bishops,[4]

---

[1] In the basilica of Sylvester. Duchesne gives his epitaph. *Op. cit.*, p. 217, n. 5.

[2] The *Apostolic Constitutions*, which represent the early Syrian usage, direct that priests and deacons shall stand during the reading of the Gospel. Sozomen, the fifth century historian, says that in his day the Alexandrian custom was peculiar in allowing the bishop to keep his seat. *Ecclesiastical History*, VII, 19, tr. Nicene and Post-Nicene Fathers, ser. 2, vol. II, p. 390. Duchesne thinks it possible that the Alexandrian custom was in this respect, as in others, a reflection of the custom at Rome. *Lib. Pont.*, vol. I, p. 218, n. 1.

[3] The site of this basilica is now unknown. It is not mentioned, at least under this name, after the fifth century. The Via Mamurtini is usually identified with the modern Via Marforio, but the latter street lies outside the Second Districts, both civil and ecclesiastical.

[4] Gregory I, in a letter to one of his bishops, gives the following injunction. "Do not on any consideration accept Africans or unknown travellers who claim admission to ecclesiastical orders, for some of the Africans are Manicheans and others rebaptised; moreover, many strangers who were actually members of the lower orders are known to have laid claim often to higher honors." *Epistolæ*, II, 37; Migne, *Patrologia Latina*, vol. 77, col. 575. The *Liber Pontificalis* demands an especially high guarantee of honesty. In ordinary circumstances an African priest or bishop on a visit to Rome took with him credentials signed simply by the primate of his province or the bishop of Carthage in order to gain access to the communion of the Roman church, but more may have been required of one who wished to be ordained at Rome. Duchesne, *op. cit.*, p. 218, n. 4.

because at that time Manicheans | on account of the Manicheans.
were found in the city of Rome. |

\*      \*      \*      \*      \*      \*      \*      \* 1

He also was buried in his own cemetery near the Ursus
Pileatus,[2] April 27.  And the bishopric was empty 21 days.


## XLII.  INNOCENT I (401–417)

Innocent, by nationality an Alban, son of Innocent, occupied
the see 15 years, 2 months and 21 days.

He made a regulation for the whole church and statutes concerning monastic rules and concerning Jews and pagans [3] and he
found many Catafrigians [4]

in the city                         |

whom he constrained to exile in a monastery.

He found Pelagius [5] and Cælestius, the heretics, and con-

---

[1] List of ordinations.

[2] The *Salzburg Itinerary*, one of the early guides for pilgrims, mentions the tomb
of Pope Anastasius on the Via Portuensis, not far from the city gate.  Duchesne, *op. cit.*,
p. 219, n. 5.  The name of the district, Ursus Pileatus, is explained by the tale that
there stood there once the image of a bear with a cap upon its head.  Gregorovius,
*History of the City of Rome*, tr. Hamilton, vol. I, bk. II, p. 256.

[3] A number of the letters and decretals of Innocent I have survived but none
dealing particularly with monastic organization, Jews or pagans.  Jaffé, *Regesta*, vol. I,
pp. 44–49, 285–327.  Migne, *Pat. Lat.*, vol. XX.

[4] *I.e.* Phrygians.  The Theodosian Code (lib. XVI, 5, 40) contains a law of Honorius, dated February 407, against Manicheans, Phrygians and Priscillianists.  The
term Phrygian is used as a synonym for Montanist.

[5] The famous heretic and exponent of the doctrines of the original soundness of
human nature and the freedom of the will as against Augustine's theories of original
sin and absolute dependence upon divine grace.  He and his friend Celestius were in
Rome for several years before the sack of Alaric, 410.  The two then crossed to Africa,
where Celestius was tried for heresy and excommunicated by a synod called by the
bishop of Carthage.  Pelagius meanwhile had gone on to Palestine, where in time he
too was summoned upon a charge of heresy before a synod at Diospolis (Lydda) but was
acquitted.  The African church felt that a reflection was thereby cast upon its action
in the case of Celestius and in 416 sent an appeal on the whole matter to Innocent at
Rome.  Innocent upheld the African position and denounced the peculiar tenets of
Pelagius.  His letters in reply to the appeal may be found summarized in Jaffé, *op. cit.*,
p. 48, 321–323.  Mansi gives the entire text.  *Amplissima Collectio*, vol. III, pp. 1071
*et seq.*

demned them. And he ordained that the child of a Christian woman must be born a second time through baptism, that is must be baptised, a doctrine which Pelagius condemned.[1]

At the same time he dedicated the basilica of the holy Gervasius and Protasius,[2] built

by bequest,                                        |

as the gift of an illustrious lady named Vestina, under the direction of the priests Ursicinus and Leopardus [3] and the deacon Livianus. And the aforesaid lady made provision in her will that the basilica of the holy martyrs should be built from the proceeds of her jewels and her pearls, which should be sold at a fair price, and that the building should be carried on until it was complete. The most blessed Innocent, by request of the illustrious lady Vestina, appointed the basilica a parish church of Rome and for that same church she offered :

> *        *        *        *        *        *        *        *[4]

three twenty-fourths and three twelfths of the Porta Nomentana, yielding 22 and one third sol.

He decreed that the sabbath should be observed as a fast day, because on the sabbath the Lord was laid in the tomb and the disciples fasted.[5]

He appointed that the basilica of the blessed Agnes, the martyr, should be administered and cared for by the priests Leopardus and Paulinus and should be roofed over and decorated at their dis-

---

[1] One corollary of Pelagius' teachings was that unbaptised infants have eternal life.

[2] The modern church of San Vitale is on the same site as this " Titulus Vestinae."

[3] This same priest helped in the construction and embellishment of the church of Santa Pudenziana under Siricius and in the restoration of San Lorenzo under Zosimus. See *infra*, p. 89, n. 3. Frothingham, *Monuments*, pp. 49, 50, 54, 55.

[4] Long list of gifts to the new basilica, precious vessels, houses, lands and finally one-eighth of the customs collected at the Porta Nomentana.

[5] Another decree with a clear basis in a genuine document. The letter of Innocent to Decentius, bishop of Gubbio, contains the following passage : "Therefore we do not deny that fast should be observed on the sixth day but we maintain that the same should be practiced on the sabbath, because both days brought grief to the apostles and those who had been with Christ." Mansi, *Amplissima Collectio*, vol. III, p. 1028; Jaffé, *Regesta*, vol. I, p. 47, 311.

cretion.[1]   The control of the aforesaid parish church of Vestina was entrusted to the priests.

\*          \*          \*          \*          \*          \*          \*          \* [2]

He also was buried in the cemetery near Ursus Pileatus,[3]

June 27.                                    | July 28.

And the bishopric was empty 22 days.

### XLIII.  Zosimus  (417–418)

Zosimus, by nationality a Greek, son of Abramius, occupied the see

7 years, 9 months and 24 days.    | 1 year, 3 months and 11 days.

He made many decrees for the church and ordained that deacons should wear napkins of wool and linen to cover their left shoulders

in all the parishes [4] and that the wax should be blessed.[5]
| and that in all the parishes permission should be granted to bless the wax.

He likewise gave order that no member of the clergy should

---

[1] The basilica of St. Agnes, being outside the walls of the city, may have suffered especially at the hands of the horde who accompanied Alaric.   For a description of the destruction that marked the sack of 410 see Lanciani, *Destruction of Ancient Rome*, ch. V, pp. 56–70; Gregorovius, *History of Rome*, tr. Hamilton, vol. I, chs. III and IV.

[2] List of ordinations.

[3] See *supra*, p. 86 and n. 2.

[4] An extension to the deacons of the "parish" or suburban churches of the right to wear the maniple bestowed by Sylvester upon the Roman deacons.  *Supra*, p. 45 and n. 6.   Neither this nor the following decrees are found among the records of Zosimus elsewhere preserved.

[5] The Latin word in the first column translated "wax" is "cera," in the second "cereus."   Duchesne suggests that the "cera" was the wax used in Roman churches for modelling little forms of the Agnus Dei to distribute to the people at Easter time. The custom of blessing this wax and moulding the lambs is described in an *Ordo Romanus* of the ninth century.   On the other hand the "cereus" is undoubtedly wax for lighting, and Duchesne conjectures that the author of the second text had in mind the blessing of the Paschal candle, formulæ for which were drawn up early in the sixth century. Duchesne, *Lib. Pont.*, vol. I, p. 225, n. 2.

drink in public, except in a chamber belonging to the faithful, preferably to the clergy.[1]

\*      \*      \*      \*      \*      \*      \*      \*[2]

He also was buried on the Via Tiburtina, near the body of blessed Lawrence, the martyr,[3] December 26.

And the bishopric was empty 11 days.

## XLIV. BONIFACE I (418–422)

Boniface, by nationality a Roman, son of Iocundus, the priest, occupied the see 3 years, 8 months and 6 days.

He was ordained by one faction on the same day as Eulalius and there was dissension among the clergy for 7 months and 15 days.[4]

[1] A similar ordinance was passed by the Council of Laodicea and the Council of Carthage in the fourth century.

[2] List of ordinations.

[3] An inscription which was visible in the ninth century near the choir of the basilica of San Lorenzo recorded the repair and rebuilding of the church by the priest Leopardus at his own expense in the time of Zosimus. *Cf. supra*, p. 87 and n. 3. Duchesne thinks that Leopardus' reconstruction may have included the sinking of the old basilica to the level of the saint's tomb and the Constantinian confession so that one did not have to be reached by a stairway from the other as in Constantine's day, but the whole structure was partially subterranean, as it is at present. *Cf. supra*, p. 61. If that was the case, the church itself was then provided with a new entrance, a flight of stairs leading from the ground outside down into a vestibule, an arrangement similar to that now to be seen at Sant' Agnese. After the small basilica was united with the larger by Honorius III the independent entrance was closed up and the small church was reached only through the larger one, as it is to-day. The three niches in the vestibule, the middle one of which is now occupied by the tomb of Pius IX, were apparently used for burial places soon after Leopardus finished them. At least De Rossi believes that Zosimus was interred in one, Xystus III and Hilary in the other two. *Infra*, pp. 97, 104. Duchesne, *op. cit.*, p. 197, n. 84.

[4] Enough of the history of this brief schism has been recovered to make clear the narrative of the *Lib. Pont.* Pope Zosimus was buried Friday, December 27, 418. On their return from his obsequies the Roman deacons, headed by Eulalius, the archdeacon, seized the basilica of the Lateran, shut out the priests and elected Eulalius as Zosimus' successor. The priests on the next day elected Boniface, one of their number, in spite of his own protests. Both parties held ordination ceremonies on Sunday, Eulalius and his adherents in the Lateran, having dragged the bishop of Ostia from a sick bed to officiate, Boniface in another church in the presence of nine other bishops. Both claimed thereafter the authority of pope. The dispute was referred to Honorius at

Eulalius was ordained in the basilica of Constantine and Boniface in the basilica of Julius.[1]

At the same time Placidia Augusta heard of it, when she was sojourning at Ravenna with her son, Valentinian Augustus, and she reported it to Honorius Augustus who was at Milan. Then both the Augusti sent authority and commanded that the two bishops should depart from the city.[2] And after they were driven out Boniface dwelt in the cemetery of the holy Felicitas, the martyr, on the Via Salaria, and Eulalius in the town of Antium[3] near the holy Hermes.

But when the next Easter came Eulalius was presumptuous, because he had been ordained in the basilica of Constantine, and he entered into the city and baptised and celebrated Easter in the basilica of Constantine; but Boniface celebrated the baptism of Easter, as was his custom, in the basilica of the holy martyr Agnes.[4]

Ravenna, who ordered both rivals to appear before a council of Italian bishops and justify their pretensions. The council met in February or early March but seemed unable to arrive at a satisfactory conclusion. It was accordingly decided to convoke another in May, to which the bishops of Gaul and Africa should also be invited. Meanwhile, in order that Easter, which fell that year on March 30, might be celebrated peaceably in Rome, the council and emperor together determined that Boniface and Eulalius should remain outside the city in places appointed for them and that Achilleus, bishop of Spoleto, should preside over the Paschal ceremonies within the city. Boniface obeyed the injunction but Eulalius made his way back to Rome, summoned his party about him, and on Good Friday took possession again of the Lateran. The prefect of the city was obliged to dislodge him by force and to station guards around the bishop of Spoleto while he performed the episcopal office. As a result of Eulalius' refractoriness Honorius sent a letter shortly to Rome declaring him a pretender and Boniface the true pope. On April 10 Boniface made his entry into the city and was received with general rejoicing. The schism had lasted a little over three months. Duchesne, *Lib. Pont.*, vol. I, p. 228, nn. 1 and 2. Jaffé, *Regesta*, vol. I, pp. 51–53.

[1] Boniface I was neither elected nor ordained in the basilica Julia. An eye-witness to his ordination says that it took place in the church of Marcellus, *i.e.* San Lorenzo in Lucina. Our author has substituted the name of the basilica where Boniface II was ordained when a rival excluded him also from the Lateran. *Infra*, p. 140.

[2] There is no other mention of the participation of the Empress Placidia in this affair. Her son Valentinian, if born at this date, was an infant of a few months only.

[3] The modern Porto d'Anzio. *Cf. supra*, p. 50, n. 2.

[4] It seems curious that Boniface should have been allowed to remain in such close proximity to the city while Eulalius was banished to Antium. It is possible that Boniface's stay in the cemetery of Felicitas is purely legendary, suggested by the fact that he restored later the oratory of Felicitas and set up an inscription of gratitude for her aid. *Cf. infra*, p. 91.

And a synod was held and Eulalius was deposed by 52 bishops, because he had not been rightfully ordained, and Boniface took the seat of bishop by general consent and Eulalius was appointed bishop for the town of Nepete.[1]

When the Augusti heard this, they both sent and expelled Eulalius by 52 bishops and by their authority they recalled Boniface into the city of Rome and appointed him bishop but they sent Eulalius away into Campania.

And after 3 years and 8 months Boniface died. The clergy and the people asked that Eulalius be recalled.[2] Nevertheless Eulalius refused to return to Rome. And in that same place in Campania, a year after the death of Boniface, Eulalius died.

Boniface decreed that no woman or nun should touch the consecrated altar cloth or wash it or offer incense in church but only the ministering attendants;[3] and that no slave should be admitted to the clergy nor any man liable to curial service or any other exaction.[4]

He built an oratory in the cemetery of the holy Felicitas near her body and beautified the sepulchre of the holy martyr, Felicitas, and of the holy Silvanus.[5]

[1] The town of Nepi on the northern border of the Roman province.

[2] In 420, a year after entering upon his office, Boniface fell seriously ill. At once dissension arose over the question of his successor. Upon his recovery he wrote to Honorius to ask that measures might be taken to prevent a fresh outbreak of the schism at his death. Honorius replied with an edict to the effect that in case of a double-election the two rival candidates should henceforth both be debarred and that a new pope should be chosen who could obtain the support of every one. Unfortunately the edict could not always be enforced. Duchesne, *op. cit.*, p. 229, n. 10. Jaffé, *Regesta*, vol. I, p. 53, 353.

[3] The exclusion of women from the ministry of the altar was already the ancient and invariable practice as early as there is any reference to the subject.

[4] There was apparently throughout this period a regulation against the ordination of slaves and "curiales." Innocent I excluded the latter class. Jaffé, *op. cit.*, p. 47, 314. Duchesne, *op. cit.*, p. 229, n. 12.

[5] De Rossi has identified the cemetery of Felicitas with a catacomb and group of tombs to the right of the Via Salaria about a mile from the city. The oratory of Boniface is mentioned in itineraries of the seventh century, although no traces of it are now to be found. His inscription, however, may be read in Duchesne. There still exists within the city, near the baths of Trajan, a chapel to the saint, dating from the time of Boniface and perhaps built also by him. It is decorated with a fresco representing the martyred Felicitas and her seven sons, among whom was the Silvanus noted in the text. Duchesne, *ibid.*, n. 13; Frothingham, *Monuments*, pp. 55–56.

\*　　\*　　\*　　\*　　\*　　\*　　\*　　\* 1

He also was buried

| | |
|---|---|
| in the cemetery of holy Felicitas, the martyr, on the Via Salaria, | on the Via Salaria, near the body of the holy Felicitas, the martyr, |

October 25.

And the bishopric was empty 9 days.

## XLV. Celestine I (422–432)

Celestine, by nationality

| | |
|---|---|
| a Campanian, | a Roman, |

son of Priscus, occupied the see 8 years, 10 months and 17 days.

He made many regulations and appointed that the 150 psalms of David should be chanted antiphonally before the sacrifice by everyone; [2] this was not done previously but only the epistle of blessed Paul, the apostle, was read and the holy gospel,

and thus masses were performed.

He made a regulation for the whole church, in particular with regard to the religious life, and to this day it is kept preserved in the archives of the church.[3]

He dedicated the basilica of Julius and offered there after the Gothic fire: [4]

a silver paten, weighing 25 lbs.;

[1] Short list of gifts to the oratory and list of ordinations.

[2] The antiphonal chanting of the Psalms was at first a feature of the liturgy of the Eastern church and thence was adopted into the service in Italy. It is known to have been the practice in Milan in 387. This, of course, is the psalmody before public mass as distinct from the psalmody of the canonical hours of prayer. With the recitation of the Psalms followed by the Epistle and Gospel the office of the mass was assuming shape. Duchesne, *Lib. Pont.*, vol. I, p. 231, n. 1.

[3] Several letters of Celestine are still in existence. They relate to ecclesiastical affairs in Gaul, Africa, Illyria and Britain and to Nestorius and the Council of Ephesus. No one of them corresponds to the description here. Jaffé, *Regesta*, vol. I, pp. 55–57, 366–388.

[4] Santa Maria in Trastevere. See *supra*, p. 73 and n. 5. This is one of the rare, surviving allusions to the damage done by Alaric's raid of 410. Orosius says that Alaric charged his soldiers to respect the sanctuaries of Peter and Paul, but churches in

\*　　\*　　\*　　\*　　\*　　\*　　　\*　　\*[1]

He also was buried in the cemetery of Priscilla on the Via Salaria, April 6.

And the bishopric was empty 21 days.

## XLVI. Xystus III (432–440)

Xystus, by nationality a Roman, son of Xystus, occupied the see 8 years and 19 days.

After one year and 8 months he was accused by a man called Bassus,[2]

| | |
|---|---|
| and by order of Valentinian Augustus a synod was held and a great trial | Then Valentinian Augustus heard it and ordered a holy synod to be called together as a council; and when it was convened there was a great trial and the synodical judgment was given |

and he was acquitted by 56 bishops

| | |
|---|---|
| and they expelled Bassus from the communion. | and Bassus was condemned by the synod but with the provision that at his death the viaticum should not be denied him<br>for the sake of mercy<br>and the compassion of the church. |

other parts of the city apparently were not spared. Orosius, *Historiarum Adversum Paganos Libri VII*, VII, 39, ed. Zangemeister (Teubner), pp. 292–293. See also *infra*, p. 95, n. 1.

[1] List of gifts offered to the churches of Julius, Peter and Paul. List of ordinations.

[2] The whole of the ensuing account of the accusation and trial of Xystus is apocryphal, taken with modifications from a narrative entitled *Gesta de Xysti Purgatione*, which was composed about the year 501, the period when the *Gesta Liberii*, the legend of Liberius, was also fabricated. See *supra*, p. 75, n. 2. Xystus III was never tried for any crime. The chief concerns of his pontificate were problems of dogma and the Pelagian and Nestorian heresies. The story here given is obviously the work of some one who aimed to create a precedent for the trial of Pope Symmachus by a church council

When Valentinian Augustus heard this and his mother, Placidia Augusta, they were filled with holy wrath and proscribed Bassus by an edict and bestowed all the lands of his estates upon the catholic church. And Bassus, by the will of God, died within 3 months. And Xystus, the bishop, with his own hands wrapped his body in linen cloths and spices and laid it near blessed Peter, the apostle, in his family burial chamber.

He built the basilica of the holy Mary, which was called by the ancients the basilica of Liberius,[1] near the Macellum of Lybia, and he offered there:

&ast; &ast; &ast; &ast; &ast; &ast; &ast; &ast;[2]

the tenements adjoining the steps of the basilica and all contained therein.

He adorned with silver the confession of blessed Peter, the apostle, to the weight of four hundred pounds. At his solicitation Valentinian Augustus offered a golden relief with 12 doors and the 12 apostles and the Savior, adorned with jewels of great price,[3]

the which as a votive gift he set up

over the confession of blessed Peter, the apostle.

at the direction of Theodoric. See *infra*, pp. 117–118. The history of Pope Damasus was also tampered with for a similar purpose. *Supra*, pp. 79, n. 3; 82, n. 2. In the narrative here Valentinian plays the part of Theodoric later. Anicius Bassus was a consul in 431 and his name was probably found in the Fasti. The two special features of this story, the confiscation of Bassus' goods for the benefit of the Roman church and his burial near the tomb of Peter, were no doubt suggested, the one by the basilica of Junius Bassus, consul in 317, which had been converted into a church before the year 500 and the other by the sarcophagus of another Junius Bassus, who died in 359, which is still one of the ornaments of the Vatican crypt. Duchesne, *Lib. Pont.*, vol. I, pp. cxxvi, cxxvii.

[1] The basilica of Santa Maria Maggiore. See *supra*, p. 77, n. 5; Gregorovius, *History of Rome*, tr. Hamilton, vol. I, pp. 184–189. Xystus did not build the basilica but restored it. He added the mosaics of the triumphal arch which proclaim the divine motherhood of Mary, the dogma enunciated by the Council of Ephesus during Xystus' pontificate. Above them his inscription may still be read, "XYSTUS EPISCOPUS PLEBI DEI," Bishop Xystus to the People of God.

[2] List of gifts to the basilica of Mary.

[3] This is one of the notable works of art mentioned by Pope Hadrian in his letter to Charlemagne on the sacred images at Rome. Mansi, *Amplissima Collectio*, vol. XIII, p. 801. It was probably destroyed during the sack of the Saracens in 846. A design showing Christ and the apostles seated beneath the arcades of a portico is found on many sarcophagi of the fourth and fifth centuries.

Likewise Valentinian Augustus, at the request of Xystus, the bishop, erected a ciborium of silver in the basilica of Constantine, which

weighed 2,000 pounds, | weighed 1,610 pounds,

in place of the one which had been destroyed by the barbarians.[1]

At this time Valentinian Augustus made the confession of blessed Paul, the apostle, out of silver, weighing 200 pounds. Also Xystus, the bishop, set up the confession of blessed Lawrence, the martyr,[2] with porphyry columns and adorned

with slabs |

the screen and the altar and the confession of holy Lawrence, the martyr, with purest silver,

he made an altar |

weighing 50 lbs. ;
silver rails over the porphyry slabs, weighing 300 lbs. ;
an apse[3] above the rails with a silver figure of blessed Lawrence, the martyr, weighing 200 lbs.

He built also the basilica to the holy Lawrence,[4] which Valentinian Augustus granted to him, where likewise he offered the following gifts :

    \*       \*       \*       \*       \*       \*      \* 5

---

[1] *I.e.* in place of the one given by Constantine and removed by the Goths of Alaric. *Supra*, p. 47, n. 2.

[2] The rich confession of St. Lawrence, built in the time of Constantine (*Supra*, p. 62), had apparently been plundered also by the Goths, so that Xystus found it necessary to restore most of the furniture. Duchesne thinks that the porphyry columns of Xystus are those which still support the ciborium and that the porphyry slabs of Xystus' screen now enclose the altar.

[3] *I.e.* a niche to hold the image of the saint.

[4] The larger basilica of San Lorenzo fuori le Mura, forming the body of the present structure and connected with the smaller and older church in the thirteenth century. *Supra*, p. 61, n. 2. This is the generally accepted view, although Mr. Frothingham claims to have grounds for maintaining that Xystus III built the church of San Lorenzo in Lucina instead of the basilica outside the city. The latter was certainly in existence before the end of the fifth century, but there is no monument or record to connect it with Xystus beyond the ambiguous notice here. Duchesne, *op. cit.*, p. 235, n. 12. Frothingham, *Monuments*, p. 407.

[5] List of precious utensils given to the basilica of St. Lawrence.

He built also a monastery at the Catacombs.[1]

He built also a baptismal font for the holy Mary and beautified it with porphyry columns.[2]

He erected in the baptistery of the basilica of Constantine the columns which had been collected in the time of Constantine Augustus, eight in number, made of porphyry; and he set them in place and decorated them with letters and verses;[3]

also a tablet in the cemetery of Callistus, where he recorded the names of the bishops.[4]

He built in the basilica of Constantine a decoration around the font, which previously had not been there; that is, he set up the marble architraves and the porphyry columns which Constantine Augustus collected and laid together and ordered to be set up and he adorned them with verses. He placed a tablet in the cemetery of Callistus on the Via Appia, where he inscribed the names of the bishops and martyrs for a memorial.

---

[1] The monastery of San Sebastiano, one of the first, if not actually the first, to be built adjoining a suburban church, in order to provide for the religious services which could no longer be adequately maintained by the clergy of the urban basilica with which the cemeterial church was connected. For the site see *supra*, p. 81 and n. 2.

[2] No trace of this baptistery now remains.

[3] The eight porphyry columns and the inscription upon the architrave may still be seen in the Lateran baptistery. *Cf. supra*, p. 50.

[4] The marble tablet was set up in the papal crypt of the catacomb of Callistus and bore the names of the martyred popes and other saints who were buried there. Duchesne gives a conjectural reading of the inscription, as made out by De Rossi:

"The Names of the Bishops, Martyrs and Confessors who are buried in the Cemetery of Callistus

| | | | |
|---|---|---|---|
| Xystus | Dionysius | Stephen | Urbanus |
| Cornelius | Felix | Lucius | Manno |
| Pontianus | Eutychianus | Anteros | Numidianus |
| Fabianus | Gaius | Laudiceus | Julianus |
| Eusebius | Miltiades | Polycarp | Optatus |

Of These the First, the Holy Xystus, Suffered with Agapitus, Felicissimus and XI Others."

The tablet itself has long disappeared but De Rossi derives his reading from two early lists of inscriptions which seem to have been copied from the original stones. Duchesne, *op. cit.*, p. 236, n. 16. It may be noticed that fourteen out of these twenty names are those of popes.

\*      \*      \*      \*      \*      \*      \*      \* 1

And in his time Peter, the bishop, built the basilica of the holy Savina in the city of Rome and erected there a font.[2]

He also was buried on the Via Tiburtina in a crypt,

near the holy Lawrence.[3]

near the body of the blessed Lawrence.

And the bishopric was empty 22 days.

From the death of Silvester to Leo I is 99 years, 5 months and 26 days.

## XLVII. Leo I (440–461)

Leo, by nationality a Tuscan, son of Quintianus, occupied the see 21 years, 1 month and 13 days.

He made a regulation for the church.

In his time Demetria, the handmaid of God, built a basilica to the holy Stephen in her own garden on the Via Latina at the third milestone.[4]

He found two heresies, Eutyches and Nestorius,[5]

the Eutychian and the Nestorian.

through the aid of some bishops.

---

[1] Minor gifts to the churches of Peter, Paul and Lawrence. List of ordinations.

[2] The basilica of Santa Sabina on the Aventine. Its graceful columns are supposed to have been taken from a neighboring temple to Juno Regina, despoiled by Alaric. Its famous carved doors of cypress wood are among the finest examples of fifth century art. According to the dedicatory inscription over the entrance the building was begun while Celestine was pope. It may have been finished under Xystus.

[3] On this place see *supra*, p. 89, n. 3.

[4] This is Anicia Demetrias, of the house of the Anicii Probi, one of the group of devout women at Rome, the friend and pupil of Augustine and Jerome. She left her property for the building of a church to St. Stephen, which was erected toward the close of Leo's pontificate. A few ruins now show where it stood and testify by their rude workmanship to the decline of Roman skill during the years that saw the invasions of Attila and Genseric. Frothingham, *Monuments*, p. 63.

[5] Nestorius was charged with holding that there were two persons as well as two

| | |
|---|---|
| and by request of Marcian Augustus, the orthodox, and at his bidding | He, by his own authority, issued precepts and he sent to Marcian Augustus, the orthodox, catholic prince, and an assemblage was called and the bishops were gathered together with the prince and |

the holy council of the bishops was held at Chalcedon

| | |
|---|---|
| in the East in the basilica of the holy martyr Euphemia;[1] and he gathered together 266 priests beside | in the confession chapel of the holy Euphemia; and 256 priests were met together, |

| | |
|---|---|
| 406 bishops | 408 bishops |

who sent their autographs,

| | |
|---|---|
| and they condemned Eutyches and Nestorius. And after 42 days, being gathered together with the autographs, those who were present, 1200 bishops, set forth the faith in the presence of Marcian, the most pious Augustus, | and they were assembled together with the Tome, that contained the declaration of faith of the apostolic, Roman church and the autograph of the holy bishop Leo. Then in the presence of the catholic prince Marcian Augustus the assembled council of bishops, in number 1200, in company with Marcian Augustus set forth the catholic faith, two natures in one Christ, God and man. |

natures in Christ, the God-man, Eutyches that there was but one person and one nature. For a good, general account of the Nestorian and Eutychian controversies see *Cambridge Medieval History*, vol. I, pp. 494–515. *Cf.* Luke Rivington, *Roman Primacy, 430–451*, (Catholic); Puller, *Primitive Saints and the See of Rome*, (Protestant); Hefele, *op. cit.*, vol. II, pp. 499–881. Ayer, *Source Book of Ancient Church History*, pp. 476–481, 504–522.

[1] The following two accounts in our text of the Council of Chalcedon are both somewhat confused, the one in the first column giving, on the whole, a slightly more accurate notion of its work than the other, as may be seen by a comparison with the facts. The council met in 451 at the summons of the emperor Marcian and contrary to the express desire of the pope. It held its sessions in the basilica of St. Euphemia

and he, together with Placidia Augusta, professed his faith publicly before the eyes of the holy bishops and Eutyches was condemned a second time.

And there the pious Marcian Augustus, together with his wife, Pulcheria Augusta, laid aside his regal majesty and professed his faith before the eyes of the holy bishops and they condemned Eutyches and Nestorius. Nestorius and Dioscorus.

Afterwards the emperor Marcian and 150 bishops sent an official letter and asked Leo, the pope, to transmit to them an exposition of the catholic and apostolic faith. Then the blessed Leo expounded it and sent the Tome and confirmed the holy synod.

And a second time the emperor Marcian with his consort, Pulcheria Augusta, set forth his faith and signed it with his own hand and demanded of the holy council that it should send his profession to the most blessed pope Leo and condemn all heresies.

He wrote many letters setting forth the true catholic faith, which are kept to this day in the archives of the Roman church, He set forth the true catholic faith in company with many bishops, and his writings are kept to this day in the archives of the

Moreover the most blessed archbishop Leo sent many letters regarding the faith, which are preserved to this day in the archives.

in Chalcedon. A confession chapel, "martyrium," would have been too small. There were probably six hundred bishops in attendance. The number of those who accepted its decisions afterwards cannot be estimated. About twenty sessions were held during the twenty-four days of its duration. At one of these sessions the emperor and empress were present and made public profession of the imperial creed. At the emperor's urgent behest the bishops drew up a declaration of orthodox doctrine, basing it to a large extent upon Leo's famous letter written two years earlier to the bishop Flavianus and known as the Tome. It contained an exposition, drawn from Tertullian, of the dual nature of Christ. Marcian then required of Leo a confirmation of the dogma as set forth by the council and Leo gave it. Jaffé, *Regesta*, vol. I, p. 62, 423. Duchesne, *Lib. Pont.*, vol. I, p. 239, n. 2.

Roman church
on account of
the Eutychian
and Nestorian
heresies which
were condemned
in his time,

likewise a decretal, which he sent
about and circulated throughout
the whole world.[1]

He confirmed the synod of Chalcedon in many letters: 12
letters to Marcian, 13 letters to Leo Augustus, 9 letters to Flavianus, the bishop, 18 letters to the bishops of the East, all of which
confirmed the faith of the synod.[2]

| | |
|---|---|
| He replaced all the conse-crated silver vessels in all the parish churches after the Vandal devastation.[3] | He replaced the vessels of the Roman church after the Vandal war. |

    *     *     *     *     *     *     *     *[4]

| | |
|---|---|
| He repaired the basilica of blessed Peter, the apostle,[5] and restored the vaulting of blessed Paul after the fire from God.[6] | He made the vaulting and dec-orated the basilica of blessed Peter and repaired the basilica of Paul, the apostle. |

[1] It is impossible to identify this decretal.  Leo wrote several of importance, ad-dressed to bishops in different countries, but no single one, so far as we are aware, with such wide application as to be described by the phrase here used, unless it be the Tome already mentioned.  In 453 that was being read in Greek by the monks of Palestine. Jaffé, *Regesta*, p. 70, 500.

[2] The *Regesta* of Jaffé enumerates in all 150 letters of Leo, of which 17 are addressed to Marcian, 8 to the emperor Leo and 7 to Flavianus, bishop of Constantinople, the last, however, anterior to the Council of Chalcedon.  There are 13 more letters to the bishops of Constantinople after Flavianus and 38 to other Eastern bishops at Alexan-dria, Antioch, Jerusalem, Thessalonica, etc.  Our author evidently knew something of the extent of the correspondence.  Duchesne, *op. cit.*, vol. I, p. cxxxii.

[3] The sack of Rome by Genseric in 455.  See Gregorovius, *History of Rome*, tr. Hamilton, vol. I, ch. VI.

[4] Short list of vessels replaced in the basilicas of Peter, Paul and John.

[5] The mosaic on the façade of old St. Peter's bore a dedicatory inscription com-memorating a restoration by the prætorian prefect Marinianus and his wife Anastasia at the request of Leo.  Duchesne, *op. cit.*, p. cxxvii, n. 4.

[6] The roof of the basilica of St. Paul had fallen in, destroyed perhaps by lightning.

He made likewise the vaulting in the basilica of Constantine.[1]

He built also a basilica to the blessed Cornelius, bishop and martyr, near the cemetery of Callistus on the Via Appia.[2]

He, for the sake of the Roman name, undertook an embassy and went to meet the king of the Huns, Atthela by name, and delivered all Italy from the peril of the enemy.[3]

He founded a monastery at the church of blessed Peter, the apostle,

> which is called the monastery of the holy John and Paul.[4]

He ordained that during the performance of mass "sanctum sacrificium," etc. should be repeated.[5]

He ordained that a nun should not receive the blessing of the veiled head until she had been tried in virginity

| 40 years.[6] | 60 years. |

---

The inscription recording the fact of its ruin and of its reparation by two priests, Felix and Adeodatus, during the pontificate of Leo is preserved in the museum of the basilica. The mosaic of the triumphal arch was also a part of Leo's reconstruction. Though badly restored, the design may still be made out and the inscription which testifies to assistance from the empress Galla Placidia. Duchesne, *op. cit.*, p. 240, n. 7.

[1] Parts of the apsidal mosaic of the Lateran basilica, the bust of Christ in the clouds and the Earthly Paradise at the foot, are perhaps work of the early fifth century. Duchesne, *op. cit.*, p. 241, n. 8. Frothingham, *Monuments*, pp. 336–338.

[2] No trace of this basilica now remains. It is mentioned in two itineraries of the seventh century but not later. Duchesne, *op. cit.*, p. 241, n. 9.

[3] The well-known story of the meeting with Attila in 452. Jaffé, *Regesta*, vol. I, p. 68; Gregorovius, *History of Rome*, vol. I, pp. 228–230; Hodgkin, *Italy and her Invaders*, vol. II.

[4] The first monastery to be attached to the Vatican basilica. By 732 there were two others. They have all, of course, disappeared now, along with every other early and medieval structure on that site. Duchesne, *op. cit.*, p. 241, n. 11.

[5] *I.e.* in the eucharistic formula ending, "quod tibi obtulit summus sacerdos tuus Melchisedech sanctum sacrificium, immaculatam hostiam." Leo seems to have added the words, "sanctum sacrificium, immaculatam hostiam," to the reference to Melchisedech's offering of bread and wine, instigated thereto possibly by the aversion of the Manicheans to wine and in particular to its use in a sacred liturgy. Duchesne, *op. cit.*, p. 241, n. 12.

[6] We have no early, authentic document that specifies the age required at Rome of a woman who wished to assume the veil of a consecrated virgin. In Africa, at the beginning of the fifth century, she was ordinarily expected to be at least twenty-five years old. The Council of Saragossa, 380 A.D., fixed forty as the minimum age in Spain. An edict of the emperor Marjorian in the time of Leo confirmed the act of the Spanish

He appointed guards from the Roman clergy over the tombs
of the apostles; they are called the "cubicularii." [1]

\*       \*       \*       \*       \*       \*       \*       \* [2]

He also was buried

| in the basilica of the blessed | in the church of blessed Peter |
| Peter,[3] | the apostle, |

April 11.

And the bishopric was empty 7 days.


## XLVIII. HILARY (461–468)

Hilary, by nationality a Sardinian, son of

| Crispinianus, | Crispinus, |

occupied the see 6 years, 3 months and 10 days.

He made a decretal and

| sent it | disseminated it |

throughout all the East [4] and letters concerning the catholic

| and apostolic | |

faith and he confirmed the three synods of Nicea, Ephesus and
Chalcedon [5] and the Tome of the holy

| bishop | archbishop |

church. None of the surviving decretals of Leo or his successors through the fifth
and sixth centuries alludes to the subject of age. Duchesne, *op. cit.*, p. 241, n. 13.
Mansi, *Amplissima Collectio*, vol. IV, p. 508.

[1] An inscription dated 533 or 544 names one Decius, "cubicularius of the basilica
of St. Paul;" another of the same period mentions a "cubicularius of blessed Peter."
The confessions before the tombs of the apostles were being filled with gifts of such
price as to demand special warders or custodians. Duchesne, *op. cit.*, p. 241, n. 14.

[2] List of ordinations.

[3] Leo was the first of the popes to be buried in the portico of St. Peter's. His
remains were brought within the sanctuary by Sergius I in 688 and now lie with those
of Leo II, Leo III and Leo IV in the left transept of the modern cathedral. Lanciani,
*Pagan and Christian Rome*, pp. 221–223.

[4] No documents survive to prove Hilary's correspondence with the Eastern branch
of the church, but it is not unlikely that they once existed. Duchesne, *Lib. Pont.*,
vol. I, p. cxxxii.

[5] Duchesne quotes this passage in support of his contention that the *Liber Pontificalis* was first compiled in the early sixth century. See *supra, Introduction*, pp. xi–xii.
Until the time of Pope Vigilius, 537–555, the Roman church recognized only the three
ecumenical councils here enumerated; afterward it acknowledged also the Council
of Constantinople of the year 381. Duchesne, *op. cit.*, p. xxxviii.

Leo and he condemned Eutyches and Nestorius and all their disciples and all heresies; and he maintained

the supremacy | the authority

and the headship of the holy catholic and apostolic see.

He made a regulation for the church in the basilica of the holy Mary during the consulship of Basiliscus and Hermenericus, November 16.[1]

He built 3 oratories in the baptistery of the basilica of Constantine, one to holy John the Baptist, one to holy John the Evangelist, and one to the Holy Cross, all decked with silver and precious stones;[2]

\*  \*  \*  \*  \*  \*  \*  \*[3]

And in the city of Rome he provided vessels for service to be carried about to the appointed stations:[4]

a golden beaker

for the station, | with handles,

[1] The Roman synod of 465. The date here given is exact. A letter of Pope Hilary, still in existence, speaks of the bishops as in session on November 19. Jaffé, *Regesta*, vol. I, p. 76. Duchesne, *op. cit.*, p. 245, n. 2.

[2] The first two oratories are still to be seen opening out of the Lateran baptistery. The former preserves the bronze doors of Hilary with the dedicatory inscription above them, "HILARUS EPISCOPUS SANCTÆ PLEBI DEI," the latter Hilary's vault mosaics. The oratory of the Holy Cross was torn down in the seventeenth century.

[3] List of rich gifts to the three oratories, especially to that of the Holy Cross, which he beautified with a court, portico and elaborate fountain. Lists of gifts to the basilicas of the Lateran, Peter, Paul and Lawrence.

[4] As early as the fifth century it was customary for the clergy of the whole Roman church to assemble from time to time in one basilica or another for a stational mass, that is, a mass where the entire city church was represented from bishop to laity. This custom, like the distribution of the leaven (*supra*, p. 41 and n. 2), was apparently intended to typify the unity of the Christian fellowship. The pope was the chief celebrant at the altar but the priests of the twenty-five parish churches stood about and assisted both in the consecration service and in the distribution of the blessed elements to the people. Hilary provided a special set of altar vessels to be used at these stational masses, to be stored during the intervals at the Lateran or at Santa Maria Maggiore. Gregory I made out a definite schedule of the churches at which these stations should be held, including the parish churches and certain oratories and cemeteries. For an eighth century ritual for the observance of the stational mass see Atchley, *Ordo Romanus Primus*, p. 32 and *passim*. Duchesne, *op. cit.*, p. 246, n. 9. *Cambridge Med. Hist.*, vol. I, pp. 158–159.

weighing 8 lbs. ;

25

silver |

beakers for the parish priests, weighing each 10 lbs. ;
25 silver pitchers, weighing each 10 lbs. ;
50 silver chalices for service, weighing each 2 lbs.

| | |
|---|---|
| All these he appointed to be kept in the basilica of Constantine or in that of holy Mary. | which he appointed to be kept in the church of holy Mary. |

He built a monastery near the church of the holy Lawrence [1]

and a bath |

and another in the open air,
and a villa

| | |
|---|---|
| to the holy Stephen. ·He built also an oratory of the holy Stephen in the Lateran baptistery. | |

He erected also two libraries in the same place, likewise a monastery within the city of Rome "ad Luna."

\* \* \* \* \* \* \* \*[2]

He also was buried near the holy Lawrence in a crypt near the body of the blessed bishop Xystus.[3]

And the bishopric was empty 10 days.

---

[1] This and the following buildings have now all disappeared. Hilary's monastery of St. Lawrence may have stood upon the site of the present convent. One of his two baths was evidently enclosed and heated like the usual Roman bath, the other was an uncovered basin of cold water. The villa or "pretorium" may have been an hospice for pilgrims or a papal residence. If the succeeding sentence in the text is an interpolation, as seems probable, the two libraries were attached to the villa. Hilary's successor, Simplicius, built a church to St. Stephen in the neighborhood (*infra*, p. 105), and for that reason a later editor may have ascribed to Hilary a shrine to the same saint. The location of the monastery within the city is unknown. Duchesne, *op. cit.*, p. 247, nn. 10, 11, 12.

[2] List of ordinations.

[3] On his burial place see *supra*, p. 89, ń. 3.

## XLIX. Simplicius (468–483)

Simplicius, by nationality a Tiburtine,[1] son of

| Castinus, | Castorius, |

occupied the see 15 years,

| 1 month and 7 days. | and 7 days. |

He dedicated the basilica of the holy Stephen on the Celian Hill in the city of Rome[2] and the basilica of the blessed apostle Andrew near the basilica of the holy Mary[3] and another basilica of the holy Stephen near the basilica of the holy Lawrence[4] and another basilica of the blessed martyr Bibiana within the city of Rome beside the Licinian palace where her body rests.[5]

He appointed weeks for holy Peter, the apostle, and for holy Paul, the apostle, and for holy Lawrence, the martyr, when priests should be in attendance

| to administer baptism and penance to those who sought them, | for administering penance and baptism, |

---

[1] *I.e.* from Tivoli.

[2] The enigmatical, round church now called San Stefano Rotondo. It is still a problem whether it was built originally for pagan or for Christian uses.

[3] Later known as Sant' Andrea in Catabarbara. Simplicius took a secular hall, erected by the consul Junius Bassus during the reign of Constantine and adorned richly with scenes from Roman mythology and history, and transformed it into a basilica by throwing out an apse on the end opposite the entrance and decorating it with a mosaic of Christ and six apostles. The structure fell into ruin and was destroyed in the seventeenth century. It stood near Santa Maria Maggiore on land now owned by the convent of Sant' Antonio. Duchesne, *Lib. Pont.*, vol. I, p. 250, n. 2. This is the first mention of a public building appropriated by the church. In the turmoil of the period of Anthemius, Ricimer and Odoacer any one was free to take possession of the decaying, civil monuments.

[4] This basilica also has been torn down, but there are remnants of an ancient oratory with three apses a little to the southeast of San Lorenzo, near the stairs by which one climbs to the upper part of the modern cemetery. Duchesne, *op. cit.*, p. 250, n. 3.

[5] The original church of Santa Bibiana was constructed perhaps out of one of the pleasure houses which decked the gardens of the emperor Gallienus. The emperor's full name was Publius Licinius Gallienus; hence the title applied to his palace. No vestige of Simplicius' church is visible in the present basilica. Duchesne, *op. cit.*, p. 250, n. 4.

throughout the 3rd district for the holy Lawrence, the first district for the holy Paul, the 6th and 7th districts for the holy Peter.[1]

During his episcopate a report was sent from Greece, from Acacius, bishop of Constantinople, to the effect that Peter of the city of Alexandria was a Eutychian heretic; and a petition came from Acacius, the bishop, drawn up by his own hand.

|  |  |
|---|---|
| Then the church acted. | At that time the church, that is the first, apostolic see, took action. |

|  |  |
|---|---|
| Then Simplicius, the bishop and | |

the head, learned of it and condemned Peter of Alexandria, against whom Acacius charged innumerable crimes, but reserved for him an opportunity for penance.

Forthwith Timotheus, a catholic, and Acacius wrote again, saying that Peter was likewise implicated in the death of Proterius, a catholic. Then

|  |  |
|---|---|
| the archbishop | the pope |

Simplicius took no heed and did not reply to Acacius but condemned Peter until such time as he should do penance.[2]

---

[1] The priests of the three great basilicas had evidently reached a point where they found themselves unable to accomplish all the various duties connected with their offices, *e.g.* the performance of sacraments and services in the basilicas, the conduct of funerals and other services in the suburban cemeteries attached to the basilicas, the administration of the cemeteries and the properties belonging to the basilicas, the care of their parishioners, especially during the troublous years of political anarchy and social upheaval. Simplicius devised a plan by which priests from the smaller churches in the neighborhood should attend the greater basilicas to help provide spiritual ministrations. In the twelfth century a similar system was still in vogue, the basilica of Santa Maria Maggiore also receiving aid from adjacent priests. At that time the priests of Santa Maria in Trastevere, Santa Cecilia and San Crisogono in the seventh ecclesiastical district and of San Lorenzo in Damaso and San Marco in the sixth officiated at stated intervals in the Vatican and priests of Santa Sabina, Santa Prisca, Santa Balbina and Santi Nereo ed Achilleo in the first district in San Paolo. The Lateran basilica was assisted by bishops from the vicinity of Rome. Duchesne, *op. cit.*, p. 250, n. 5.

[2] This brief and obscure narrative is an account of the part played by the pope in the events of the Monophysite insurrection which followed the Council of Chalcedon. See *supra*, pp. 97–99. The disciples of Eutyches and Cyril of Alexandria saw in the

\* \* \* \* \* \* \* \* 1

He was buried

| near the blessed Peter, | in the basilica of blessed Peter, the apostle, |

March 2.

And the bishopric was empty 6 days.

## L. FELIX III (483–492)

Felix, by nationality a Roman, son of Felix, priest of the parish church of Fasciola,[2] occupied the see 8 years, 11 months and 17 days.

Chalcedon decree another form of the Nestorian heresy, ascribing a dual personality as well as a dual nature to Christ, and broke into a revolt that disturbed both church and empire for a century. The struggle was most violent in Alexandria. There the orthodox patriarch, Proterius, was assassinated in 457 and for some years the Mono-physites held the see. The accession of Emperor Zeno to the throne, however, in 477 turned the tide temporarily in favor of the orthodox party. Peter Mongius, the heretic patriarch, was deposed by imperial order and Timotheus Solofaciolus installed in his stead. Acacius, bishop of Constantinople, was already in correspondence with Simplicius regarding the lamentable state of affairs in Alexandria. Timotheus now also sent a deputation to the pope to complain of Peter's unceasing intrigues against him and to urge Simplicius to use his influence with the emperor to have Peter banished to a distance. The letters of Simplicius to Zeno and Acacius on the subject may be found summarised in Jaffé's *Regesta*, vol. I, pp. 78–79, 579–582. He seems to have made no impression on the emperor, for Peter remained free as before until the death of Timotheus in 482. The latter's orthodox successor proved to be unacceptable to both Zeno and Acacius and negotiations were straightway undertaken by them for a com-promise with the indomitable Peter. The result was the Henotikon Edict issued by Zeno in 482, which condemned both extremists, Eutyches and Nestorius, ignored the Chalcedon decree and attempted to formulate a doctrine to which Catholics and Monophysites might all subscribe. Simplicius, learning of this change of face, wrote to protest against the restoration of Peter, but with no more effect than before. Neither Zeno nor Acacius replied to him. Jaffé, *ibid.*, 586–589. The controversy was resumed by Simplicius' successors, as we shall see. Duchesne, *op. cit.*, p. 251, n. 6. On Zeno's policy see *Cambridge Med. Hist.*, vol. I, pp. 515–520.

[1] Lists of gifts to the Vatican basilica and of ordinations.

[2] An ancient name for the church now called Santi Nereo ed Achilleo. Duchesne prints the text of several epitaphs, found in the basilica of San Paolo, which are prob-ably those of the father of Felix III and of the latter's wife and two children. Petronia, wife of Felix, died in 472, while her husband was only a deacon. Gregory the Great was one of their descendants. In his Dialogues he recounts the vision which his aunt, a consecrated virgin, had of their ancestor, Pope Felix, shortly before her own death. Duchesne, *Lib. Pont.*, vol. I, pp. 240, n. 7, 253, n. 2. Gregory I, *Dialogi*, IV, 16; Migne, *Pat. Lat.*, vol. 77, col. 348.

He was bishop in the time of Odobacer,[1] the king, until the time of Theodoric,

the king.

He built the basilica of the holy Agapitus near the basilica of the holy Lawrence, the martyr.[2]

During his episcopate there came another report

| from the region of Greece | from Greece |

that Peter of Alexandria had been reinstated

in the communion

by Acacius, bishop of Constantinople.[3]  Then the venerable

| pope Felix | Felix, archbishop of the apostolic see of the city of Rome, |

sent an advocate

| by resolution of the synod | by advice |

of his see and held a council and condemned Acacius together with Peter.

---

[1] Odoacer.  Theodoric did not take Ravenna until 493 but by 491 he was able to send Faustus, prince of the Senate, as his ambassador to Emperor Zeno, a fact which indicates that by this time he was pretty well master of Rome.  Duchesne points out that our author here resumes the imperial synchronisms which had been discontinued since the period covered by the Liberian Catalogue.  He argues that the author is now competent to supply them from memory.  Duchesne, *op. cit.*, pp. xlv, 253, n. 4.

[2] The situation of this church is now unknown, although it is mentioned in several early itineraries.  Duchesne, *op. cit.*, p. 253, n. 5.

[3] The controversy of Simplicius with Acacius of Constantinople over Peter, the Monophysite bishop of Alexandria (*supra*, p. 106 and n. 2), was promptly taken up by Felix.  The arrival in Rome of the orthodox claimant of the Alexandrian see, John Talaia, entreating the pope's assistance, was the signal for him to put forth every effort to induce Acacius to abandon Peter.  The subsequent events are told in the main correctly in our text but their order has been inverted.  The first step in Felix' proceedings was the sending in 483 of the envoys, Misenus, bishop of Cumæ, and Vitalis, bishop of Truentum, to summon Acacius to appear before the pope and his council to answer for his contumacy.  On their return in the following year Felix held a synod which condemned and anathematised Acacius and sent an advocate, "defensorem," with notification of the sentence to Acacius, to the emperor Zeno and to the clergy and people of Constantinople.  The documents may be found in Jaffé, *Regesta*, vol. I, pp. 80–81, 591–595, 599–603.  *Cf.* Puller, *Primitive Saints and the See of Rome*, pp. 376 ff.

After 3 years another report came from the emperor Zeno that Acacius had returned and was penitent.[1]  Then Pope Felix

held a council by agreement and |

sent two bishops, Mesenus and Vitalis, so that if they found Acacius to be a confederate of Peter

| they might condemn them again but if not they might offer him the code of penance.[2] | they might condemn them. |

But they, when they had arrived at

| the city of Constantinople, | Constantinople, | the city of Heraclea, |

were corrupted with bribes given them by the aforesaid bishop and they did not carry out the injunctions of the apostolic see.[3]

And when they returned to Rome to the apostolic see,

| Pope Felix called a council and held an inquiry and | at that time the venerable pope Felix called a synod and held a discussion and |

he found both bishops, that is Mesenus and Vitalis, guilty before the court and corrupted with bribes; and he expelled Mesenus and Vitalis, the bishops, from the communion.  Then Mesenus confessed that he had been corrupted by a bribe

and the council granted him an | opportunity for penance.[4]

---

[1] This statement is quite fictitious.  It was perhaps introduced by our author to give ground for the sending of Misenus and Vitalis.

[2] Misenus and Vitalis were given no such discretion in the affair as this account implies.  They were commissioned simply to cite Acacius to a trial before the pope. A code of penance, "libellus pænitentiæ," was, however, in existence long before this time.  The African synods of 251 and 255 referred to a "libellus," where the divers penalties for sins were written down.  Schmitz, *Die Bussbücher und die Bussdisciplin der Kirche*, vol. I, pp. 17, 45, 107.

[3] In the documents published by Jaffé (*supra*, p. 108, n. 3), the pope accuses his envoys of disobedience to instructions in communicating with the heretical party, in acknowledging the authority of Peter and in accepting bribes.

[4] Misenus and Vitalis were both deposed and excommunicated.  Misenus was pardoned in after years by Pope Gelasius but Vitalis died before that time.  Duchesne, *op. cit.*, p. 254, nn. 12 and 13.

This took place in the time of Odobacer, the king.

\*        \*        \*        \*        \*        \*        \*        \* 1

He was buried

| in the church of the blessed Paul.[2] | in the basilica of blessed Paul, the apostle. |

And the bishopric was empty 5 days.

And after his death a regulation was made by the priests and deacons for the whole church

> that no one should ever presume to show himself hasty in a matter which must sometime come up for examination.[3]


## LI. GELASIUS (492–496)

Gelasius, by nationality an African, son of Valerius, occupied the see 4 years, 8 months and 18 days. He was bishop in the time of Theodoric, the king, and Zeno Augustus.[4]

> In his time was found the church of the holy Angel on Mount Garganus.[5]

---

[1] List of ordinations.

[2] Felix III is the only pope buried at San Paolo. He may have chosen the spot in order to lie with his family. *Supra*, p. 107, n. 2.

[3] There is no other record of any action by the clergy during the interval between Felix' death and the consecration of Gelasius, but in the days between the death of Simplicius and the accession of Felix there had been an assembly of the Senate and clergy of Rome in the mausoleum of Santa Petronilla, adjoining the Vatican basilica. There it had been decided that no pope in the future should have power to alienate property belonging to the church as a whole. The decision was declared null by the Roman synod of 502 on account of the irregularity of the proceeding but Pope Symmachus issued a decree to the same effect during the sessions of the same synod and with its approval. The obscure clause of our text may be a reference to the decision which was annulled. Duchesne, *op. cit.*, p. 254, n. 16.

[4] The synchronism is inexact. Zeno died in 491 and Anastasius was emperor during the pontificate of Gelasius.

[5] This sentence is found in only one manuscript and is undoubtedly a late interpolation. The earliest existing description of the miraculous discovery of the sanctuary of St. Michael on Monte Gargano dates from the ninth century, although it purports

In his time Manicheans were discovered in the city of Rome, whom he transported into exile and whose books he burned with fire before the doors of the basilica of the holy Mary.[1]

He, in accordance with a decree of the synod, after the laws of penance had been fulfilled, reinstated the purified bishop Mesenus with weeping and restored him to his church. This Mesenus had sinned in the matter of Acacius and Peter.[2]

He, in accordance with a synodical decree, reinstated Mesenus, the bishop, in the communion and restored him to his church, after the laws of penance had been fulfilled and Mesenus was purified and received again.

He was a lover

of the clergy and

of the poor [3] and he increased the clergy.

He delivered the city of Rome from the peril of famine.[4]

to be taken from a "libellus" or record contained in the shrine itself. Waitz, *Scriptores Rerum Langobardicarum*, p. 541. Paul the Deacon mentions an oracle of the holy archangel on Monte Gargano which was plundered by the Greeks in the seventh century. *History of the Lombards*, tr. Foulke, *Univ. of Penn. Transls. and Reprints*, New Series, vol. 3, p. 200.

[1] There is no other reference in contemporary historians to the episode here narrated. If Duchesne's theory as to the date of the composition of the first part of the *Lib. Pont.* be correct, the author may either have witnessed the burning of the Manichean books or have heard of it from witnesses. *Supra, Introduction*, p. xi.

[2] We still possess the report of this synod, held in March, 495, and two "libelli" or declarations of Misenus which he presented to the assemblage, prostrating himself to the earth. On Misenus see *supra*, p. 108, n. 3; p. 109 and nn. 1–4. It is a satisfaction to find that in 499 Misenus attended another council at Rome once more in his capacity of bishop of Cumæ. Duchesne, *Lib. Pont.*, vol. I, p. 256, n. 4. Jaffé, *Regesta*, vol. I, p. 88.

[3] Dionysius Exiguus, who knew of Gelasius through the priests he had trained, writes of him that he spent all his substance on the poor and died himself in poverty, that he looked upon his office as an opportunity to serve rather than to rule. Quoted by Duchesne, *op. cit.*, p. 256, n. 5.

[4] About 494 Gelasius wrote a tractate in denunciation of the Lupercalia and the party that wished to revive the celebration of the pagan rites. In the course of it he asked, "As for your Castors, whose worship you refuse to abandon, why did they not give you tranquil seas so that the ships might reach here with grain in winter and the city suffer less with want?" He wrote also to Firmina, a lady of rank, to request that lands belonging to St. Peter, which had been seized by the barbarian and Roman armies, should be restored to the church. They were needed, he said, for the support of the hungry multitudes who were flocking to Rome from the provinces which had been devastated by the wars. Jaffé, *Regesta*, pp. 89, 90, 672, 685.

He made a regulation for the whole church.[1]   In his time another report came from Greece to the effect that many crimes and murders were being committed through Peter and Acacius in Constantinople.[2]

At that time John of Alexandria, the catholic bishop, fled and came to Rome to the apostolic see

| and the blessed Gelasius received him with honor and bestowed upon him also a second bishopric.[3] Then he held a synod and sent throughout the countries of the East | Then the blessed Gelasius received John |

and he sent again and condemned eternally Acacius and Peter,[4]

| if they should not do penance in accordance with the code and seek for absolution. | if they did not repent; notwithstanding he allowed them opportunity for satisfying the apostolic see and displayed the clemency of the first see of the church. |

He dedicated the basilica of the holy Euphemia, the martyr, in the town of Tibur,[5]

[1] There exists a comprehensive decretal by Gelasius in twenty-eight chapters on a variety of questions of church administration and discipline addressed to "all the bishops in Lucania, Bruttium and Sicily." Jaffé, *Regesta*, p. 85, 636.

[2] Both Acacius and Peter died before the accession of Gelasius.  The reference here must be to parties of their adherents, unless the author is simply confusing his chronology, as he does below.  On this whole controversy see *supra*, pp. 106–109 and notes.  Duchesne, *op. cit.*, p. 256, n. 8.

[3] John Talaia, orthodox bishop of Alexandria, had taken refuge in Rome ten years earlier, in 482, just as Felix III became pope.  *Supra*, p. 108, n. 3.  Gelasius continued to support John's cause.

[4] Gelasius held three synods at Rome, no one of which, so far as we know, concerned itself particularly with Acacius and Peter, whose case was regarded as settled.  Gelasius instead wrote letters to various Eastern prelates, condemning all who did not concur in the sentence passed by his predecessor.  Jaffé, *Regesta*, pp. 83–88, 620, 622, 638, 639, 664, 665, 669.  The clauses in our text, granting opportunity for penance, are obviously interpolations, Acacius and Peter being both dead.

[5] The basilica of St. Euphemia at Tivoli disappeared early.  Duchesne, *op. cit.*, p. 256, n. 11.

twenty miles from the city,

and other basilicas       | He dedicated also the basilica

of the holy Nicander, Eleutherius

and Andrew       |

on the Via Lavicana in the village Pertusa.[1]

    He built also the       | and another

basilica of Holy Mary on the Via Laurentina in the estate Crispinis,

twenty miles from the city.[2]       |

He wrote 5 books against Nestorius and Eutyches; he wrote also hymns after the manner of the blessed Ambrose; likewise two books against Arius; he wrote also prefaces to the sacraments and prayers in careful language and many eloquent epistles regarding the faith.[3]

He wrote treatises and hymns, as did blessed Ambrose, the bishop, and books against Eutyches and Nestorius, which to-day are kept preserved in the library of the archives of the church.

    During his bishopric the clergy waxed greater.

    *     *     *     *     *     *     *    *[4]

[1] Sergius I, at the end of the seventh century, is said to have rebuilt an oratory to St. Andrew on the Via Labicana. It was perhaps the basilica or group of basilicas mentioned here. The site is now lost. Duchesne, *op. cit.*, p. 256, n. 12.

[2] This church also is now unknown.

[3] The hymns of Gelasius have all been lost, as also his refutations of Arianism. Jaffé lists among his writings one treatise on the dual nature of Christ "against Eutyches and Nestorius." *Regesta*, p. 89, 670. The prefaces and prayers were evidently parts of a liturgy. In the ninth century the *Liber Sacramentorum* or office of Gelasius was distinguished from that of St. Gregory. Duchesne, *op. cit.*, p. 257, n. 14. Jaffé enumerates over one hundred letters of Gelasius dealing with matters of doctrine, ecclesiastical government, morality and the temporal needs of his flock. *Op. cit.*, pp. 83–95, 619–743. One of the most striking was written in 494 to the emperor Anastasius, setting forth the superiority of the priestly to the civil power. "There are two powers which for the most part control this world, the sacred authority of priests and the might of kings. Of these two the office of the priests is the greater, inasmuch as they must give account to the Lord even for the kings before the divine judgment. . . . You know, therefore, that you are dependent upon their decision and that they will not submit to your will." Jaffé, *op. cit.*, p. 85, 632. Ayer, *Source Book*, p. 531.

[4] List of ordinations.

He also was buried

| | |
|---|---|
| in the church of blessed Peter, | in the basilica of blessed Peter, the apostle, |

November 21.

And

after his death                    |

the bishopric was empty 7 days.

## LII. ANASTASIUS II (496–498)

Anastasius, by nationality a Roman, son of Peter,[1] from the 5th district,

Tauma,                             |

of the Caput Tauri,[2] occupied the see 1 year, 11 months and 24 days. He was bishop in the time of Theodoric, the king.

He set up the confession of blessed Lawrence, the martyr, of silver,

| | |
|---|---|
| weighing 80 lbs. | which weighed 100 lbs. |

At that time many of the clergy and of the priests withdrew themselves from communion with him, because without consulting

| | |
|---|---|
| the priests or the bishops or the clergy of all the catholic church | them |

he had communicated with a deacon of Thessalonica, Photinus by name, who was of the party of Acacius, and because he desired secretly to reinstate Acacius and could not. And he was struck dead by divine will.[3]

---

[1] The epitaph of Anastasius states that his father was a priest. Duchesne, *Lib. Pont.*, vol. I, p. 259, n. 5.

[2] For this district see *supra*, p. 10, n. 3.

[3] This notice of Anastasius is bitter with the feeling engendered by the controversy with the Eastern church, which had begun under Pope Simplicius and which under Felix III and Gelasius had resulted in an open schism between the Western branch, led by Rome, and the Eastern patriarchates and the emperor. See *supra*, pp. 106, 108, 109, 112. Anastasius II, upon his accession, sent two bishops to the emperor to beg that the seamless tunic of the Savior be no longer rent for the sake of a single dead man. He did not propose to retract the censure of Felix III upon Acacius and his tenets but  suggested

\*      \*      \*      \*      \*      \*      \*      \* 1

And he also was buried

| in the church of blessed Peter in the Vatican,[2] | in the basilica of blessed Peter, the apostle, |

November 19.

And the bishopric was empty 4 days.

## LIII. Symmachus (498–514)

Symmachus, by nationality a Sardinian,[3] son of Fortunatus, occupied the see 15 years, 7 months and 27 days.

He was bishop in the time of Theodoric,

| the heretic, [4] | the king, |

and Anastasius Augustus,

the Eutychian,

from November 22 to July 19.

---

that Acacius' name be allowed to drop and assured the emperor that the baptisms and ordinations performed by Acacius and his followers would be accepted as valid at Rome. Jaffé, *Regesta*, vol. I, p. 95, 744. These overtures produced an effect at least upon the bishop of Thessalonica, who thereupon had the letter of Gelasius denouncing Acacius read publicly in the churches of his diocese and who dispatched a deacon, Photinus, to renew in his behalf communion with the Roman see. Jaffé, *ibid.*, 746. Unfortunately a zealot party at Rome disapproved of the pope's conciliatory attitude and ascribed to him, as in the text, a design to abandon the principles and to rescind the acts of Felix III and Gelasius. Thus arose a schism within the Roman church itself which was to break out violently after Anastasius' death. The fact that Anastasius died soon after his resumption of relations with the church at Thessalonica was looked upon by his opponents as a clear proof of divine displeasure. Duchesne, *op. cit.*, pp. xliii and 258, n. 3.

[1] List of ordinations.

[2] Duchesne gives his epitaph. *Op. cit.*, p. 259, n. 5.

[3] Symmachus said of himself that he came out of paganism and learned the catholic faith at Rome. Duchesne, *Lib. Pont.*, vol. I, p. 263, n. 1.

[4] Mommsen argues that if the *Lib. Pont.* had been composed early in the sixth century under Ostrogothic rule, as Duchesne maintains that it was, the derogatory epithet of "heretic" could not have been applied to Theodoric. Mommsen, *Lib. Pont.*, p. xvii. On Theodoric's relations with the Roman Church see Gregorovius, *History of Rome*, tr. Hamilton, vol. I, pp. 311–333.

| | |
|---|---|
| He loved the clergy and the poor; he was a good man and sagacious, kindly and courteous, and at the time of his ordination Laurentius also was ordained because of a dissension in the bishopric,[1] | He was ordained on the same day with Laurentius because there was a dissension, |

Symmachus in the basilica of Constantine and Laurentius in the basilica of the blessed Mary.

Wherefore

| | |
|---|---|
| one party of the clergy and also of the senators was divided from the rest | the clergy was separated into parties and the senate also was divided |

and some supported Symmachus and others Laurentius. And after the dissension had arisen

| | |
|---|---|
| they all alike | the parties |

decided that both factions should betake themselves to Ravenna for the judgment of Theodoric.[2] And

| | |
|---|---|
| when they had come | when they had both arrived at Ravenna |

they received this righteous judgment, that he who had been first ordained or who

| | |
|---|---|
| was supported by | was known to have |

the largest party should occupy the apostolic see. Thus through justice and perception of the truth Symmachus was selected and made bishop. At that time Pope Symmachus assembled a synod and appointed Laurentius bishop of the town of Nuceria out of compassion.[3]

[1] There is no mention here of the theological and political reasons underlying the split in the Roman church but the situation may be better appreciated if the reader recalls the beginning of discord under Anastasius II. *Supra*, p. 114 and n. 3. Laurentius seems to have been the candidate of the party that desired more compromise with the Eastern church.

[2] Other versions of the story say that the contending parties were forced to accept the arbitration of Theodoric. Duchesne, *op. cit.*, p. 263, n. 4.

[3] The acts of the synod of Italian bishops, held under the presidency of Symmachus in 499, have been preserved. They consist chiefly of measures to prevent confusion in

But after 4 years[1] some of the clergy and some of the senate, in particular Festus and Probinus, full of zeal and craft,

brought charges against Symmachus and suborned false witnesses whom they sent to King Theodoric, the heretic,

at Ravenna to accuse the blessed Symmachus; and they recalled Laurentius stealthily to Rome,

after the accusation had been drawn up at Rome; and they created a schism and

| a party withdrew itself from communion with Symmachus.[2] | the clergy was divided again and some communicated with Symmachus and some with Laurentius. |
|---|---|

Then the senators Festus and Probinus sent a report to the king

| and asked King Theodoric to send Peter of Altinum[3] as an inspector to the apostolic see. | and began to negotiate with the king to send an inspector to the apostolic see. Then the king sent Peter, bishop of the town of Altinum, although the canons forbade it. |
|---|---|

future papal elections. During the synod Laurentius was appointed bishop of Nocera. Jaffé, *Regesta*, vol. I, p. 96. Hefele, *op. cit.*, vol. II, p. 958.

[1] In fact early in 501.

[2] The first accusation brought by the malcontents against Symmachus concerned the date of Easter. Symmachus had celebrated that festival in 501 on March 25, following the old Roman calendar. Jaffé, *Regesta*, p. 97, 754. His adversaries complained that he should have adopted the Greek reckoning, which brought the date to April 22. Symmachus went to Rimini to lay his case before Theodoric and while there learned of other and graver charges which were being preferred against him: viz., violation of chastity and misuse of church property. Thereupon, without waiting to face Theodoric, he fled back to Rome by night and entrenched himself in the buildings of the Vatican. The hostile party took advantage of his flight to prevail upon Theodoric to send a "visitor" or inspector to Rome in order to celebrate Easter at the proper season, as the emperor Honorius had done at the time of the dissension between Boniface I and Eulalius. *Supra*, p. 89, n. 4; p. 90. The act, however, was tantamount to a declaration that the see of Rome was vacant or contested. Symmachus was bound to resent it as a negation of all his rights. Duchesne, *op. cit.*, p. 264, n. 8. Jaffé, *ibid.*, p. 97.

[3] The modern Altino near Venice.

Then the blessed Symmachus assembled 115 bishops and in the synod was acquitted of the false accusation and Peter of Altinum, the intruder upon the apostolic see, and Laurentius of Nuceria were condemned, because during the lifetime of the bishop Symmachus they had invaded his see.[1] Then the blessed Symmachus was reinstated with glory in the apostolic see by all the bishops, priests and deacons and all the clergy and the people, to sit as bishop in the church of the blessed Peter.

Then Festus, the patrician, began to slaughter in the city the clergy who were communicating with the blessed Symmachus [3] and he expelled consecrated women from their dwell- At that time Festus, the exconsul and leader of the senate,[2] and Probinus, the exconsul, began to fight in the city of Rome with other senators, in particular with Faustus, the exconsul,

[1] The Roman synod of 501 was convened to pass on the whole situation by order of Theodoric and with the consent of Symmachus. It held three sessions, the first during the spring or early summer at the church of Santa Maria in Trastevere. At this session Symmachus agreed to appear, waiving the claim of his see not to be judged by inferiors and overlooking the fact that Theodoric had seized the lands and buildings of the church, leaving him only St. Peter's. The second session met in September at the basilica of Santa Croce in Gerusalemme on the farther side of the city. Symmachus set out to cross from the Vatican but was attacked by a band of enemies on the way and many of the priests accompanying him were killed. Thereafter Symmachus remained shut up in the Vatican and refused to attend another session of the synod. Nevertheless in October the assembled bishops declared that they could find no reason why he should not continue in full enjoyment of his office and left the accusations against him to the judgment of God. They solemnly condemned both Laurentius and Peter of Altino, Theodoric's "visitor." In November, 502, Symmachus on his own initiative called another synod of bishops, which proceeded to annul an irregular decree forbidding the pope to alienate church property, that seems to have been employed by Symmachus' opponents as a basis for their charges against him. *Supra*, p. 110, n. 3. The synod indeed passed other ordinances prohibiting the pope to dispose of rural property but allowing him to sell city houses which cost too much to maintain. In 505 Symmachus petitioned Theodoric to compel the patrician Festus, the instigator of the violence which continued to harass the city, to abstain from further opposition and to order Laurentius to leave Rome. Dioscorus, a young deacon from Alexandria, was able to persuade Theodoric to take this step and Symmachus resumed possession of all the churches and ecclesiastical estates. Duchesne, *op. cit.*, p. 264, n. 10. Jaffé, *Regesta*, pp. 97–98. Hefele, *loc. cit.* Dioscorus' powers of eloquence served the Roman church even more conspicuously later. *Infra*, pp. 127–130.

[2] Festus was consul in 472, Probinus in 489 and Faustus in 490. They are all three mentioned as persons of high reputation in a contemporary work by Ennodius. *Opusc.* VI. Quoted by Duchesne, *op. cit.*, p. 265, n. 12.

[3] This passage is not probably descriptive of any one occasion but of the general

ings, and stripped women of their clothing and beat them with clubs and he killed many priests there, and, in their hatred, to commit slaughter and murder upon the clergy who rightfully communicated with the blessed Symmachus and they killed with the sword publicly those who were found within the city. Also they expelled consecrated women and virgins from their convents and their dwellings and they stripped women of their clothing and wounded them with blows and stripes; and daily they waged war against the church in the midst of the city. Likewise they slew many priests,

among them Dignissimus and Gordianus,[1] priests of Saint [2] Peter, the apostle, "ad Vincula," and of Saints John and Paul, whom they did to death with cudgels and sword; also many other Christians, so that it was unsafe for one of the clergy to walk abroad in the city by day or by night. Only Faustus, the exconsul, fought for the church.

After all this the blessed Symmachus found Manicheans in the city of Rome and burned with fire all their images and books before

state of lawlessness and tumult which lasted during the years before Symmachus was finally and decisively reinstated. The people as a whole seem to have supported Symmachus but a party of the clergy and a majority of the Senate were bitter against him.

[1] The name of Dignissimus does not appear on the list of parish priests who took part in the synod of 499, perhaps because the basilica which he served was not counted among the parish churches. Gordianus is registered as priest of Santi Giovanni e Paolo. He was the father of Pope Agapitus. *Infra*, p. 143 and n. 6. Both undoubtedly perished early in the disturbances, for neither was among the priests loyal to Symmachus who attended the synod of November, 502. Duchesne, *op. cit.*, p. 265, n. 13.

[2] From the sixth century onward the word "sanctus" was an official title, applied only to the distinguished dead who were publicly venerated in the churches, no longer a general epithet for all bishops or even, as in primitive times, for all believers, living or dead. Hereafter, therefore, in our text the word will usually be translated "saint," instead of the vaguer "holy."

[3] The church of San Pietro in Vincoli was built during the fifth century by the empress Eudoxia to receive the relic of the chains of Peter.

the doors of the basilica of Constantine and condemned them to exile.[1]

He was bishop from the consulship of Paulinus (A.D. 498) to the consulship of Senator (A.D. 514).[2]

He built the basilica of Saint Andrew, the apostle, near the basilica of the blessed Peter.[3]

    \*     \*     \*     \*     \*     \*     \*     \*[4]

Also he adorned with marbles the basilica of blessed Peter.

The fountain of blessed Peter with the square portico around it he beautified with marble work and with lambs and crosses and palms of mosaic. Likewise he enclosed the whole atrium; and he widened the steps before the doors of the basilica of Saint Peter, the apostle, and he made other steps of wood on the right and on the left. Also he built palaces in the same place on the right and on the left. Also, below the steps into the atrium, outside in the

---

[1] This event must have taken place after the emperor Anastasius accused Symmachus himself of being a Manichean, probably during the latter half of his pontificate. Symmachus wrote an *Apologeticus* in his own defence. Duchesne, *op. cit.*, p. 265, n. 14. Jaffé, *Regesta*, p. 99, 761.

[2] This is the first consular synchronism since the close of the *Liberian Catalogue*. Synchronisms are given for the three following popes as well. Duchesne regards their appearance here as another proof that the *Lib. Pont.* was first compiled between 514 and 530. *Op. cit.*, p. xlv.

[3] Symmachus was peculiarly concerned to enlarge and beautify the basilica of St. Peter, perhaps out of gratitude for the shelter it afforded him during his years of struggle, 501–506. The basilica of St. Andrew was a rotonda which stood beside the church of St. Peter until it was demolished by Pius VI to make room for the present sacristy. It seems to have been built originally during the fifth century, together with a second circular structure which stood behind it and was connected with it and with St. Peter's by a gallery. The two were apparently intended as mausoleums for the family of Theodosius and the rear building actually contained some imperial tombs. It was called in the Middle Ages the chapel of Santa Petronilla. The rotonda which Symmachus now converted into a church and dedicated to St. Andrew had presumably never been used as a mausoleum and was empty until he furnished it. Duchesne, *op. cit.*, p. 265, n. 16.

[4] List of gifts to the shrine of St. Andrew and of four oratories constructed within the rotonda ; also of three oratories built about the baptistery of St. Peter, which stood at the end of the north transept of the basilica. These last three oratories were dedicated to the Holy Cross, St. John the Baptist and St. John the Evangelist respectively, as were the oratories attached to the baptistery of the Lateran. *Supra*, p. 103. Symmachus may have equipped the Vatican baptistery to serve instead of the Lateran during his exclusion from the latter.

square, he set another fountain and an accommodation for human necessity.[1]

And he built other steps for ascent into the church of blessed Andrew and set up a fountain.

He built the basilica of the holy martyr Agatha on the Via Aurelia on the estate Lardarium;[2] from the foundation he built it and offered there 2 silver coffers.[3]

At that time he built the basilica of Saint Pancratius,[4] where also he set a silver coffer, weighing 15 lbs.; he built likewise in the same place a bath.

Also in the church of blessed Paul, the apostle, he rebuilt the apse of the basilica, which was falling into ruin, and he embellished it with a picture behind the confession and he made a vaulting and a transept; and over the confession he erected a silver image of the Savior and the 12 apostles, which weighed 120 lbs.; and before the doors of the basilica he built steps into the atrium and a fountain; and behind the apse he brought down water and built there a bath from the foundation.[5]

---

[1] This account of the completion and adornment of the atrium before St. Peter's is not altogether clear. One gathers that Symmachus finished and decorated the famous fountain of the bronze pine cone and the walls of the atrium, widened the stairway leading up to the atrium and built a palace or papal residence on either side. It is not plain what was the purpose of the steps that went to right and left, unless they were approaches to the palaces. The second fountain was shaped like a shell and stood apparently before the entrance to the atrium. Of course there is now no trace of these arrangements. Only the bronze pine cone is preserved in a courtyard of the Vatican palace.

[2] It is uncertain where this basilica stood.

[3] Boxes or coffers of hammered silver were used as reliquaries. Some few examples from this period are still preserved. See for illustration Lowrie, *Christian Art and Archæology*, pp. 360–361; Dalton, *Byzantine Art and Archæology*, pp. 563–564.

[4] San Pancrazio on the Via Aurelia over the martyr's tomb. The modern church has been much restored. After the Gothic wars the city gate which led to this basilica was called Porta San Pancrazio instead of Porta Aurelia. The last years of Symmachus were passed in the comparative peace and order of Theodoric's reign. The civil government took up vigorously the work of repairing public buildings, palaces, theatres, aqueducts, etc., and furnished bricks and other materials to the church for its restorations and new enterprises. Frothingham, *Monuments*, pp. 69–71. Gregorovius, *History of Rome*, tr. Hamilton, vol. I, pp. 290–308.

[5] San Paolo has passed through so many vicissitudes that it is impossible now to identify any handiwork of Symmachus. Behind the apse of the basilica is the public street and beyond that on the hill the cemetery of Lucina. An inscription of the sixth or seventh century, however, speaks of a bath built in a cemetery and of water brought

Within the city of Rome he built the basilica of Saints Silvester and Martin from its foundation, near

the baths                   |

of Trajan [1] and there also he set a silver ciborium above the altar, which weighed 120 lbs.; 12 silver coffers, which weighed each 10 lbs.; a silver confession, which weighed 15 lbs.

For the blessed John and Paul he built steps behind the apse.[2]

Also he enlarged the basilica of the archangel Michael and built steps and brought in water.[3]

Also he erected from its foundation an oratory of Saints Cosma and Damian beside Saint Mary.[4]

Also on the Via Trivana, 27 miles from the city of Rome, on the estate Pacinianum, he dedicated a basilica to blessed Peter at the request of Albinus and Glaphyra, the illustrious prætorian prefects, who built it from the foundation at their own expense.[5]

Also near blessed Peter and blessed Paul,

the apostles,               |

and near Saint Lawrence,

the martyr,                |

he erected lodging houses for the poor.[6]

---

in by means of wheels and pulleys. The reference may be to the bath of Symmachus. Duchesne, *op. cit.*, p. 267, n. 34.

[1] A church had been built on this site two hundred years before by Pope Sylvester. *Supra*, p. 42, n. 1. It seems likely that Symmachus restored or enriched the earlier structure and added another close beside it, dedicated to St. Martin of Tours. The two basilicas were later spoken of as one under the title Sts. Sylvester and Martin. In course of time the name of St. Martin predominated and the modern church is known as San Martino ai Monti. Duchesne, *op. cit.*, p. 267. n. 35.

[2] The flight of steps down the hill behind the apse is a feature of Santi Giovanni e Paolo to-day.

[3] The tomb of Hadrian was not consecrated to the archangel until the seventh century. It is not known what basilica to St. Michael existed as early as the age of Symmachus, although three are said to have stood within the city at the beginning of the ninth century. Duchesne, *op. cit.*, p. 268, n. 36.

[4] Now disappeared.

[5] The site is unknown. Via Trivana may be a corruption for Via Tiberina, the road which branches off from the Via Flaminia at Saxa Rubra. Duchesne, *op. cit.*, p. 268, n. 37.

[6] Whether these lodgings were for impoverished citizens of Rome or for impecunious pilgrims from a distance, they testify to the increasing scope of church activity.

\*     \*     \*     \*     \*     \*     \*     \*[1]

He appointed that on every Lord's day and anniversary of the martyrs the hymn, "Gloria in excelsis," should be repeated.[2]

He set in order the cemetery of the Jordani for the sake of the body of Saint Alexander.[3]

He every year sent relief of money and garments to the bishops who had been driven into exile throughout Africa and Sardinia.[4]

He redeemed with money captives in Liguria and Milan and divers provinces and bestowed gifts upon them and let them go free.[5]

\*     \*     \*     \*     \*     \*     \*     \*[6]

He also was buried

| | |
|---|---|
| in the church of the blessed Peter,[7] July 19, in peace. | in the basilica of blessed Peter, the apostle. |

And the bishopric was empty 7 days. And he slept in peace as a confessor.[8]

He was buried the 19th day of the month of July.

---

[1] List of gifts to St. Peter and of repairs to the basilicas of St. Felicitas and St. Agnes, both of which are said to have been falling into ruin.

[2] Before the time of Symmachus the angelic hymn was chanted only at the papal mass on Christmas night. *Supra*, p. 13 and n. 2.

[3] This cemetery is on the Via Salaria Nova, not far from the church of St. Agnes. It contained the tomb of the martyr Alexander, one of the sons of St. Felicitas, and sepulchres of other saints. The discovery of this cemetery in 1578 led to the opening up of the other catacombs of Rome. Lanciani, *Pagan and Christian Rome*, ch. VII.

[4] Trasamond, king of the Vandals, about 508 drove the African bishops into exile in Sardinia. For a letter of Symmachus to these refugees see Jaffé, *Regesta*, vol. I, p. 99, 762.

[5] We possess no other information regarding the captives said to have been ransomed by Symmachus in Northern Italy but the country was overrun by Gothic bands and life and liberty must have been precarious.

[6] List of ordinations.

[7] John the Deacon in the ninth century mentions the tombs of Leo I, Simplicius and Symmachus which he had seen in the portico of the Vatican. *Vita Sancti Gregorii*, IV, 68; Migne, *Pat. Lat.*, vol. 75. Both tombs and epitaphs have disappeared.

[8] Duchesne remarks that this epithet, like the other laudatory terms applied to Symmachus, show that our author felt a particular sympathy for and interest in this pope as one with whose difficulties he had been himself acquainted. *Op. cit.*, p. 268, n. 46. Mommsen is of the opinion that the author was merely following a good source which has since been lost. *Lib. Pont.*, p. xvii.

## LIV. Hormisdas (514–523)

Hormisdas, by nationality a Campanian, son of Justus, from the town of Frisino,[1] occupied the see 9 years and 17 days. He was bishop in the time of Theodoric, the king, and Anastasius Augustus,[2] from the consulship of Senator (A.D. 514) to the consulship of Symmachus and Boethius (A.D. 522). He set the clergy in order [3] and taught them from the Psalms. He built a basilica in the Alban district on the estate Mefontis.[4]

By authority of his bishopric and by decree of a synod and in accordance with the clemency of the apostolic see he sent to Greece and reconciled the Greeks who had been in bondage of the anathema, because of Peter of Alexandria and Acacius of Constantinople.[5]

At that time by a decree of a synod he sent to Greece and displayed the clemency of the apostolic see, for the Greeks had been bound by the chain of the anathema, because of Peter of Alexandria and Acacius, bishop of Constantinople, under John, bishop of Constantinople.[6]

This pope sent to King

By advice of King Theo-

---

[1] A town in ancient Latium, the modern Frosinone. The name Campania is here applied in the medieval sense to the region around Rome.

[2] To be quite exact the author should have added the name of Justin, who was emperor from 518 to 523.

[3] This may mean that Hormisdas did his utmost to efface the vestiges of the schism which had rent the church under his predecessor. His epitaph says that he restored "the members torn from their wonted places." Duchesne, *Lib. Pont.*, vol. I, p. 272, n. 4.

[4] The spot is now unknown.

[5] The following account of the negotiations of Hormisdas with the Eastern emperor and the final reconciliation of the Eastern church is substantially correct, the version in the first column from the Felician Epitome being in the main more accurate than that in the second. The insurrection of Vitalian in 514 forced the emperor to propitiate orthodox opinion and to propose the settlement of differences at a general council to be held at Heraclea under the presidency of the pope. Hormisdas agreed to participate in the council, provided that the Eutychian heresy should be expressly anathematised during the proceedings and the acts of the Council of Chalcedon should be ratified. *Supra*, p. 106, n. 2. In the summer of 515 he sent the legates mentioned in the text to discuss with the emperor the conditions of church reunion. Jaffé, *Regesta*, vol. I, p. 101, 771, 773, 777.

[6] John was not bishop at Constantinople until 518, toward the close of the events about to be narrated. Timotheus was his predecessor. Duchesne, *op. cit.*, p. 272, n. 6.

Theodoric at Ravenna and by advice of the king he dispatched Ennodius, bishop of Ticinum,[1] and Fortunatus, bishop of Cathena,[2] and Evantius, a priest of the city, and Vitalis, a deacon of the city.

They went to Anastasius Augustus and proposed that the Greeks should do penance according to the code and be reinstated but they effected nothing.[3]

Likewise a second time [4] Hormisdas sent Ennodius and Peregrinus, the bishops, and Pollio, a subdeacon of the city, and they carried with them secret letters and arguments for the faith, 19 in number, and the code of penance, by means of which the Greeks might be

doric he dispatched Ennodius, bishop of Ticinum, and Fortunatus, bishop of Catina, and Venantius, a priest of the city of Rome, and Vitalis, a deacon of the apostolic see, and Hilary, a notary of the aforesaid see.

They went to Anastasius Augustus

but effected nothing.

Likewise a second time he sent the same Ennodius and Peregrinus, bishop of Mesena,[5] carrying secret letters and arguments in support of the faith, 19 in number, and the text of the code of penance.

---

[1] The modern Pavia.

[2] A corruption for Catina, the modern Catania in Sicily.

[3] By 516 Anastasius was no longer afraid of Vitalian and accordingly sent the pope's embassy home with a letter declining his proposal.

[4] Anastasius, not wishing to appear to discourage altogether the agitation for ecclesiastical reunion, next sent an embassy of his own to the pope and the Roman senate with counter propositions. In February, 517, Hormisdas was writing in an irritated and despondent tone about the hollowness of the Greek professions. In April of that same year, however, he had been himself persuaded to send a second deputation to Constantinople. It carried with it letters to the emperor, to Timotheus, bishop of Constantinople, to Possessor, an African bishop sojourning at the capital, to the orthodox clergy, monks and populace of the city, to the orthodox bishops of the Orient and finally to all Eastern bishops without distinction of party. The orthodox were approved and urged to remain constant; the rest reminded that they must return to the rock on which the church was built. Jaffé, *Regesta*, pp. 102–103, 784, 789–794. The *Lib. Pont.* also speaks of an argument in nineteen headings and a code of penance. No copy of the argument is known to exist. The copies distributed in the East were destroyed, as our text relates. Felix III had already offered the penitential code to the erring Greeks. *Supra*, p. 108 and n. 3; p. 109.

[5] Messina.

restored; and if the Greeks refused to receive the arguments of the letters, the bishops were to distribute them among the cities.

And Anastasius Augustus refused to accept their offer, because he believed in the heresy of Euthices.[1]  Therefore he tried to corrupt the bishops with a bribe but they despised the prince and would not take the money.

And Anastasius Augustus refused to accept the code of penance, because he himself shared in the Euthycian heresy. Therefore he tried to corrupt the legates with a bribe but the legates of the apostolic see despised Anastasius Augustus and would not take the money, unless he would render satisfaction to the apostolic see.  Then the emperor, full of wrath, sent them forth by a back way and embarked them on a dangerous ship with soldiers and captains and prefects, Heliodorus and Demetrius.

The emperor, hot with anger, sent them forth by a dangerous place and embarked them on a ship in peril of death with a captain and a prefect, Heliodorus and Demetrius.  And the emperor gave command that they should not enter any city.

And the emperor Anastasius gave command that they should not enter any city.

Nevertheless the bishops secretly dispatched the above mentioned 19 letters on the faith through all the cities by the hands of catholic monks.

Nevertheless the legates of the apostolic see secretly dispatched the above mentioned 19 letters on the faith through all the cities by the hands of orthodox monks.

But these letters were received by bishops of the cities who agreed with Anastasius Augustus, the heretic, and in fear they forwarded them all to

But these letters were received by bishops of the cities who were of the party of Anastasius Augustus and in fear forwarded all the letters on the

---

[1] The details of the failure of the second mission to Anastasius are recorded only in the *Lib. Pont.*

Constantinople to the hands of Anastasius.

Anastasius in rage wrote to Pope Hormisdas and said among other impious things: "We wish to command you not to lay commands upon us."[1] Then, struck by a blow from the divine thunderbolt, Anastasius perished.[2]

So Justin, the orthodox, succeeded to the empire and he sent to the apostolic see, to Pope Hormisdas, Gratus, a man of illustrious name, and asked that legates might be commissioned by the apostolic see.[3]

Then, by advice of King Theodoric, Hormisdas sent Germanus, bishop of Capua, and John, the bishop, and Blandus, a priest, and Felix, a deacon of the apostolic see, and Dioscorus, a deacon of the aforesaid see,[4] and he fortified them on every

faith as criminal to Constantinople.

Full of rage Anastasius wrote against Pope Hormisdas and among other impious things said this: "We wish to command you not to lay commands upon us." At that time by the will of God Anastasius was struck by the divine thunderbolt and died.

So Justin, the orthodox, succeeded to the empire and he sent with his authority to Pope Hormisdas and the apostolic see Gratus, a man of illustrious name, to request of the apostolic see that the peace of the churches might be restored.

Then Hormisdas, the bishop, by advice of King Theodoric, sent from the apostolic see Germanus, bishop of Capua, and John and Blandus, a priest, and Felix and Dioscorus, deacons of the apostolic see, and Peter, a notary, and he instructed them

[1] The text of the imperial letter is printed in Thiel, *Epistolæ Romanorum Pontificum*, vol. I, p. 813. It is dated July 11, 517, and ends with the words, "We can endure to be insulted and to be made of no effect; we cannot endure to be commanded." Duchesne, *op. cit.*, p. 273, n. 12.

[2] Several writers of the time mention a great storm on the day of the death of Anastasius. Duchesne, *op. cit.*, p. 273, n. 13.

[3] August 1, 518, Justin wrote to Hormisdas to announce his accession, and in September of the same year he sent Gratus, "vir clarissimus," to reopen the question of reuniting the divided church. The emperor's letter is in Thiel, *Epistolæ*, vol. I, p. 831. Hormisdas' answers are summarized in Jaffé, *Regesta*, vol. I, p. 104, 801, 802.

[4] This Dioscorus had already proved his talents of eloquence and persuasion. *Supra*, p. 118, n. 1. Being an Alexandrian he, of course, was familiar with the Greek language and point of view and was especially qualified for a part in the mission.

point of faith and gave them the code of penance, by means of which the Greeks might return to communion with the apostolic see.[1]

And when they drew near to Constantinople

there came out to meet them a multitude of monks and a host of distinguished men, among whom were the emperor Justin and Vitalianus, master of the soldiery, and they escorted them from the so-called Round Castle into the city of Constantinople.[2]

With glory and praise they entered the city together with the illustrious Gratus.

So after their entrance into the city they were gloriously received by Justin Augustus, the orthodox.

Then all the clergy of Constantinople and John, the bishop, knowing that these men had been joyfully received,

on every point of faith and gave them the text of the code of penance.

And when they drew near to Constantinople they were so radiant with the grace of faith that a multitude of orthodox monks and a vast host of distinguished men, among whom were the emperor Justin and the consul Vitalianus, came to meet them and escorted them from the so-called Round Castle into the city of Constantinople.

With glory and praise they entered the city together with the illustrious Gratus.

And they were gloriously received by Justin Augustus, the orthodox.

Then all the clergy and John, the bishop of Constantinople, knowing that these men had been joyously received, also they

[1] The instructions given by Hormisdas to the legates have been preserved and may be found in Mansi, *Amplissima Collectio*, vol. VIII, p. 441, and in Migne, *Pat. Lat.*, vol. 63, p. 433. Jaffé, *Regesta*, p. 104, 805.

[2] An official report from the envoys to the pope, describing their enthusiastic reception at Constantinople, and a special report from the deacon Dioscorus on the same topic are printed in Thiel, *op. cit.*, vol. I, pp. 857–859. They mention among the grandees who met them and escorted them to the gates the count Justinian, then an influential minister of the emperor Justin. The author of the *Lib. Pont.* has taken the name for that of the emperor and has therefore mistakenly represented Justin himself as being among the escorts. A sentence or two later he explicitly says that Justin received the Romans after their arrival in the city.

shut themselves up in the great church which is called Santa Sophia and held a council and sent word unto the emperor, saying, "Unless the reason be expounded to us why Acacius, the bishop of our city, was condemned, we make no agreement with the apostolic see."

And a council was held before Justin Augustus, in the presence of all the nobility, and the legates of the apostolic see chose Dioscorus, the deacon, from among themselves to expound the reason. And he set forth to them the guilt of Acacius so clearly that they all, even Justin Augustus, cried out together, saying, "Damnation to Acacius here and in eternity!" At that time Justin Augustus accepted the truth and gave command that every bishop within the realm of Justin should satisfy the code of penance without delay and return to communion with the apostolic see. And this came to pass and there was harmony from the East unto the West and the peace of the church prevailed. And the text of the code of penance is kept laid up in the archives of the church unto this day.[1]

who had been associated with Anastasius, | Acacius, shut themselves up in the great church which is called Santa Sophia and held a council and sent word unto the emperor, saying, "Unless the reason be expounded to us why our bishop Acacius was condemned, we make no agreement with the apostolic see."

[1] An extract from Dioscorus' account of the hearing given to the envoys before

This pope Hormisdas sent to King Theodoric at Ravenna[1] and by his advice delivered authority to Justin and restored him to unity with the apostolic see through the seal of his autograph and the code of penance and condemned Peter and Acacius and all heresies.

He found Manicheans and shattered them

| | |
|---|---|
| with a multitude of | and tried them by |
| blows and sent them into exile; and | |
| he destroyed | he burned |

their books with fire before the doors of the basilica of Constantine.[2]

In his days the bishopric

| | |
|---|---|
| of Africa, which had been abolished by the heretics in the time of persecution, was reestablished after 74 years.[3] | in Africa, which had been abolished by the heretics, was restored after 74 years. |

At that time there came

| | |
|---|---|
| a golden crown, | a diadem, |

the emperor, the Byzantine senate and the leaders of the church is quoted by Duchesne, *op. cit.*, p. 273–274, n. 19. Dioscorus says that the reading of the pope's letters and the code of penance produced conviction at once and modestly makes nothing of his own part in bringing about the happy termination. A letter from Hormisdas, however, written to Dioscorus in December of the same year, expresses his thankfulness for what God had done through him and his own intention of asking the emperor to bestow on Dioscorus the bishopric of Alexandria as a reward for his labors. Jaffé, *Regesta*, p. 107, 842. A "libellus pænitentiæ" or penitential code of the year 517 is printed in Thiel, *Epistolæ*, vol. I, p. 755.

[1] The author of this second text places the expedition of Hormisdas to Ravenna during the reign of Justin and connects it with the successful negotiations of 519. The author of the first text places it under Anastasius as a part of the fruitless ventures of 515–517.

[2] This episode is mentioned only in the *Lib. Pont.*

[3] The reëstablishment of the orthodox church in the Vandal kingdom of Africa took place immediately on the death of Trasamond, May, 523. News of the event must have reached Rome shortly before the death of Hormisdas in August of the same year. The figure 74, given here for the duration of the term of Catholic persecution,

set with precious stones, from the king of the Franks, Cloduveus, for a gift to blessed Peter, the apostle.[1]

During his episcopate many gold and silver vessels came from Greece, and the gospels with golden covers and precious stones, which weighed 15 lbs. ;[2]

\*      \*      \*      \*      \*      \*      \*      \* 3

These all were sent as a thank offering by Justin Augustus, the orthodox.

\*      \*      \*      \*      \*      \*      \*      \* 4

He also was buried

| | |
|---|---|
| in the church of blessed Peter,[5] | in the basilica of blessed Peter, the apostle, |

August 6, in the consulship of Maximus,

the younger (A.D. 523).    |

And the bishopric was empty 6 days.

## LV. JOHN I (523–526)

| | |
|---|---|
| John, by nationality a Tuscan, son of Constantius, occupied the see 2 years, 9 months | John, by nationality a Tuscan, son of Constantius, occupied the see 2 years, 9 months |

should probably be 84.  The latter would carry one back to 439, the year when Carthage was captured by Genseric and the clergy of the city were driven into exile.  Duchesne, *op. cit.*, p. 274, n. 22.

[1] Clovis died in 511, three years before the accession of Hormisdas.  It is possible, however, that there had been a delay in the transportation of his votive crown to Rome.

[2] A letter has been preserved, sent in 521 by Hormisdas to Epiphanius, bishop of Constantinople, to which is added a note in the pope's own handwriting.  "We have received the golden, jewelled chalice, the silver paten and a second silver chalice and two curtains sent by your charity to serve in the ministry of the basilica of blessed Peter."  Jaffé, *Regesta*, p. 108, 858.

[3] List of rich vessels and other objects.

[4] Lists of gifts from Theodoric and Hormisdas to the great basilicas.  List of ordinations.

[5] His epitaph, written by his son Silverius, who himself became pope in 536, is given by Duchesne; *op. cit.*, p. 274, n. 25.  It ascribes to Hormisdas the credit not only for the healing of the schisms at home and abroad but also for the restoration of the Catholic church in Africa.

and 15 days, from the consulship of Maximus (A.D. 523) to the consulship of Olybrius, the younger (A.D. 526).

He was summoned by King Theodoric to Ravenna and the king commissioned him and sent him on an embassy to Constantinople to Justin, the emperor. For Justin was a devout man and in his great love for the Christian religion he tried to root out heretics.

With great fervor he dedicated the churches of the Arians to the catholic faith.[1]

Therefore Theodoric, the Arian, was angered and threatened to put all Italy to the sword.

Then John, the venerable pope, set forth and journeyed with weeping and lamentation and certain devout men, ex-

and 16 days. He was bishop from the consulship of Maximus (A.D. 523) to the consulship of Olybrius (A.D. 526), in the days of Theodoric and of Justin Augustus, the Christian. He was summoned by King Theodoric to Ravenna and the same king commissioned him and sent him on an embassy to Constantinople to Justin, the orthodox emperor. For at that time Justin, the emperor, a devout man, in his ardent love for the Christian religion was trying to root out the heretics.

With great fervor for Christianity he adopted a plan to consecrate the churches of the Arians as catholic. Hence the heretic king, Theodoric, was incensed, when he heard of it, and threatened to destroy all Italy with the sword.

Then John, the pope, ill with infirmity, journeyed weeping, and certain senators and ex-consuls with him, namely The-

[1] The Anonymous Chronicle of Valois, compiled apparently after the death of Theodoric, tells practically the same story; viz. that Theodoric believed that "Justin was afraid of him" and therefore he charged John to tell him "among other things not to readmit to the catholic religion the heretics who had been reconciled." "And when he came (to Constantinople) the emperor Justin met him as if he had been the blessed Peter; and when he had delivered his message the emperor promised to do everything, except that he could never restore to the Arians those who had been reconciled and had adopted the catholic faith." Ch. 88–93. Quoted by Duchesne, *Lib. Pont.*, vol. I, p. 277, n. 2. The proscription of the Arians by Justin took place in 523. Theodoric may have felt that this action was a menace to the safety of the Gothic tribes in Italy and jeopardised the policy of general peace and toleration which he himself had labored to enforce. On the *Anon. Valesianus*, see Mommsen, *Chronica Minora*, I.

consuls and patricians, went with him, Theodorus, Importunus, Agapitus and another Agapitus.

And they took this for the message of their embassy, that the churches of the heretics in the dominions of Greece should be returned to them and that if it were not done

| Justin Augustus | King Theodoric |

would put all Italy to the sword.

When all the aforesaid envoys had arrived at Constantinople with John, the pope, the people came to meet them at the 12th milestone in honor of the apostles, for from the days of the blessed Silvester, the pope, in the time of Constantine, they had desired to be accounted worthy to receive in Greece the vicar of Saint Peter,

and Justin Augustus adored the blessed John,

odorus, Importunus, Agapitus, the exconsuls,[1] and another Agapitus, a patrician.

And they took this for their message as ambassadors, that the churches should be returned to the heretics in the dominions of the East and that otherwise Theodoric would put all Italy to the sword.

When they had journeyed with John, the pope, the whole city with candles and crosses came to meet them at the 15th milestone in honor of the blessed apostles, Peter and Paul, and the ancients among the Greeks bore witness, saying that in the time of Constantine Greece had been accounted worthy to receive the blessed Silvester, bishop of the apostolic see, and again in the time of Justin Augustus it had received the vicar of blessed Peter, the apostle, with glory.[2] Then Justin Augustus gave honor to God and bowed himself to the ground

---

[1] Flavius Theodorus was consul in 505, Importunus in 509, Agapitus in 517. Duchesne, *op. cit.*, p. 277, n. 3.

[2] As a matter of fact John I was the first pope to visit Constantinople. The reference to Sylvester in the first column of our text, taken from the Felician Epitome, probably means that since the time of Sylvester, *i.e.* since the official recognition of Christianity and the establishment of the state church at Constantinople, no such honor had been paid to the Eastern capital. The author of the later version in the second column has misunderstood the passage and interpreted it as a statement that Sylvester himself had once been in Greece. The contemporary chronicle of Marcellinus says,

and adored John, the most blessed pope. At that time blessed John, the pope, and the aforesaid senators with many tears besought of Justin Augustus that their embassy might be favored in his sight. And Pope John and the senators, devout men, obtained all their requests and Italy was delivered from King Theodoric, the heretic.[1] Moreover Justin, the emperor, was filled with joy because he had been accounted worthy to behold the vicar of blessed Peter, the apostle, during his lifetime within his realm and Justin Augustus was crowned gloriously by the pope's hands.

and he was crowned by his hands.

At that time, when the aforesaid envoys, that is Pope John and the senators,

| | | |
|---|---|---|
| Likewise the emperor granted all the request of the pope and the noble senators, exconsuls and patricians of the city of Rome, Flavius Theodorus, who excelled the other digni- | Then the emperor granted the requests | |
| of the illustrious Theodorus and of the other nobles | Theodorus, the exconsul, | |

"He (John) was received with extraordinary honor; he sat upon a throne on the right side of the church and he celebrated the day of our Lord's resurrection with Roman prayers in a loud voice." Migne, *Pat. Lat.*, vol. 51, p. 941.

[1] The *Lib. Pont.* does not mention the demand of Theodoric already cited, that Justin should compel the converted Arians to return to their old faith. *Supra*, p. 132, n. 1. Justin did apparently consent to restore the confiscated Arian churches.

taries in splendor and distinction, the illustrious Importunus, also an exconsul, the illustrious Agapitus, an exconsul, and the other Agapitus, the patrician, and to save the blood of the Romans he returned the churches to the heretics.

But while this was taking place in the dominion of Greece, in accordance with the will of King Theodoric, the heretic, many priests and Christians were being put to the sword. Even while King Theodoric kept the blessed bishop John and the other illustrious men sojourning in

who came with the blessed pope John,

and to save the blood of the Romans he returned the churches of the heretics to them.

But while King Theodoric kept the bishop John and the other illustrious men sojourning at

Importunus, the exconsul,

Agapitus, the exconsul,

and Agapitus, the patrician, who died at Thessalonica,

were kept sojourning at Constantinople by King Theodoric, the heretic,

Constantinople he slew two senators, exconsuls and patricians, Boethius and Symmachus, with the sword and commanded that their bodies should be concealed.[1]

Then when everything had been accomplished in due order and Agapitus, the patrician, was dead in Greece, the aforesaid illustrious men with John, the bishop, returned and

Constantinople he slew two senators, Boethius and Symmachus, the patrician, with the sword and commanded that their bodies should be concealed.

Then Pope John and the aforesaid illustrious men on their return

he put to death two illustrious senators and exconsuls, Symmachus and Boethius, slaying them with the sword.

At that time the venerable pope John and the senators returned with glory, having obtained all their requests of Justin Augustus,

were received by King Theodoric craftily; in great hatred he received John, the bishop, and the illustrious and devout senators and in the heaviness of his wrath he would have punished them with the sword but he feared the

but King Theodoric, the heretic, received them, that is Pope John and the senators, with craft and hatred and would even have slain them with the sword but he feared the indignation of Justin Augustus.

[1] The Anonymous Chronicle of Valois says that Boethius was strangled by Theodoric before the pope was sent to Constantinople but that Symmachus was put to death in John's absence. "For the king feared that his grief for his father-in-law (Boethius) might cause him to plot against the government and he accused him of crime and ordered him to be executed." Ch. 92. A third chronicle of the time, *Chronicon Cuspinianeum*, arranges these events still differently. "In that year Theodoric slew Symmachus and Boethius and died himself eighteen days later." Quoted by Duchesne, *op. cit.*, p. 277, n. 7.

indignation of Justin Augustus, the orthodox, and did it not.

However, he confined them all cruelly in prison, so that the blessed pope John, worn by illness, gave up the ghost and died in prison.[1] He died at Ravenna gloriously, May 18, in the prison of King Theodoric. On the 98th day after Bishop John had died in prison, by the will of omnipotent God, King Theodoric suddenly was struck down by divine power and perished.[3]

However, he confined them all miserably in prison, so that the blessed John, bishop and pope of the chief of sees, sickened in prison and gave up the ghost and died. He died a martyr at Ravenna in prison, May 18.[2] Then it came to pass, by the will of omnipotent God, that on the 98th day after blessed John died in prison King Theodoric, the heretic, suddenly perished.

was struck by a thunderbolt and perished.

This pope John rebuilt the cemetery of the blessed martyrs, Nereus and Achilleus, on the Via Ardeatina;[4] he likewise restored the cemetery of Saints Felix and Adauctus;[5] he likewise restored the cemetery of Priscilla.[6]

[1] The events here related all followed each other in rapid succession. At the end of 525 or the opening of 526 Pope John was in Rome, conferring with Dionysius the Less, over the celebration of the approaching Easter. Migne, *Pat. Lat.*, vol. 67, p. 517. When that Easter came, April 19, he was in Constantinople. *Supra*, p. 133, n. 2. On May 18 he died in confinement under Theodoric's displeasure. The king was in a frame of mind that brooked no delays.

[2] The author of the text in the second column calls John a martyr. The Anonymous Chronicle of Valois tells how a man possessed by a devil was healed as the pope's bier passed him in the street and how the senators and the populace thereupon tore off fragments of the dead man's vestments to preserve as relics. Ch. 93. Duchesne, *op. cit.*, p. 277, n. 9.

[3] Theodoric died on August 30, one hundred and four days after the pope.

[4] John restored the basilica of Santi Nereo ed Achilleo in the cemetery of Domitilla. It is possible still to distinguish between the remains of the original basilica, built about 390 under Pope Siricius, and the renovations of John.

[5] This cemetery was also known as the cemetery of Commodilla. It stood a little to the east of the basilica of St. Paul, near the Via Ostiensis. Frothingham thinks that John decorated with frescos the subterranean chapel recently unearthed there. *Monuments*, pp. 73, 74, 279–281.

[6] He probably restored the basilica of St. Sylvester, which stood over the catacomb of Priscilla. Duchesne, *op. cit.*, p. 277, n. 13.

\*      \*      \*      \*      \*      \*      \*      \*1

His body was brought from Ravenna and buried in the basilica
of the blessed Peter, May 27, in the consulship of Olybrius (A.D.
526).[2]

And the bishopric was empty 58 days.


## LVI.  FELIX IV (526–530)

Felix, by nationality a Samnite, son of Castorius, occupied the
see 4 years, 2 months and 13 days.   He was bishop in the time of
King Theodoric and Justin Augustus, from the consulship of Ma-
burtius (A.D.  527) to the consulship of Lampadius and Horestes
(A.D.  530), from July 12 to October 12.[3]

He built the basilica of Saints Cosma and Damian in the city
of Rome, in the region which is called the Via Sacra, near the
temple of the city of Rome.[4]

[1] Short list of gifts to Roman basilicas, contributed principally by Emperor Justin.
List of ordinations.

[2] An epitaph copied from the ancient atrium of St. Peter, which perhaps marked
the tomb of John I, is given by Duchesne.  *Op. cit.*, p. 278, n. 15.   The seventh line
runs,

"Priest of the Lord, thou art fallen a victim for Christ."

[3] The dates recorded here for the pontificate of Felix IV are not quite exact.   Theodoric died seven weeks after his installation and Justin a year later.   Accordingly the
greater part of his term of office was passed under Athalaric and Justinian.   Boniface
II was ordained September 22, 530, so that Felix must have died during the same month.
A calculation based upon the length of the pontificate as given in the first sentence of
our biography brings one to September 21 as the date of Felix' death.   The Latin text
for this passage is "a die IV id. Jul. usque in IV id. Octub."   It is possible that a copyist
may have repeated the "IV id." by mistake in the second phrase and that it originally
read "in X kal. Octub."   Duchesne, *Lib. Pont.*, vol. I, p. 279, nn. 1, 2.   Mommsen
suggests that the inaccuracy in date, which is noticeable from time to time through this
part of the narrative and is explained by Duchesne as copyist's error or later interpolation, is due to the fact that the author is not a contemporary of the events he is
describing but is introducing dates at his own discretion into a narrative of an earlier
age.   Mommsen, *Lib. Pont.*, p. xvii.

[4] This is, of course, the church now known as Santi Cosma e Damiano.   It was
originally a pagan hall, dedicated by Vespasian, restored by Severus and Caracalla
and employed as a storehouse for census reports and survey records.   On its eastern
wall was set up the marble plan of Rome, of which fragments are now preserved in
the Capitoline Museum.   Felix constructed an apse on this eastern end and adorned
it with a mosaic of Christ among the clouds, attended by saints and apostles, and inscribed the dedicatory verses which may be still read beneath it.   The hall itself stood

In his time the basilica of the holy martyr Saturninus on the Via Salaria was burned with fire and he rebuilt it from its foundation.[1]

| | |
|---|---|
| He was ordained by order of King Theodoric [2] and he died in the time of King Athalaric, October 12. | He was ordained peaceably and he lived to the time of Athalaric. |

  *  *  *  *  *  *  *  *[3]

He also was buried in the basilica of blessed Peter, the apostle, October 15.[4]

And the bishopric was empty 3 days.

---

a little back from the Via Sacra, from which it was separated by a small, circular temple, erected by Maxentius in honor of his son Romulus. Either Felix or some later builder threw the new church and the round temple together, so that the latter served as a vestibule for the former and gave it an entrance upon the Via Sacra. There is considerable uncertainty as to the edifice referred to here as the "temple of the city of Rome." The *Lib. Pont.* relates of Pope Honorius that he covered the whole basilica of St. Peter with bronze tiles taken by permission of the emperor Heraclius from the "temple which is called the temple of Rome." Duchesne opines that the building thus denoted was the civil basilica of Constantine, which stood near Felix' church. Frothingham and others think it rather the temple of Venus and Rome. The cult of the Cilician martyrs, Cosma and Damian, was especially popular at Rome at this period. Symmachus had already built an oratory in their honor. *Supra*, p. 122. Duchesne, *op. cit.*, p. 279, n. 3. Frothingham, *Monuments*, pp. 73–74, 89–90. Gregorovius, *History of Rome*, tr. Hamilton, vol. I, pp. 339–346.

[1] A cemeterial basilica over the catacomb of Thrason on the Via Salaria. It has long since disappeared. Duchesne, *op. cit.*, p. 280, n. 4.

[2] A letter has survived, written by Athalaric to the Roman senate, in which he expresses his pleasure that they had so obediently elected the pope chosen for them by his predecessor, Theodoric. He assures them that Theodoric, "although of a different faith," had taken pains to select a pontiff who would be satisfactory to any upright man. Cassiodorus, *Variæ*, VIII, 15; tr. Hodgkin, *Letters of Cassiodorus*, pp. 360–361.

[3] List of ordinations.

[4] Duchesne (*op. cit.*, p. 280, n. 7) gives his epitaph. The last four lines may be translated as follows:

> "For his humble piety he was preferred to many of the proud
> And by singleness of heart he won a lofty place;
> He was bountiful to the poor, he comforted the wretched,
> He increased the wealth of the apostolic see."

## LVII. Boniface II (530–532)

Boniface, by nationality a Roman, son of Sigibuld,[1] occupied the see 2 years and 26 days. He was bishop in the time of King Athalaric, the heretic, and of Justin[2] Augustus,

the catholic.

He was ordained by one faction at the same time as Dioscorus.[3] Dioscorus was ordained in the basilica of Constantine and Boniface in the basilica of Julius;[4] and there was strife among the clergy and in the senate for 28 days.[5] At that time Dioscorus died, Octo-

---

[1] The first Germanic name to appear in the lists of the popes or their forbears. A consul of the year 437 was called Sigisbuld. Duchesne, *Lib. Pont.*, vol. I, p. 282, n. 2.

[2] This name should, of course, be Justinian.

[3] For the previous career of Dioscorus see *supra*, p. 118, n. 1 and p. 127 *et seq.* The history of this brief schism in the church has been recently illuminated by the discovery in the chapter library at Novara of three documents now published by Duchesne. *Op. cit.*, p. 282, nn. 4 and 8. The first is a mandate addressed by Felix IV on his deathbed to the bishops and clergy, the senate and people of Rome, announcing the selection and ordination by himself of Boniface, the archdeacon, to succeed him in the government of the church and bidding them all accept Boniface and avoid dissension on pain of suspension from the communion of the Lord's body. Felix, we may recollect, had been an appointee of Theodoric and apparently wished to ensure the succession of a pope who would continue to favor the Goths. Dioscorus, on the other hand, had more connection with the Greek party in church and state. The second document is a general order from the Roman senate to the clergy to refrain during the lifetime of a pope from planning for the ordination of his successor. The edict is impartial in its phraseology and applies equally to the partisans of Boniface and those of Dioscorus. The third document is entitled, "The Paper Which the 60 Priests Presented to Pope Boniface after the Death of Dioscorus." It is a formula of repudiation and anathematization of Dioscorus, " who in opposition to the decree of your (Boniface's) predecessor, Pope Felix, of blessed memory, aspired to the bishopric of the Roman church." It contains a confession of error in having espoused the cause of Dioscorus and a promise never again to be guilty of such wickedness. It closes with a declaration that it is signed by the offender's own hand. The copies of this instrument deposited by Boniface in the Roman church were burned five or six years later by Pope Agapitus. *Infra*, p. 144. It is interesting to observe that the emperor Justinian in 551 used the condemnation of Dioscorus as a precedent to prove that it was lawful to anathematize the dead.

[4] The basilica of Constantine is, of course, San Giovanni in Laterano. Duchesne thinks that the basilica of Julius is not Santa Maria in Trastevere, often known under this title, but a hall in the Lateran palace which also bore the designation. *Op. cit.*, p. 282, n. 5.

[5] The number of the priests who adhered to Dioscorus was at least sixty, as may be inferred from the title of the formula of repudiation described above. *Supra*,

ber 14. Then Boniface, full of ambition and guile, commanded
with much bitterness the clergy to return to him under bond of an
anathema in their own handwriting and the anathema in their
own hand he deposited in the archives of the church, as if for condemnation of Dioscorus; and he gathered the clergy together.
Nevertheless no one subscribed to his episcopate,[1] for the great
majority had been with Dioscorus.[2]

He gave the priests, deacons, subdeacons and notaries plates of
metal which were bequeathed to him [3] and succored the clergy with
lavish alms when in danger of famine. He held a synod in the
basilica of blessed Peter, the apostle,[4] and made a decree that he
should ordain his own successor. This decree he ratified by the
signatures of the priests and an oath before the confession of the
apostle Peter and he appointed the deacon Vigilius. Then a second
synod of all the priests was held out of reverence for the holy see,
because the decree had been contrary to the canons and because
Boniface repented of his sin in that he wished to appoint his successor; and Pope Boniface confessed that he had been guilty of
sacrilege and

had confirmed                          |

the decree with his own signature in behalf of the deacon Vigilius
and before the confession of blessed Peter, the apostle, in the
presence of all the priests and clergy and senators he burned the
decree with fire.

At that time a communication came from the bishops of Africa

n. 3. At the synod of 499, which all the Roman priests would naturally have attended,
there were only sixty-seven present. It therefore seems clear that Dioscorus was the
favorite candidate with the great majority of the clergy, who disliked the domination
of the Goths. Duchesne, *op. cit.*, p. 282, n. 6.

[1] This probably means that Boniface did not require the followers of Dioscorus to
sign the decree attesting his election, but satisfied himself with the form of recantation already described.

[2] In 553 one of the members of the fifth ecumenical council at Constantinople alluded
to Dioscorus as pope and declared that the officials in Constantinople had been in communion with him up to the time of his death. Duchesne, *op. cit.*, p. 283, n. 10.

[3] A letter of Gregory the Great mentions a silver plate or platter (scutella), which
had been bequeathed to a monastery. Gregory I, *Epistolæ* II, 32; Migne, *Pat. Lat.*,
vol. 77, col. 569.

[4] The *Lib. Pont.* is the only source for the following events.

regarding their government, saying also that the bishop of Carthage would in every act take counsel of the apostolic see.[1]

He (Boniface) also was buried in the basilica of blessed Peter, the apostle,[2]

| | | |
|---|---|---|
| October 18, in the consulship of Lampadius and Orestes.[3] | October 17, in the consulship of Lampadius. | on the 17th day of the month of October, in the consulship of Lampadius. |

And the bishopric was empty 2 months and 15 days [4] in the eleventh indiction.

## LVIII.  JOHN II (533-535)

John,

the younger,

who was also called

Mercurius,                    | Martyrius,

by nationality a Roman, son of Projectus, from the Caelian Hill,[5]

---

[1] The orthodox church of Africa had been given its freedom by the Vandal king Hilderic in 523.  *Supra*, p. 130 and n. 3.  For some years thereafter it was divided over certain problems of reorganisation, two in particular, viz.: the character and extent of the primacy of the see of Carthage and the relation of that see to the bishopric of Rome.  Duchesne, *op. cit.*, pp. xli, 283, n. 13.

[2] His epitaph is given by Duchesne.  Its tone is different from that of our text.

. . .  "The gentle shepherd reunited his divided flock,
        Folding again his distressed sheep as the enemy fell;
        With meek heart he abated his anger against the suppliants
        And overcame all wiles by the simplicity of his spirit."

It also records his aid to the city in a year of famine.  Duchesne, *op. cit.*, p. 283, n. 14.

[3] Lampadius and Orestes were consuls in 530, the year of the death of Felix IV.  *Supra*, p. 138.  Through an error their names have been inserted in the text again here.

[4] The unusual length of this interregnum was apparently due to a series of scandalous party-intrigues and efforts to purchase the see by simony.  A letter of King Athalaric to John II speaks of these deplorable machinations and says that during this course some of the sacred vessels were offered for public sale.  The Roman senate about this time issued a decree to the effect that any one who attempted to buy the papacy by any kind of bribery should be considered guilty of sacrilege.  Cassiodorus, *Variæ*, IX, 15; tr. Hodgkin, *Letters of Cassiodorus*, pp. 398-400.  Duchesne, *op. cit.*, pp. 283-284, n. 16.

[5] John was a priest of San Clemente on the Cælian Hill before his elevation to the pontificate.  A votive inscription still existing in the church of San Pietro in Vincoli

occupied the see 2 years, 4 months and 6 days. He was bishop in the time of King Athalaric [1] and Justinian Augustus,

the catholic.                    |

In his time the emperor, a devout man and ardent lover of the Christian religion, sent a statement of his faith, written in his own hand, to the apostolic see by the bishops Epatius and Demetrius.[2]

* * * * * * * * [3]

He also was buried in the basilica of blessed Peter, the apostle,[4] May 27, in the second consulship of Lampadius.[5]

And the bishopric was empty 6 days.

## LIX. AGAPITUS (535–536)

Agapitus, by nationality a Roman, son of the priest Gordianus, one of the clergy of the church of Saints John and Paul,[6] occupied the see

gives the name of the reigning pope as John, surnamed Mercurius, "promoted from the parish church of San Clemente to the pontifical glory." The present choir screen and ambones at San Clemente, with their decorations in low relief, two columns and a fragment of the epistyle of the ciborium are relics of the gifts of John to the basilica. His monogram may be seen on the screen. Duchesne, *Lib. Pont.*, vol. I, p. 285, n. 1; Frothingham, *Monuments*, pp. 74–75.

[1] Athalaric died in 534 and was succeeded by Theodatus or Theodahad, of whom we shall hear more under the ensuing pontificates.

[2] The disturbing problem of the dual nature of Christ had been raised again in the East by a monkish party who inclined to the Nestorian view. *Supra*, p. 97, n. 5. Justinian sent Hypatius and Demetrius, bishops of Ephesus and Philippi respectively, with a letter to the pope setting forth his own position and asking to have it approved. That letter, with the answer of the pope endorsing it, was published in the first chapter of the first book of the Code of Justinian, issued in November 534. Duchesne, *op. cit.*, p. 285, n. 3. Jaffé, *Regesta*, p. 113, 884, 885. For an account of Justinian's relations with the church and the papacy see *Cambridge Med. Hist.*, vol. II, pp. 43–49.

[3] List of gifts from Justinian. List of ordinations.

[4] His epitaph is given by Duchesne, *op. cit.*, p. 286, n. 4.

[5] These dates are both wrong. John II died May 8. May 27 was the date of the burial of John I. The second consulship of Lampadius fell in 532. Duchesne, *op. cit.*, p. 286, n. 5.

[6] Gordianus signed his name to the proceedings of the Roman synod of 499 as priest of Santi Giovanni e Paolo and lost his life in 501 during the disturbances of the pontificate of Symmachus. His house stood near the church which he served and his son Agapitus founded there a library of Greek and Latin theology. A dedicatory inscription was painted upon the wall above the bookcases and the frescoed portraits

11 months and 18 days.     | 8 months and 10 days.

He, at the opening of his episcopate, assembled everyone into a church and burned with fire the book of the anathema which Boniface in anger and guile had extorted from the priests and bishops contrary to the canons and in condemnation of Dioscorus, and he absolved the whole church from the guilt of perfidy.[1]

He was sent by Theodatus, king of the Goths, on an embassy to the lord emperor Justinian,[2] because at that time the lord emperor Justinian was wroth against King Theodatus for killing Queen Amalasuenta, daughter of King Theodoric, who had been put under the protection of Justinian and who had made Theodatus king.[3] Therefore Agapitus journeyed to Constantinople; on April 22 [4] Agapitus, the bishop, entered Constantinople and was received with glory.[5] And first he began a discussion with the most pious

---

of the church fathers. The inscription was copied in after years and may be found in Duchesne, *Lib. Pont.*, vol. I, p. 288, n. 1. Gregory I converted the house into a monastery.

[1] *Supra*, p. 140, n. 3; p. 141. This episode is recorded only in the *Lib. Pont.*

[2] Procopius does not mention the embassy of the pope to Constantinople but other chroniclers of the period refer to it. In the *Variæ* of Cassiodorus we hear that the pope, whose revenues were scanty at this hard time, was forced to pawn sacred vessels in order to raise the money for the expedition. *Letters of Cassiodorus*, tr. Hodgkin, pp. 510–511.

[3] Amalasuntha was the mother of Athalaric and Theodahad was her consort. He resented his wife's activity and energy and shut her up on an island in the lake of Bolsena. When she appealed to Justinian he had her strangled.

[4] Another instance of the transference of dates, which occurs so frequently in this part of the *Lib. Pont.* This date is given again below as the date of the death of Agapitus. The latter passage is where it rightfully belongs.

[5] "At this time Theodatus, king of the Goths, wrote to the pope and to the senate at Rome and threatened to put not only the senators but also their wives and sons and daughters to the sword, unless they should prevail with the emperor to recall from Italy the army which he was sending against him; and the pope for this reason undertook the embassy and journeyed to Constantinople. First of all he received honorably the men whom the emperor sent to him but refused to see Anthemius and would not accept his salutation; then he appeared before the prince and pled the cause of the embassy which he had undertaken. But on account of the great expense to the treasury (*fisc*) the emperor would not withdraw from Italy the army which he was sending and he refused to heed the supplications of the pope." Liberatus, *Breviarium*, 21; Migne, *Pat. Lat.*, vol. 68, col. 1039. Jaffé, *Regesta*, vol. I, p. 114. Duchesne, *op. cit.*, p. 288, n. 6. Liberatus describes the deposition of Anthemius by Agapitus on the ground not only of unorthodoxy but also of irregular transference from another see. Our own author passes over Agapitus' failure to deter the emperor from sending

Pope St. Simplicius

Pope St. Silverius

prince and emperor, Lord Justinian Augustus, concerning the faith. And the blessed bishop Agapitus set forth most steadfastly the apostolic doctrine of the Lord Jesus Christ, God and man, that is of two natures in one Christ.    Then a contention arose but the Lord aided Agapitus and he found the bishop of Constantinople, Anthemius by name, to be a heretic.

And when the contention arose between Augustus and Agapitus, the pope,                                |

the emperor Justinian said to him: "Either you agree with us or I dispatch you into exile."   Then the most blessed pope Agapitus answered joyfully and said to the emperor: "I indeed am a sinner, yet I have desired to come unto the most Christian emperor, Justinian; now, however, I have found Diocletian; nevertheless, I fear not your threats."   And Agapitus, the venerable pope, said to him a second time: "Notwithstanding, that you may know you are unworthy of the Christian faith, bid your bishop confess the two natures in Christ."   Then, by order of Augustus, the bishop of Constantinople, Anthemius by name, was summoned and the argument was begun but in response to the questions of the blessed pope Agapitus he refused to confess the catholic dogma of two natures in one Lord Jesus Christ.   And the holy pope Agapitus convicted him of error and was glorified by all the Christians.   Then the most pious emperor Justinian rejoiced and prostrated himself before the apostolic see and adored the most blessed pope Agapitus. And straightway he expelled Anthemius from the communion and sent him into exile.   Then the most pious emperor Justinian asked of the most blessed pope Agapitus that he would consecrate in place of Anthemius a catholic bishop, by name Menas.[1]

Furthermore Pope Agapitus obtained all that he had been sent to request.[2]   But after some days he fell ill and died at Constanti-

Belisarius to Italy but makes much of his achievement in upholding orthodoxy and ecclesiastical discipline in the Eastern capital.

[1] The Vatican manuscript 4961 contains a copy of a "Book of Menas, priest and head of the hospice, who was created bishop of Constantinople, March 13, after the second consulship of the distinguished Paulinus, the younger (536)." Duchesne, *op. cit.*, p. 280, n. 8.

[2] As we have already remarked, Agapitus failed entirely to secure what Theodahad and the Romans expected of him.

nople, April 22.[1]   And his body was carried in a leaden coffin
to Rome,                              |

to the basilica of blessed Peter, the apostle, where it was buried,
September 20.[2]

\*        \*        \*        \*        \*        \*        \*        \* [3]

And the bishopric was empty 1 month and 28 days.


## LX.  SILVERIUS (536-537)

Silverius, by nationality a Campanian, son of Hormisdas, bishop
of Rome,[4] occupied the see 1 year, 5 months and 11 days.   He was
appointed bishop by the tyrant Theodatus without discussion of
the appointment.   For Theodatus had been corrupted by bribes
and he terrified the clergy so that they believed that whoever did
not support the ordination of Silverius would suffer by the sword.
Accordingly the priests did not accept him in the ancient way and
confirm his appointment before his ordination;  but after he had
been ordained by force of fear, then for the sake of the unity of the
church and of the faith, when the ordination was ended, the priests
accepted Silverius.[5]

But after 2 months the tyrant Theodatus perished by the will
of God and King Witiges reigned.[6]   Then Witiges journeyed to

---

[1] Before Agapitus' death he appointed Pelagius, his deacon, as legate to represent
the Roman church at the imperial court.   Duchesne, *op. cit.*, p. 289, n. 10.   This
Pelagius figures again later.   *Infra*, p. 159 *et seq.*

[2] His epitaph has been lost.

[3] List of ordinations.

[4] *Supra*, p. 131, n. 5.

[5] These details as to the manner of Silverius' elevation are found only in the *Lib.
Pont.*   Liberatus in his *Brevarium* (ch. 22) tells us merely that the city of Rome chose
Silverius, a subdeacon and son of the former pope Hormisdas, to be ordained in Agapitus' stead.   It is curious, however, that the choice should have fallen upon one so
low in rank as a subdeacon if there were no pressure from outside in favor of Silverius,
and it is not unlikely that Theodahad, who determined the fate of Pope Agapitus,
insisted now on placing his own candidate in the papal chair, as Theodoric had done in
the case of Felix IV after the death of John I.   *Supra*, p. 139.   The tone of our narrative,
together with the imputation of simony, indicates some resentment on the part of the
Roman clergy against the Gothic interference.   Duchesne, *Lib. Pont.*, vol. I, p. 293, n. 2.

[6] Silverius was ordained June 8, 536.   The revolt of the Gothic armies, which set
Vitiges upon the throne, took place probably early in August.

Ravenna and by violence took the daughter of Queen Amalasuenta to be his wife. But thereupon the lord emperor, Justinian Augustus, being angry because Theodatus had murdered the queen who had been put under his protection, sent Vilisarius,[1] the patrician, with an army to free all Italy from the bondage of the Goths. And the aforesaid patrician came into Sicily and abode

there                           |

some time.

Then he heard that the Goths had chosen them a king contrary to the will of Lord Justinian Augustus and he marched into Campania toward the city of Naples and began to besiege the city with his army, because the citizens of Naples refused to open to him.[2] At that time the patrician fought against the city and entered it; and in his fury he slew both the Goths and all the inhabitants of Naples and sacked it and spared not even the churches from the sack. He killed husbands with the sword in the presence of their wives and he put to death the captive sons and wives of the nobles; he spared none, neither priests nor servants of God nor consecrated virgins.[3]

Then there was a terrible war, for Witiges marched against the patrician Vilisarius and against the city of Rome. For the patrician Vilisarius entered the city of Rome, December 10, and he surrounded the city with guards and fortifications and walls and repaired the trenches and strengthened it. The very night when the patrician Vilisarius entered, the Goths who were in the city or outside the walls fled and left all the gates open and escaped to Ravenna.[4] Then King Witiges collected a vast army of the Goths

---

[1] A form, of course, of the well-known name Belisarius. It is also spelt Velisarius, Bisilarius, etc., in the manuscripts. For Justinian's determination to avenge the death of Amalasuntha see *supra*, p. 144. On Belisarius' relations with the Romans see Gregorovius, *History of Rome*, tr. Hamilton, vol. I, pp. 363–450.

[2] The order of events here is uncertain. Procopius and the continuator of the *Chronicle of Marcellinus* describe the siege of Naples before the accession of Vitiges. Jordanes does the same in the *Romana* but in the *Getica* he keeps the order of the *Lib. Pont.* Duchesne, *op. cit.*, p. 293, n. 5.

[3] Procopius says that the Massagetæ, who fought in the army of Belisarius, were chiefly guilty of the loot and sacrilege, that they cut down even the inhabitants who fled to the churches for shelter and that Belisarius went up and down the city restraining them. *De Bello Gothico*, I, 11; ed. Haury, vol. II, pp. 58–62.

[4] Procopius says that Belisarius entered Rome by the gate called Asinaria on the

and marched back against Rome, February 21, and pitched his camp by the Molbian bridge [1] and began to besiege the city of Rome. And the patrician Vilisarius, who defended the Roman name, shut himself up within the city

and kept the city.          |

In those days the city was besieged so that no man might go out or come in. And all the buildings, private and imperial and ecclesiastic, were consumed by fire and men died by the sword; some perished by the sword, some by famine and some by pestilence.[2] Likewise the churches and the bodies of the holy martyrs were destroyed by the Goths.[3] Within the city there was a great famine, so that water would have been sold for a price if the springs had not furnished deliverance.[4] And the battles were fierce about the city. In those days the patrician Vilisarius fought against King Witiges and the host of the Goths and defended the Romans and with his army saved the city and the Roman name. Then the city and the harbor of Rome were besieged one year by the Goths.[5] But the patrician Vilisarius fought and conquered the Goths and at last, after one year, the Goths fled to Ravenna.

same day that the Goths marched out by the Flaminian Gate. *De Bello Gothico*, I, 14; p. 77.

[1] The Mulvian bridge.

[2] Rome had suffered in the fifth century from barbarian invasions but without losing much of the outer semblance of her grandeur. With this terrible siege begins the real destruction of her orderliness and beauty, the transformation of the splendid capital of the ancient world into the scarred, crumbling, poverty-stricken, medieval city of the popes. Lanciani, *Destruction of Ancient Rome*, pp. 70–71, 79–87. Frothingham, *Monuments*, pp. 76–85. Gregorovius, *History of Rome*, tr. Hamilton, vol. II, *passim*.

[3] Duchesne prints selections from inscriptions taken from martyrs' tombs and cemeteries along the Via Salaria, where the Gothic assaults were heaviest, recording the restoration of sacred monuments wrecked or damaged by the enemy. In one or two cases remains have been found both of the original epitaphs shattered by the Gothic soldiers and of the sixth century reproductions of the originals erected to fill the empty places. *Op. cit.*, pp. 293–294, n. 11.

[4] Procopius tells us that the aqueducts, which ordinarily gave the city its abundant supply of water, were cut by the invaders but that the springs within the walls together with the stream of the Tiber furnished enough for the reduced population. *De Bello Gothico*, I, 19, ed. Haury, vol. II, pp. 96–100. Lanciani, *Destruction of Ancient Rome*, pp. 79–82.

[5] According to Procopius the siege lasted one year and nine days and ended just before the vernal equinox of 538. *De Bello Gothico*, II, 10, ed. Haury, vol. II, p. 192.

At that time there was a heavy famine throughout the whole world, as Datius, bishop of the city of Milan, has related fully in his report, so that in Liguria women ate their own children for hunger and want; some of them, he has said, were of the family of his own church.[1]

At that time the patrician Vilisarius went to Naples and set it in order and afterwards came to Rome.[2] And he was received graciously by Lord Silverius;[3] and the patrician Vilisarius removed to the Pincian palace, May 11,[4] in the 15th indiction. At that time Vigilius, the deacon, was delegate to Constantinople. And

---

[1] Procopius speaks of the desolating famine that fell upon Italy in 538 and of instances of cannibalism due to starvation. *De Bello Gothico*, II, 20, ed. Haury, vol. II, pp. 236–239. He also says that Datius, bishop of Milan, and some of the leading citizens of the city came to Rome during that year to ask of Belisarius a small force of soldiers, with whose aid they proposed to reëstablish the imperial government in the province of Liguria and to drive out the Goths. During his stay at Rome Datius may have reported on the famine in his diocese. Belisarius furnished the desired support, but in spite of it the Goths took and sacked Milan the following year. Datius escaped and fled to Constantinople, where he died in 552. The *Variæ* of Cassiodorus contain a letter, written by himself as pretorian prefect to Datius between 534 and 539, regarding the opening of granaries for the relief of famine sufferers. Procopius, *ibid.*, II, 7; pp. 180–185. *Letters of Cassiodorus*, tr. Hodgkin, pp. 521–522.

[2] With this sentence, in the judgment of Duchesne, begins a later account by a new writer of the deposition of Pope Silverius, which took place in 537, before the Gothic siege was over. Up to this point, in his opinion, the narrative has been that of a contemporary, as were the lives of the popes immediately preceding. It is vivid and, on the whole, accurate, mentioning often details which are given by no other history and showing intense party spirit in the references to the conflicts between the Gothic and imperial parties. It is hostile to Silverius as the creature of Theodahad and is interested less in strictly ecclesiastical questions than in the military and political situation. This narrative now ceases abruptly and the history of the pope is continued by another and more sympathetic biographer to whom the recital of his cruel misfortunes seems more important than that of the fall of cities. The first sentence in this second narrative merely recounts again the events already more fully described, the capture of Naples and the coming of Belisarius to Rome. Duchesne, *op. cit.*, pp. xxxix–xl, 294, n. 15. Mommsen, of course, is convinced that our seventh century author has simply been making use of two different sources and pieces the two together here. *Lib. Pont.*, p. xvii.

[3] Procopius tells us that Silverius persuaded the Romans to open their gates to Belisarius. *De Bello Gothico*, I, 14; pp. 75–76.

[4] Another instance of an interpolated date. Belisarius fixed his headquarters at the Pincian palace immediately on his entry into Rome toward the close of 536. Possibly the name of the month here has been changed by a clerical error from March to May and the date is really that of Silverius' deposition. Vigilius was ordained March 29, 537. Duchesne, *op. cit.*, p. 294, n. 17.

the empress was vexed for the patriarch Anthemius, because he had
been deposed by the most holy pope Agapitus, who had found him
to be a heretic and had appointed Menas, the servant of God, in
his stead.[1]  So Augustus took counsel with Vigilius, the deacon,
and sent a letter to Rome to Pope Silverius with the request:
"Be not slow to come to us or else fail not to restore Anthemius
to his place." [2]  And when the blessed Silverius read the letter he
groaned and said: "Now I know that this affair has put an end to
my life."  But the most blessed Silverius had trust in God and in
blessed Peter, the apostle, and he wrote to the empress: "Lady
Augusta, I will never do this thing, to recall a heretic condemned
in his iniquity."

Then Augusta was wroth and she sent instructions to Vilisarius,
the patrician, by Vigilius, the deacon,

as follows:                                 |

"Find some occasion to accuse Pope Silverius and depose him
from the bishopric or else send him surely and speedily to us.
See, you have with you Vigilius, the archdeacon and legate, our
well beloved, who has promised us to restore the patriarch Anthemius."  And Vilisarius, the patrician, received the instructions
and said: "I forsooth will perform these instructions; but as for
him who brings about the overthrow of Pope Silverius he shall

---

[1] The intrigue of Theodora, by means of which Silverius was deposed, is described
by Liberatus even more minutely than it is here.  Liberatus says: "Augusta summoned
Vigilius, deacon of Agapitus, and asked him secretly to promise her that if he were
made pope he would annul the synod of Chalcedon, where the dual nature of Christ
had been maintained, and would write to Theodosius, Anthemius and Severus and in
his letters approve their faith, and she offered to give him an order to Belisarius to make
him pope and to bestow on him seven hundred thousand sesterces.  So Vigilius gladly
gave his promise, desiring the bishopric and the gold, and after making his pledge he
went to Rome; but when he arrived there he found that Silverius had been ordained
pope.  Also he found Belisarius at Ravenna (this should be Naples), besieging and
capturing the city, and he delivered to him the command of Augusta and promised
to give him two hundred thousand sesterces of gold if he would remove Silverius and
ordain him (Vigilius) instead." *Breviarium,* 22; Migne, *Pat. Lat.,* vol. 68, col. 1039.
Quoted by Duchesne, *op. cit.,* p. 294, n. 18.

[2] Liberatus says nothing of any correspondence between Byzantium and Silverius.
He rather gives the impression that Theodora ignored Silverius and his ordination
altogether but adds that Belisarius and his wife tried to persuade Silverius to do what
the empress demanded, implying that she cared little who was pope so long as Anthemius was reinstated. *Breviarium,* 22; *Migne, ibid.,* col. 1040.

render an account of his deeds to our Lord Jesus Christ."[1] And certain false witnesses, encouraged by these instructions, came forward and said: "We have found Pope Silverius sending letters to the king of the Goths, saying: 'Come to the gate which is called the Asinaria, near the Lateran, and I will deliver to you the city and Vilisarius, the patrician.'" And Vilisarius, the patrician, heard this and did not believe it; for he knew that it was spoken out of malice. Nevertheless, since many persisted in that same accusation, he was afraid.

Then he bade Pope Silverius come to him in the Pincian palace and he had all the clergy wait at the first and second portals.[2] And Silverius went alone with Vigilius into the mausoleum and Antonina, the patrician, was lying upon a couch and Vilisarius, the patrician, was sitting at her feet. And when Antonina,

the patrician, |

saw him she said to him: "Tell us, Lord Pope Silverius, what we have done to you and to the Romans that you should wish to betray us into the hands of the Goths." While she was yet speaking John, the subdeacon of the first district, took the pallium from his neck and carried it into an inner chamber and stripped him of his vestments and put on him a monk's robe and led him into hiding. Then Xystus, the subdeacon of the sixth district, when he saw him as a monk, went outside and proclaimed to the clergy that the lord pope had been deposed and had become a monk. And when they heard it they all fled. But Vigilius, the archdeacon, took

[1] The *Lib. Pont.* represents Belisarius as feeling more compunction than Liberatus ascribes to him. The latter says: "Belisarius returned to Rome and summoned Silverius to the palace and accused him calumniously on the ground that he had written to the Goths that they might enter Rome. And it was reported that one Marcus, a clerk, and one Julianus, a pretorian, had composed fraudulent letters under the name of Silverius and addressed them to the king of the Goths, by means of which Silverius was convicted of the intention to betray the city of Rome." *Breviarium,* 22; Migne, *ibid.* Jaffé, *Regesta,* vol. I, p. 116.

[2] Liberatus says that Silverius first took refuge in the basilica of Santa Sabina but that Photius, son of Antonina, prevailed upon him to come to the palace, pledging his safety by an oath. Silverius' companions urged him "not to believe the oaths of the Greeks" but he went and returned safely that day. Again Belisarius commanded him to appear and he prayed and committed his cause to the Lord and went and was never seen again by his friends. The scene inside the palace is described only in the *Lib. Pont. Breviarium,* 22; Migne, *ibid.*

Silverius as if in his own charge, and sent him into exile to Pontiæ and fed him with the bread of tribulation and the water of bitterness.  And he fell ill and died a confessor.[1]  And he was buried in that place, June 20, and a multitude of those who were diseased came to his sepulchre and were healed.[2]

*     *     *     *     *     *     *     * [3]

And the bishopric was empty.[4]

[1] The *Lib. Pont.* omits here some interesting details of Silverius' latter days.  He was sent first into exile not to Ponza, where he was in the power of Vigilius, but to Patara, a city of Lycia.  The bishop of Patara took up his cause and went himself to the emperor, declaring that it was wrong to expel the bishop of the mighty Roman see, "that there were many kings in the world but not one who was unique like the pope, who ruled the church of all the world and had been driven from his see."  The emperor was moved by this argument and ordered a fresh trial and a reëxamination of the forged letters.  Silverius was brought back to Italy, but before the trial could be held Vigilius, in dread of losing his position, sent word to Belisarius: "Deliver Silverius to me; otherwise I cannot perform what you expect of me."  So Silverius was turned over to the guards of Vigilius, who transported him to the island of "Palmaria," where he died of starvation.  Thus Liberatus.  *Breviarium*, 22; Migne, *ibid.*  Procopius in his *Secret History* says that Antonina, wife of Belisarius, the pliant tool of Theodora, was instrumental in bringing about Silverius' death before he could be tried a second time.  Ch. I; ed. Dindorf, pp. 13–16.  The guilt seems to rest partly upon her and partly upon Vigilius.  The islands of Pontiæ, now called Ponza, are in the Tuscan Sea.  One of the group is named Palmaria.  Duchesne, *op. cit.*, p. 295, nn. 21, 22.

[2] The remains of Silverius were never moved from Palmaria.  No other notice of veneration paid to him at Rome is known to exist earlier than the martyrology of Peter de Natalibus, which was drawn up in 1371.  For the reference *cf*. Duchesne, *op. cit.*, p. 295, n. 23.

[3] List of ordinations.

[4] There was perhaps some doubt in the mind of our author as to the time when Silverius' pontificate ended, whether with his deposition or with his death.  Therefore he does not give, as is usually the case, the exact duration of the vacancy in the papal see.

It may be urged by some historians that, if the translation of the *Liber Pontificalis* is to be broken at all, the break should occur here.  See first note on the following page.  Since, however, the question of the sources for the following pontificates is at best obscure, it seems better for practical purposes to carry the text through to the pontificate of Gregory I, as that important date in papal history is so close at hand.  [Ed.]

## LXI. Vigilius (537-555)

Vigilius,[1] by nationality a Roman, son of John, the consul,[2] occupied the see 17 years, 6 months and 26 days. At that time Vilisarius, the patrician, made war on Witiges, king of the Goths. And the king fled by night and John, the master of the soldiery, who was surnamed the Bloody, pursued after him and he seized him and brought him to Vilisarius and to Vigilius at Rome.[3] Then they pledged him their oaths in the basilica of Julius that they would conduct him safely to the emperor Justinian.[4] And when they had brought him to Constantinople the emperor rejoiced and created him patrician and count and sent him into the borders of

[1] Duchesne believes that with the biography of Silverius we come to the end of the first recension of the *Lib. Pont.*, and that with Vigilius we begin the first continuation. At a casual glance the account of Vigilius seems as likely to be contemporary work as that of Silverius. On examination, however, it is found to be full of inaccuracies and mistakes. For example, the two occupations of Rome by Totila in 546 and 549 are treated as one. The defeat of the Vandals by Belisarius in 533-534 is confused with the suppression of the revolt of Guntarith in 547. Other errors are pointed out in the notes. The lives of Pelagius I and John III contain further slips. In the latter the two Frankish expeditions of 552 and 562 are combined into one. Duchesne argues that the author of the four biographies after Silverius did not write earlier than the time of Pelagius II. *Lib. Pont.*, vol. I, pp. ccxxxi-ccxxxii. Mommsen rejoins that the style of all the sixth century lives is too barbarous to have been employed by a church official of the age of Theodoric and that the inaccuracies in the first portion, while not so numerous as those in the second, are frequent enough to make it improbable that they were the work of a contemporary. *Lib. Pont.*, p. xvii.

[2] The father of Vigilius may have been an honorary or codicillary consul. There are no consuls for the West listed in the Fasti by the name of John during this period. Vigilius' brother, Reparatus, was among the Roman hostages sent to Ravenna by Vitiges in 536 and barely escaped death when in the following year Vitiges dispatched orders to Ravenna to have the hostages massacred. Procopius, Liberatus and Marcellinus all state that Vigilius was ordained pope through the influence of Belisarius. Duchesne, *op. cit.*, p. 299, n. 1. Jaffé, *Regesta*, p. 117.

[3] The text is faulty in the part it assigns to John, "magister militum." He had been fighting in the North and was pushing down at this time toward Ravenna. His advance forced Vitiges to withdraw his army from the attack on Rome and fall back to protect Ravenna. He surrendered there in 539 to Belisarius, not to John.

[4] There is no other record of this interview. It is possible that Belisarius brought Vitiges to Rome and took ship at Porto for the East. The basilica of Julia is undoubtedly the great hall of the Lateran palace, used for state receptions and other ceremonies. *Supra*, p. 140 and n. 4. Duchesne, *op. cit.*, p. 300, n. 3.

Persia, where he died.[1]   The emperor also asked Vilisarius how he
himself fared with the Romans and how he had set Vigilius in the
place of Silverius.   Then the emperor and Augusta thanked
Vilisarius and conferred authority upon him and sent him back
into Africa

against Gundarit, king of the
Vandals, that he might do in
Africa what he had done in
Italy.[2]

And Vilisarius went into Africa under pretext of peace and
slew Guintarit, king of the Vandals, and brought Africa into sub-
mission to the empire.   Then Vilisarius, the patrician, came to
Rome and offered to blessed Peter, the apostle, by the hand of
Pope Vigilius out of the spoils of the Vandals a golden cross, set
with jewels, weighing 100 lbs.,

inscribed with                                    on which he inscribed
his victories,[3] and 2 large, gilded,
silver

candelabra, which stand to this day before the body of blessed Peter,
the apostle.   He gave likewise many other gifts and alms to the
poor.   For Vilisarius, the patrician, built a hospice on the Via
Lata [4] and on the Via Flaminia, near the town of Hortæ, he established a monastery of Saint Juvenal, which he endowed with lands
and many gifts.[5]

[1] Procopius does not say that Vitiges was sent to Persia but that Belisarius was
commissioned to carry on the Persian war.   *De Bello Gothico*, III, 1; ed. Haury, vol.
II, p. 297.

[2] Our author here confuses Belisarius' expedition against the Vandals in 533 with
the suppression of the revolt of Guntarith by Artabanes in 547.   Belisarius at this time
was in Italy, defending Rome against the assault of Totila.   Guntarith was assassinated by order of Artabanes.

[3] Belisarius' cross is mentioned again in the life of Stephen V.   It was saved from
the sack of the papal residence in 885.   Duchesne, *op. cit.*, p. 300, n. 6.

[4] The church of Santa Maria di Trevi, near the fountain of Trevi, was known in the
Middle Ages as Santa Maria in Xenodochio, because it adjoined the hospice of Belisarius.   A tablet, bearing an early inscription referring to the hospice, may still be seen
embedded in the outer wall of the church.   Duchesne, *op. cit.*, p. 300, n. 7.

[5] St. Juvenal was the first bishop of Narni, a town eight miles from Hortæ or Orta.
There was a church of St. Juvenal in Orta as late as the sixteenth century.   Duchesne,
*op. cit.*, p. 300, n. 8.

Then Theodora Augusta wrote to Pope Vigilius: "Come, fulfill for us what you promised of your

own |

freewill concerning our father Anthemius and restore him to his office." [1]

But Vigilius replied: "Far be this from me, Lady Augusta. I spoke beforetime wrongly and foolishly; now I do assuredly refuse to restore a man who is a heretic and under the anathema. Although unworthy, I am the vicar of blessed Peter, the apostle, as were my predecessors, the most holy Agapitus and Silverius, who condemned him."

Then the Romans brought

an accusation | their accusations

against Vigilius, because he had advised the deposition of the blessed pope Silverius: "We accuse him to your Holiness for he has done ill to your servants, the Romans, and to their people. We declare him to be a murderer, for he abandoned himself to rage and struck his notary a blow which felled him straightway to his feet where he died. Also he gave his niece, Vigilia, to the consul Asterius, son of a widow woman; then, making an occasion, he had Asterius

[1] Our author has probably misrepresented the demand made upon Vigilius by the Monophysite party at the imperial court. It is true that through their influence Vigilius had secured his office and that they undoubtedly expected of him some return in the way of endorsement of their peculiar views of the nature of Christ and of disparagement, if not denunciation, of the Council of Chalcedon and the Tome of Leo. *Supra*, p. 98, n. 1; p. 106, n. 2. That they required the reinstatement of Anthemius seems unlikely. His condemnation by Agapitus had been ratified by a synod held at Constantinople in 536 and by an edict of Justinian. Menas, who held the bishopric, was in high favor with the emperor. *Supra*, p. 145. Jaffé gives a letter purporting to have been written by Vigilius to Anthemius and other bishops of the heterodox party, professing his secret agreement with them but asserting the necessity of keeping the fact hidden, "so that I may more readily perform and achieve the things which I have undertaken." A declaration of faith, however, drawn up at about the same time, perhaps to satisfy suspicion at Rome, and letters to Justinian and Menas all explicitly and solemnly protest the pope's orthodoxy and loyalty to the acts of his predecessors and the Council of Chalcedon. *Regesta*, p. 118, 908, 909, 910, 911. Unless Vigilius be regarded as an absolutely unscrupulous doubledealer, the letter to Anthemius must be classed as a forgery. It might easily have been concocted by some of his opponents who desired to avenge his treatment of Silverius. Duchesne, *op. cit.*, p. 300, n. 9.

seized by night and beaten until he died."[1]  And when Augusta
heard this she sent Anthemius, the scribe, with orders and great
authority to Rome, saying: "If you find him in the basilica of
Saint Peter, let him go.  But if you find Vigilius in the Lateran or
in the palace or in any other church, set him immediately upon a
ship and bring him to us.  Else, by Him who liveth forever, I will
have you flayed."[2]  And Anthemius, the scribe, came to Rome and
found Vigilius in the church of Saint Cecilia, November 22; for
it was her birthday;[3] and Anthemius took him while he was dis-
tributing gifts to the people and brought him down to the Tiber
and set him on a ship.  The people and the multitude followed him,
calling out that they would have a prayer from him.  And when
he had spoken a prayer, all the people

said:                                    | answered:

"Amen"; and the ship began to move.  The Romans saw that
the ship in which Vigilius was seated had begun to move and
then the people commenced to throw stones after him and sticks
and dirty vessels and to cry out: "Your hunger go with you!
Your pestilence go with you![4]  You have done evil to the Romans;
may you find evil where you go!"  Yet some who loved him followed him from the church.

And when he reached Sicily and the city of Catania, he was
allowed to hold an ordination of priests and deacons in the month
of December.  Of these he sent back to Rome Ampliatus, the
priest and his vicar, and Valentinus, bishop of Saints Rufina and
Secunda, to guard the Lateran and preside over the clergy.[5]  Then

---

[1] There is no other account of the accusation against Vigilius and we know nothing
of the incidents herein mentioned.

[2] The circumstances of Vigilius' departure from Rome are described nowhere else.
Other historians say simply that he was summoned by the emperor and forcibly com-
pelled to go.  Only one adds that all Rome drove him out by public acclamation.
Facundus, *Defensio Trium Capitum*, IV, 3; Migne, *Pat. Lat.*, vol. 67, col. 624.

[3] November 22 is the day of the festival of Santa Cecilia in Trastevere.  The
gifts, "munera," here noted Duchesne understands to be the eucharistic wafers.  *Op.
cit.*, p. 300, nn. 12 and 13.

[4] Vigilius left Rome in 544 or 545.  At that time Totila had already begun to
reduce the city by cutting off supplies.  In 543 a severe pestilence had swept over the
disordered country.  Duchesne, *op. cit.*, p. 300, n. 14.  Jaffé, *Regesta*, p. 119.

[5] The word here translated vicar is "vicedominus" or " vidame," later a feudal title.
Ducange, *Glossarium*, Vicedominus.  The basilica of Sante Rufina e Seconda stood

he bade them all farewell and arrived at Constantinople on the
vigils of our Lord Jesus Christ. The emperor came to meet him
and they kissed each other and began to weep. And the people
sang psalms before him to the church of Saint Sophia: "Lo he
cometh, the Lord, the Lord," etc. Then for two years there were
dissensions over Anthemius, the patriarch, how Vigilius had
promised and had pledged with his hand to restore him to his place.[1]
But Vigilius would not yield to them but preferred to die virtu-
ously than to live. And Pope Vigilius said: "I perceive that it
was not the devout princes, Justinian and Theodora, who summoned me to them; rather I know to-day that I have met Diocletian and Eleutheria.[2] Do with me as you will; I am receiving

formerly on the Via Cornelia, not far from the Vatican. The foundation was laid by
Pope Julius I and the building was completed, if tradition be correct, by Pope Damasus.
Procopius gives us further information regarding the journey of Vigilius' envoys back
to Rome. They embarked with a convoy of vessels filled with food for the relief of the
suffering population of the city but at the entrance to the Tiber the fleet was captured
by the Goths and the bishop Valentinus was brought before Totila for examination.
The king for some reason suspected that the bishop was answering his questions falsely
and cut off both his hands. *De Bello Gothico*, III, 15; ed. Haury, vol. II, pp. 360-361.
In 554, when Vigilius left Constantinople, the archdeacon Pelagius seems to have been
performing the functions of the head of the church. *Infra*, p. 159.

[1] As has been said before (*supra*, p. 155, n. 1), the struggle was not to induce
Vigilius to restore Anthemius but to effect a compromise with the Monophysite party
in general. Justinian had already yielded to them and to the empress so far as to issue
an edict denouncing three Nestorian writers, Theodore of Mopsuestia, Theodoret and
Ibas, who the Monophysites claimed had received the tacit approval of the Council of
Chalcedon. Justinian took the step in the hope of thereby prevailing upon the party
to accept the decrees of the council and of restoring harmony to the church. The edict
was accepted, though reluctantly, by most of the orthodox Eastern bishops but met
with determined resistance in the West, where any concession to Eutychianism was
regarded as direct heresy. Vigilius was commanded in Constantinople to give the edict
his approval. He resisted stubbornly for a while, knowing that such an act would
ruin his position at Rome. But at length, in 548, he issued a document, commonly
called the Judicatum, anathematizing the three Nestorians but stoutly maintaining his
adherence to the Council of Chalcedon. Jaffé, *Regesta*, p. 121, 922. He was not
allowed to return home but was detained in the East until the meeting of the council
convened at his suggestion by Justinian in 553. Jaffé, *Regesta*, p. 121. The council
supported the emperor and found Vigilius' position unsatisfactory. His banishment
apparently was the result of his appearance before it. Jaffé, *ibid.*, p. 123, 935. The
controversy over the condemnation of the three Nestorian writers is known as that
of the Three Chapters. It brought about a new schism between East and West, which
lasted seventy years.

[2] The words are copied from the biography of Pope Agapitus. *Supra*, p. 145. It is
not known that Diocletian had a wife Eleutheria.

the reward of my deeds." Thereupon one struck him in the face, saying: "Murderer, do you not know to whom you speak? do you not know that you slew Pope Silverius and killed the son of a widow woman with kicks and blows?" Then he fled to the basilica of Saint Euphemia and laid hold of

| a column | a horn |

of the altar.[1] But he was dragged away from it and cast outside the church and a rope was put about his neck and they haled him through all the city until evening and then thrust him into prison and gave him a little bread and water. And the Roman clergy who were with him were sent into exile to work in different mines.

At that time the Goths chose for their king Badua, who was called Totila.[2] He descended upon Rome and besieged it; and there was a famine in the city of Rome so that the people ate their own children. And one day he made an entrance into Rome by the gate of St. Paul, in the 13th indiction.[3] All night long he had the trumpet blown until every inhabitant fled or concealed himself in the churches, for fear that the Romans would perish by the sword. But the king dwelt with the Romans as a father with his sons. Then some of the senators, Citheus, Albinus and Basilius, patricians and exconsuls, went to Constantinople and appeared before the emperor in their distress and desolation.[4] And the

---

[1] This account of the maltreatment of Vigilius is partly legendary. The actual facts are given in some detail in an encyclical letter written by himself in 552 relating his sufferings. Mansi, *Amplissima Collectio*, vol. IX, p. 50. Migne, *Pat. Lat.*, vol. 69, col. 53. It is true that Vigilius was dragged from an altar but the incident occurred in the church of St. Peter in Hormisda in Constantinople. Later he fled for refuge to the church of St. Euphemia in Chalcedon.

[2] Totila had become king before the departure of Vigilius. He is called Badua and Baduila in other chronicles. Duchesne, *op. cit.*, p. 301, n. 24.

[3] Our author here confounds the two sieges of Rome by Totila in 546 and in 549. The date given, the 13th indiction (549–550), and the entering by the gate of San Paolo belong to the second siege but the severe famine and the flight of the patricians were features of the first. On these events see Gregorovius, *History of Rome*, tr. Hamilton, vol. I, pp. 451–476.

[4] Procopius says that on the night that Totila entered Rome in 546 the patricians Decius, Basilius and others escaped from the city in the train of Bessas, the commander of the Byzantine garrison. Cethegus, the leader of the senate, had retired to Centum-cellæ earlier under suspicion of favoring the Gothic party. *De Bello Gothico*, III, 13 and 20; ed. Haury, pp. 349, 384.

emperor comforted them and enriched them as befitted Roman consuls.

Thereupon the emperor Justinian sent Narses, the eunuch and his chamberlain, into Italy. And he gave battle to the Goths and

| God awarded him the victory and the king was slain | won the victory and Totila, king of the Goths, was killed |

and a multitude of the Goths were killed also.[1] Then

| the assembled clergy | the Romans |

asked Narses that with his consent they might request the prince that, if Pope Vigilius still lived and the priests and deacons and clergy who had been sent into exile with Vigilius, they might return home. And when the emperor received the report of Narses and of the whole Roman clergy, he rejoiced and all his senate because God had given rest to the Romans.[2] And immediately the emperor sent instructions to the divers places whither the exiles had been transported, to Gypsum and Proconisius,[3] and he summoned them before him and said: "Are you willing to accept Vigilius, who was your pope? I thank you. If not, you have here your archdeacon Pelagius and my hand will be with you." They all replied: "May God direct your Holiness! Restore to us now Vigilius and when God wills that he shall pass from this world then let Pelagius, our archdeacon, be given to us according to your command." Then he sent them all away.

[1] Totila was defeated and killed in the battle of Tegina or Tadini in Tuscany in 552 and Rome was reoccupied finally by the imperial forces. The following year, 553, Teias, successor of Totila, was slain in the battle of Vesuvius and the long contest of Ostrogoths and Byzantines for the possession of Italy was ended.

[2] The story of the restoration of Vigilius savors somewhat of the legendary. It is possible that the Roman church appealed to Justinian on behalf of the banished pope and his attendant clergy and that they were assisted by Narses. It is certain, however, that Vigilius' final release was the result of his ultimate, unqualified condemnation of the three Nestorians and of all their supporters and his recantation of anything he had previously said in their defence. Jaffé, *Regesta*, pp. 123–124, 936, 937. Pelagius, who had also been exiled or imprisoned by the emperor, refused to concur in the condemnation and persisted in his resistance for some time after Vigilius had yielded. It is, therefore, extremely unlikely that Justinian should have suggested him at this time for Vigilius' place. Duchesne, *op. cit.*, p. 301, n. 28.

[3] Proconnesus, an island in the Propontis, now called Marmora, famous for its quarries.

They came with Vigilius to Sicily, to the city of Syracuse. And he suffered from the malady of the stone and died.[1] And his body was carried to Rome and buried in the church of Saint Marcellus on the Via Salaria.

\*     \*     \*     \*     \*     \*     \*     \*[2]

And the bishopric was empty 3 months and 5 days.[3]

## LXII. PELAGIUS I (556-561)

Pelagius,[4] by nationality a Roman, son of John, the vicar,[5] occupied the see 4 years, 10 months and 18 days. And there was no bishop to ordain him but two bishops were found, John of Perusia and Bonus of Ferentinum, and Andrew, priest of Ostia, and they ordained him pontiff.[6] At that time there was no one

---

[1] A contemporary record says of Vigilius' death : "He died in Syracuse, the second day of the week, at night, the seventh day before the Ides of June in the third indiction (June 7, 555)." Duchesne, *op. cit.*, p. 302, n. 33.

[2] List of ordinations.

[3] The vacancy was longer, for Pelagius was not ordained until April 16, 556.

[4] We know more of Pelagius' career previous to his accession than we do of that of most popes at this early period. Under Silverius he had been sent with Vigilius to Constantinople as apocrisarius and while there had intrigued in favor of the appointment of Vigilius and the deposition of Silverius. *Supra*, p. 146, n. 1; pp. 149-150. On Vigilius' ordination he had been sent by Justinian to Antioch on ecclesiastical business and had been active in other church affairs. Returning to Rome he had distributed his wealth among the poor of the city and after the departure of Vigilius had played the part of the leading citizen, negotiating with Totila in 546 and obtaining from him a promise to refrain from murder and outrage when he captured Rome. Procopius says that he was at this time the most illustrious man in Italy. Later he returned to Constantinople and was punished along with Vigilius for refusing to anathematize the Three Chapters in obedience to the decision of the ecumenical council just held. *Supra*, pp. 157, n. 1 and 159, n. 2. He did not continue obstinate, however, for a year later after the death of Vigilius he accepted the decrees of the council and was designated by the emperor as Vigilius' successor. *De Bello Gothico*, III, 16-21; ed. Haury, vol. II, pp. 362-393.

[5] The word is "vicarianus." Pelagius came apparently of aristocratic family. His father may have held the office of vicar in one of the two Italian dioceses. Duchesne, *Lib. Pont.*, vol. I, p. 303, n. 1.

[6] The regular conduct of ordinations in the suburban diocese must necessarily have been much interfered with during the ten years absence of Vigilius and the disorder of the Gothic wars. That conditions were little better in the metropolitan diocese of Milan is proved by a letter written by the clergy of that city in 551. Datius, their bishop, had then been absent in the East twelve or thirteen years and they complain that most of the bishops whom he had ordained were dead and that a vast number of

among the clergy who could be promoted. The monasteries and the multitude of wise and noble devout withdrew from communion with Pelagius, saying that he had had a part in the death of Pope Vigilius and therefore was punished with such troubles.[1] Then Narses and Pope Pelagius took counsel and when the litany had been said at Saint Pancratius they proceeded with hymns and spiritual songs to Saint Peter, the apostle.[2] And Pelagius, holding the Gospels and the cross of the Lord above his head, mounted the pulpit and thus he satisfied all the people

and the populace |

that he had done no harm to Vigilius. Likewise Pope Pelagius continued and said: "I beg of you to grant my request, that whoever deserves promotion in the holy church

and is worthy of it, |

people were dying without baptism. *Supra*, p. 149 and n. 1. Migne, *Pat. Lat.*, vol. 69, col. 118. A few episcopal ordinations had, nevertheless, taken place without the pope, in the suburban district, as is proved by the fact that Pelagius was ordained by a bishop from Perugia. Herculanus, bishop of that city, had been massacred by the soldiers of Totila, when they sacked Perugia in 549. John must have been ordained since that date. It is probable that the scarcity of bishops was not the only reason why Pelagius had but three at his ordination. Our text speaks of the widespread hostility to him in all ranks of the church.

[1] Duchesne is of the opinion that our author is mistaken in assigning this reason for the prejudice against Pelagius. It is certainly difficult to see how he could have been blamed in any way for Vigilius' death, when he was left by Vigilius in confinement in the East and had been for so long a fellow sufferer with him. *Op. cit.*, p. 304, n. 3.

[2] The ceremonies at San Pancrazio and the Vatican are described here in more detail than anywhere else. That, however, the charges of which Pelagius cleared himself were heresy and betrayal of the faith of the fathers rather than complicity in Vigilius' death is established by the encyclical which he issued at the same time. It is addressed to all the people of God and sets forth his position, "in order to remove suspicion." He declares solemnly that he accepts the statutes of the "four councils" (*i.e.* the four first councils, excluding the one called by Justinian) and the apostolic canons and that "he holds in condemnation all those whom they (his predecessors) condemned and reverences as orthodox all whom they approved, in particular the venerable bishops Theodoret and Ibas." Jaffé, *Regesta*, vol. I, p. 125, 938. Mansi, *Amplissima Collectio*, vol. IX, p. 717. By this purgation Pelagius seems to have won toleration from his own diocese but the other Western bishops for the most part still refused their fellowship. Pelagius vainly endeavored to prevail upon Narses and upon Childebert, king of the Franks, to interfere and end the schism by force. We have a letter by him addressed to Valerianus, a patrician, arguing that the decrees of the synod of Chalcedon and the writings of the blessed Augustine prove that schismatics should be suppressed by secular authority. Jaffé, *ibid.*, pp. 126, 946; 133, 1019; 135, 1038.

from a doorkeeper even to a bishop, should accept advancement, though not for gold nor any promises; you all know that that is simony. But whoever is taught in the works of God and leads a good life we bid him, not by bribes but by honest conversation, to rise unto the first rank."

At that time Pelagius appointed Valentinus, who feared God, as his notary and had all the gold and silver vessels and the vestments restored in all the churches.[1] Then he began to build the basilica of the apostles Philip and James;[2] but when the building was begun he died and was buried in the basilica of blessed Peter, the apostle,[3]

March 2.                                    |

*          *          *          *          *          *          *          *[4]

And the bishopric was empty 2 months and 25 days.

[1] Pelagius' correspondence is full of allusions to the impoverished state of the Roman church and of directions for collecting the rents and other revenues which had long been unpaid. In one instance he orders that a slave, the son of a slave woman belonging to the church, who was attempting to escape from servitude by calling himself a curial, should be returned to the ecclesiastical estates. He writes to the bishop of Arles, commending to his protection various Romans who had fled from their homes for fear of the enemy and asking that the garments bought with the dues paid by the local church should be sent by ship to Rome, "because there is such poverty and destitution in this city that we cannot look without grief and anguish of heart upon men whom we know to be meritorious and born to honorable position." Jaffé, *Regesta*, pp. 126–134, 943, 947, 949, 950, 951, 953, 956, 963, 1022, 1023. There is no mention of church furniture in the letters now extant but Pelagius may probably have tried to replace what had been lost and destroyed.

[2] The basilica of the Santi Apostoli. The first church on the site was erected by Julius I. *Supra*, p. 73, n. 4. A new one was now begun by Pelagius with the aid of Narses and finished by John III. It contained two metrical inscriptions set up by John, who claimed to have contributed the larger share of the edifice. The apsidal inscription began as follows:

> "Here the priest before me has left his slight traces;
> Pope John has completed the work which he began.
> Standing the more erect in a season of cramping distress,
> The bishop scorns to be depressed by a failing world."

Duchesne, *op. cit.*, p. 306, n. 2. The basilica was rebuilt in the fifteenth and again in the eighteenth century and shows now no remains of sixth century work. See Gregorovius, *History of Rome*, tr. Hamilton, vol. I, pp. 489–495.

[3] Duchesne prints Pelagius' epitaph, taken like others from the portico of the old basilica. *Op. cit.*, p. 304, n. 7. It is unusually long and makes much of his virtues and his title to blessedness in heaven. We give an extract:

## LXIII. John III (561-574)

John, by nationality a Roman, son of the illustrious Anastasius, occupied the see 12 years, 11 months and 26 days. He loved and restored the cemeteries of the holy martyrs.[1] He ordered that consecrated bread and flagons of wine should be supplied and lights should be lit in those cemeteries on every Lord's day by the priests of the Lateran. He finished the church of the apostles Philip and James and dedicated it.[2]

At that time the Heruli revolted and chose for their king Sinduald and oppressed all Italy. And Narses went out against him and slew the king and subdued the whole tribe of the Heruli.[3]

"As guardian of the apostolic faith he preserved the venerable dogmas
    Which were set forth by our illustrious fathers.
By eloquence he recovered those who had fallen into the errors of schism,
    That with hearts reconciled they might hold the true faith.
He consecrated many ministers of the divine law,
    Staining not his immaculate hands with gold.
He redeemed captives, he was quick to succor the afflicted,
    He never refused to share his goods with the poor."

[4] List of ordinations.

[1] During the eighteen years of the Gothic wars the suburban cemeteries had suffered from both pillage and neglect. They had ceased to be used as places of burial, new cemeteries having been opened within the city walls. The dwindling population no longer crowded the enclosed area, the old sanitary regulations were not enforced and graves outside the walls were exposed to desecration. The catacombs were, therefore hardly visited, except for the purpose of honoring the saints whose bodies were there interred. They were coming to be regarded not as ordinary burying grounds but as "the cemeteries of the martyrs," as they are called here, *i.e.* as shrines or holy places, objects of pilgrimage. Parish priests found it increasingly difficult to provide for services in those ancient sites, to which their common duties no longer brought them. John attempted to prevent their complete abandonment by laying upon the Lateran church, the centre of ecclesiastical administration, the responsibility of supplying materials for the mass. Some of the earlier Byzantine frescoes in the catacombs may have been executed by workmen in his employ. Duchesne, *Lib. Pont.*, vol. I, p. 306, n. 1. Frothingham, *Monuments*, pp. 86-87.

[2] *Supra*, p. 162 and n. 2.

[3] The events here noted belong to the obscure period between the Gothic wars and the Lombard invasion. Sinduald or Sindbal had been one of the chiefs enrolled by Narses to serve as heads of the barbarian auxiliaries. Two letters are extant addressed to Sindula, "magister militum," by Pelagius I. From them one may gather that the military leader acted as judge to settle civil cases involving questions of liability for damage and rights of inheritance and that he applied to the pope for instruction in a

Then came Ammingus, leader of the Franks, and Buccillinus; they also in like manner wasted Italy. But with the help of the Lord they too were destroyed by Narses.[1] And all Italy was joyful.[2]

Then the Romans, inspired by malice, sent an accusation to Justinian and Sophia, saying: "It were better for the Romans to serve the Goths than the Greeks, for Narses, the eunuch, governs us and reduces us to slavery; and our most devout prince is ignorant of it. Either free us from his hand or we and the city of Rome will serve the Gentiles." [3] When Narses heard this he said: "If I have done evil to the Romans may evil fall on me!" Then Narses departed from Rome and went to Campania and wrote to the tribe of the Lombards that they might come and possess Italy.[4] But

knotty suit. Jaffé, *Regesta*, vol. I, pp. 130 and 135, 990, 1031. Paul the Deacon, who probably had access to sources now lost, gives the best account of Sinduald's revolt. "Nevertheless Narses waged war against Sinduald, king of the Brenti, who came of the stock of the Heruli, whom Odoacer brought with him when he descended into Italy. He at first was faithful to Narses and received many benefits from him, but at last he rebelled arrogantly and endeavored to make himself king and Narses conquered him and took him prisoner and hung him from a high beam." *History of the Lombards*, tr. Foulke, pp. 55–56.

[1] The history of the struggle against the Frankish inroads at this period is far from clear. Bucelinus or Buccelin was apparently one of two brothers who led a host of Frankish marauders across the Alps in 553 and were repulsed and overwhelmed the following year by the imperial army. It is an error to couple his name here with that of Amingus. The latter seems to have figured in the Gothic raids of 561–563, which resulted in the temporary occupation of the province of Aquileia and of the cities of Verona and Brescia. Narses recaptured Verona and drove the Franks once more out of Italy. There is no satisfactory account of these years in any of the surviving sources. Duchesne, *op. cit.*, pp. 306–307, n. 4; Gregorovius, *History of Rome*, tr. Hamilton, vol. I, pp. 476–485.

[2] "Narses, the patrician, . . . gave Italy back to the Roman empire, rebuilt the ruined cities and by expelling the Goths restored the people throughout Italy to their ancient happiness." *Prosperi Aquit. Continuator Havniensis*, in *Mon. Ger. Hist.*, *Auctorum Antiquiss.*, *Chronica Minora*, vol. I, p. 337. Quoted by Duchesne, *op. cit.*, p. 307, n. 5.

[3] No other record gives us more than the bare statement that Narses was recalled from Italy in 568 by the emperor Justin II. The name of Justinian in our text is, of course, an error. It is impossible to verify or to disprove our narrative at this point.

[4] All historians from the seventh century onward unite in ascribing to Narses an invitation to the Lombards to enter Italy. Agathias and Marius, however, who were contemporaries of Narses, do not allude to it. The *Origo Gentis Langobardorum*, which Mommsen pronounces an extract from the lost history of Secundus of Trent, written about 612, says expressly that Alboin led his Lombards into Italy upon invita-

when Pope John learned that the Romans had sent an accusation against Narses to the emperor he went hastily to Naples. And Pope John began to entreat Narses to return to Rome. Then Narses said: "Tell me, most holy Father, what evil have I done to the Romans? I shall go back to the feet of him that sent me and all Italy shall know how I have toiled for her with all my strength." Pope John answered and said: "I myself shall go to him sooner than you shall leave this land." And Narses returned to Rome with the most holy pope John.[1]

Then the most holy pope withdrew to the cemetery of Saints Tiburtius and Valerian and abode there a long time, so that he even consecrated bishops there.[2] But Narses entered Rome and after a long time he died. And his body was laid in a leaden coffin and was carried with all his riches to Constantinople.[3]

Then Pope John likewise died and was buried in the basilica of blessed Peter, the apostle,[4]

July 13.

\*      \*      \*      \*      \*      \*      \*      \* 5

And the bishopric was empty 10 months and 3 days on the 13th day of July.

---

tion from Narses. Isidore of Seville (560–636) hints at a disagreement between Narses and the empress. The chronicle that passes under the name of Fredegarius, composed probably about 640, is the first to relate the famous story of the golden distaff sent by Sophia to Narses to show her scorn for his effeminacy. Duchesne, *op. cit.*, p. 307, n. 7; Hodgkin, *Italy and her Invaders*, vol. V, *passim*. The Lombard invasion occurred in 568.

[1] The return of Narses to Rome was in 571. There is no other account of the intercession of the pope.

[2] The little church of SS. Tiburtius and Valerian stood over the catacomb of Pretextatus on the Via Appia, about two miles from the city. The retirement of the pope to this secluded spot seems to have had some connection with the situation at Rome at the time of the disgrace and return of Narses but we lack the information to determine what the connection was.

[3] Narses died in 572 or 573. He is said to have been in his ninety-fifth year. There are various references in the chronicles to his great wealth. The imperial system of taxation seemed cruel to the impoverished Italians, and there appears to have been a widespread feeling that Narses had enriched himself by his relentless exactions. Ideas of the kind may have prompted the complaint to the emperor. Later there arose legends of the hidden treasure of Narses.

[4] His epitaph has been lost.

[5] List of ordinations.

## LXIV. Benedict I (575–579)

Benedict, by nationality a Roman, son of Boniface, occupied the see 4 years, 1 month and 28 days.

At that time the tribe of the Lombards invaded all Italy and there was also a great famine, so that many fortified towns surrendered to the Lombards in order that they might be spared the rigor of the famine.[1]  And when Justinian, the

most devout                              |

emperor, heard that Rome was endangered by the famine

and by the pestilence                    |

he sent to Egypt and dispatched ships laden with corn to Rome;[2] and thus God had compassion on the land of Italy.

In the midst of these hardships and afflictions the most holy pope Benedict died.  And he was buried in the basilica of blessed Peter, the apostle, in the vestry,[3]

July 31.                                 |

   *     *     *     *     *     *     *    *[4]

And the bishopric was empty 3 months and 10 days

on the 30th day of July.                 |

[1] Paul the Deacon, who bases his account partly upon the *Lib. Pont.* and partly upon the lost history of Secundus of Trent, gives the following description of the misery at this time.  "In these days many Roman nobles were killed through avarice (Lombard avarice).  And the rest were distributed among the invaders to pay a third part of their produce to the Lombards and were made tributary.  In the seventh year after the arrival of Alboin and all his nation the churches had been despoiled by the Lombard dukes, the priests slaughtered, the cities ravaged and the people exterminated who lived by the cultivation of crops, except in those regions which Alboin had conquered, and Italy for the most part was taken and subdued by the sword."  *History of the Lombards*, tr. Foulke, ṛ. 68.

[2] The emperor's name should be Justin, not Justinian.  Justin II died in 578.  Other sources say nothing of grain ships sent by him to Italy, but the records are all so scanty that the omission casts no doubt upon the statement of the *Lib. Pont.*

[3] The word translated vestry is "secretarium."  The name was applied to a small chamber opening to the left of the portico of old St. Peter's, originally used by the popes as a robing room.  Later it was converted into a chapel and the tomb of Benedict was beneath the altar.  His epitaph is lost.

[4] List of ordinations.

## LXV. Pelagius II (579–590)

Pelagius, by nationality a Roman, son of Unigild, occupied the see 10 years, 2 months and 10 days. He was ordained without commission from the emperor, because the Lombards were besieging the city of Rome and were working much havoc in Italy.[1]

At that time there were such heavy rains that every one said that the waters of the flood had overflowed;[2] and such fearful carnage that no one remembered that its like had ever been in the world.

At that time Pelagius enclosed the body of blessed Peter, the apostle, in plates of gilded silver.[3] He made of his own house

---

[1] The siege of Rome in 579 is not mentioned by any other contemporary historian. We have, however, a letter written by Pelagius in 580 to Aunarius, bishop of Auxerre, in which he laments the shedding of innocent blood, the violation of the holy altars and the insults offered to the catholic faith by "the idolaters." Already he turns his eyes toward the Franks as possible deliverers, "the divinely appointed neighbors and helpers of this city and all Italy," and bids Aunarius warn them to refrain from alliance with the Lombards. He sends Aunarius certain sacred relics, and adds : "We urge you to hasten, so far as you are able, to free from the pollution of the Gentiles the shrines of the saints whose merits you seek." Jaffé, *Regesta*, vol. I, p. 138, 580. Migne, *Pat. Lat.*, vol. 72, col. 705. In 584 Pelagius writes that he has sent envoys to Constantinople to beseech the aid of the emperor before the Lombards seize the few places that are left to the imperial government. "The district about Rome is," he says, "in the main destitute of any defenders and the exarch writes that he can provide no remedy." In 585 he sends several letters to the bishops of Aquileia and Istria, who were at odds with him over the question of the Three Chapters. *Supra*, p. 157, n. 1 ; p. 161, n. 2. He says that he has been prevented from writing before by the stress of events and the pressure of the enemy but that at last through the efforts of the exarch Smaragdus they are enjoying an interval of peace and quiet. Jaffé, *ibid.*, pp. 138 and 139, 1052, 1054–1056.

[2] The great flood of the Tiber occurred in the autumn of 589 and was followed by a pestilence which brought about Pelagius' death. Gregory I, writing five years later, says that the waters flowed in over the walls of the city and flooded most of it. *Dialogi*, III, 19; Migne, *Pat. Lat.*, vol. 77, cols. 268, 269. Gregory of Tours also relates the story. "Now in the fifteenth year of King Childebert (590), our deacon came from the city of Rome with relics of the saints and reported that in the ninth month (November) of the previous year the waters of the Tiber had overspread Rome in such a flood that the ancient buildings had been destroyed and the storehouses of the church wrecked, within which some thousands of measures of wheat had been lost. . . . Thereupon followed a pestilence, which they call ' inguinaria '; it broke out in the middle of the eleventh month (January, 590) and first of all . . . it attacked Pelagius, the pope, and speedily he died; and after his death there was great mortality among the people by reason of this plague." *History of the Franks*, X, 1 ; ed. Poupardin, p. 409. An English translation of Gregory's *History* by Brehaut will be found in another volume of the *Records of Civilization*.

[3] The sarcophagus of the apostle had been interred by Constantine too deep to be

| an almshouse | a hostelry |

for aged poor.  He constructed the cemetery of blessed Hermes, the martyr.[1]  He built from its foundations a basilica over the body of blessed Lawrence, the martyr, and beautified his sepulchre with silver plates.[2]  And he died and was buried in the church of blessed Peter, the apostle,[3]

February 7. |

disturbed or to need protection.  *Supra*, p. 53 and n. 3.  Our author may be describing rather inaccurately some new reliefs for the decoration of the confession.  Gregory I says in one of his letters: "When my predecessor of blessed memory thought to change the silver which was over the most sacred body of blessed Peter, the apostle, though it was distant about fifteen feet from the body, a sign of great terror appeared to him." *Epistolæ*, IV, 30; Migne, *Pat. Lat.*, vol. 77, col. 701.  That Pelagius actually made some innovations in the furniture of the basilica is evidenced by two sets of inscriptions, both of which were visible in the ninth century, one on the altar, the other on an ambone. The last lines of the former may be translated as follows:

"For which (the Roman state) the priest offers these gifts and prays
    That a season of rest be granted to the princes,
That the enemy be conquered throughout the world by the power of Peter
    And peace and our faith be with the Gentiles and the people."

Duchesne, *Lib. Pont.*, vol. I, p. 310, n. 3.

[1] The basilica at the cemetery of St. Hermes on the Via Salaria Vetus, of which vestiges may still be seen.

[2] The repairs which Pelagius executed in the smaller and older basilica of San Lorenzo remain for the most part to this day.  *Supra*, p. 61, n. 2.  The Goths had apparently done considerable damage to the building and a hill or bank close by threatened to crush it.  Pelagius rebuilt it, using original materials as far as he could, but enlarging its capacity and improving the lighting by raising the roof, adding the galleries and piercing the upper walls with numerous windows.  The columns of the galleries and the architraves on which they rest were taken from ancient buildings in the vicinity. They are of all sizes and styles and are pieced together with no attempt at artistic unity or workmanlike effect.  A little original carving in the Byzantine manner was done by stone-cutters, brought perhaps from Ravenna.  Pelagius also dug away and removed the hill which overhung the basilica and adorned the apse with the mosaic, the upper portion of which may still be seen over the triumphal arch.  The portrait of Pelagius himself is on the extreme left and the face has not been altered since his day.  Duchesne prints the metrical inscription which enumerates these various improvements.  *Op. cit.*, p. 310, n. 5.  Frothingham, *Monuments*, pp. 87–88, 281–282. The silver plates or reliefs of the confession have, of course, disappeared.  Gregory I has another anecdote to show how unsafe Pelagius found it to approach too near a holy tomb, even with the zeal of the restorer.  "My predecessor of holy memory likewise wished to make some restorations about the body of Saint Lawrence, the martyr. But since it was not known where the venerable body lay, he searched for it by digging and of a sudden in their ignorance the sepulchre was laid open.  Those who were present and took part in the work, monks and attendants, who saw the body of the martyr, although they did not presume to touch it, all died within ten days." *Epistolæ*, IV, 30; Migne, *Pat. Lat.*, vol. 77, col. 701.

[3] His epitaph has not been preserved.

*      *      *      *      *      *      *      * 1

And the bishopric was empty 3 months and 25 days

on the 7th day of February in
the 5th indiction.

From the death of Saint Silvester to the first Gregory was
246 years.

1 List of ordinations.

Also available in the Christian Roman Empire Series

*The Life of Belisarius*
    by Lord Mahon (1848)

*The Gothic History of Jordanes*
    by Charles Christopher Mierow (1915)

*The Book of the Popes (Liber Pontificalis)*
    by Louise Ropes Loomis (1916)

*For more information on this series, see our website at:*
**http://www.evolpub.com/CRE/CREseries.html**

LaVergne, TN USA
17 August 2009
155088LV00002B/34/A

9 781889 758862